READINGS IN EASTERN RELIGIOUS THOUGHT
CHINESE AND JAPANESE
RELIGIONS

READINGS IN EASTERN RELIGIOUS THOUGHT

Volume III
CHINESE AND JAPANESE RELIGIONS

Edited by
Allie M. Frazier

THE WESTMINSTER PRESS
PHILADELPHIA

STANDARD BOOK No. 664-24848-9

LIBRARY OF CONGRESS CATALOG CARD No. 69-14197

BOOK DESIGN BY
DOROTHY ALDEN SMITH

PUBLISHED BY THE WESTMINSTER PRESS ®
PHILADELPHIA, PENNSYLVANIA

PRINTED IN THE UNITED STATES OF AMERICA

To
my Mother and Father

Preface

In this book of readings on Chinese and Japanese religious thought and experience, the editor has been mainly concerned with the major movements in China and Japan rather than with the many subsidiary groups and factions that arose in those countries. The book is designed to bring together in one volume the primary religious texts of China and Japan along with significant readings in secondary materials that shed valuable light upon these traditions. The book is fundamentally constructed for Westerners who are approaching the Eastern traditions for the first time, and, hence, the supplementary material becomes invaluable for a higher comprehension of a remote and distant culture. The beginner, attempting to understand the East and its traditions for the first time, needs such auxiliary help if he is to have an appropriate understanding of the riches involved in Eastern thought. On the other hand, it would be meaningless to read about traditions and not have at hand the primary substance of those traditions. Thus this book purports to combine, for the Westerner, primary and secondary reading material, assuming that only this approach deals adequately with the subject matter and truly meets the present need with respect to Eastern thought.

In an introductory volume, a full and complete representation of the Chinese and Japanese traditions is not possible, so that the principle governing selectivity has been to present to the reader the mainstream of the traditions and the major movements in both countries as presented in original sources and commentaries.

I would like to express my sincere appreciation to Mrs. Leslie

Seyfried Roberts, who assisted me throughout my work on this book. I would also like to thank my wife, Ruth, who helped at every stage in the preparation of this volume. Finally I owe a debt of gratitude to Hollins College and my colleagues and students, who have given me every encouragement during my work on this project.

A. M. F.

Hollins College

Contents

CHAPTER I

The Religions
of China

Confucianism, Taoism, and Buddhism are the major religions of China. Traditionally referred to as san-chiao, the three teachings or creeds, these faiths have shaped the spiritual history of the Chinese people and created that unusual sense of moral order and propriety which is generally associated with Chinese society. Each of these faiths has enjoyed periods of dominance at various stages of Chinese history, but they have usually managed to live amicably together in a spirit of toleration and mutual respect. Of course, Chinese society has experienced episodes of religious persecution and harassment, but the pervasive relationship between the major religions in China has been cooperation and tolerance. None of these religious movements requires dogmatic adherence to creed or to inflexible moral systems. Nothing prohibits a Confucian from participating fully in Buddhist ceremonies or Taoist festivals.

Although these faiths have dominated the religious history of China, a popular religion, practiced in the earliest days of their civilization, exercised an important influence upon the development of the Chinese. Throughout their history, the Chinese have shown themselves to be susceptible to superstition, and this disposition fostered the popular religion of ancient China (ca. 1750–800 B.C.). Ancestor worship constituted the fundamental concern of primitive Chinese religion. It was frequently referred to as the "worship of heaven." For the ancient Chinese, there was a plethora of deities including nature spirits and the spirits of ancestors. In primitive Chinese religion as in most primitive religions, the boundaries separating the spirit world from the human world tended to oscillate dramatically. Despite the inclination of the Chinese to elevate departed humans to the status of holy powers, they maintained a sharp division between the secular and the sacred, between the "earth dwellers" and the "heaven dwellers." The ancestral spirits exercised an immense range of influence over the affairs of man. They were thought to be responsible for good luck, misfortune, ill omens, bountiful harvests, prolific wives, handsome heirs, and so on. Moreover, as the most ancient members of the human family or clan, they were possessed of the complete history of the ancestral tree and indeed of all humanity. Their knowledge encompassed all of the past and gave them special powers for knowing how the future would grow out of the present. A significant portion of ancestor worship was devoted to "sciences" designed to tap the ancestral fount of its wisdom through all forms of divination.

The universal moral commandment of this popular religion was that man must follow the "way of heaven." To do so, he must maintain the system of sacrifice and offerings to the ancestral spirits. Individual identity and happiness, as well as the weal of society, depended upon all men submerging their private egos or selves in the rites of the group. Without the maintenance of offerings to ancestor spirits, group identity and cohesion was lost. Thus, the sustenance of the sacrificial system was the goal of every institution in primitive Chinese society. By such sacrificial rites, these ancient people believed they confirmed, nurtured, and preserved the unity of self, family, and clan.

Two areas of perplexity and concern occupied the attention of these ancient Chinese. First, there was the world of nature, the macrocosm, displaying itself in the changes of season, the dramatic cycles of growth and decay, the pleasures and infirmities of the body, and so forth. Living in the midst of a maelstrom of change, primitive man confronted the task of deciphering the portents of natural events. Because he was so helpless in the face of nature, he tried to learn how to read nature's "signs" in order to discover whether the future held disaster or good luck for him.

Every event, no matter what its scale, from rainstorms to warts, could be viewed as an omen, prefiguring one's luck or fate. Popular religion occupied itself with discovering how to read, or divine, events in the macrocosm so that man could avert disaster and court good fortune. In a crude way, the "science" of divination, with all the rituals and sacrifices associated with it, gave the ancient Chinese the illusion of having some control over their own destiny.

A second area of perplexity and concern was the sphere of human affairs and the problems relating to the achievement of order in social relationships. Although the Chinese felt they had but limited control over the "things that happened to them," they viewed themselves as masters of those "things that they caused to happen." How then was a man to order his individual and social life to produce the greatest possible harmony and power? A man was morally upright if he kept the "way of heaven," conforming to the traditional ancestor worship and maintaining the sacrificial offerings.

About 400 B.C., a radical change in attitude occurred regarding ancestor worship and its rituals. Gradually there emerged in the popular religion of China in the fifth century B.C. a new purpose for sacrificial offerings. It was as though the man of the fifth century B.C. decided that the "way of man" was just as important, if not more so, than the "way of heaven." Sacrifice to the spirits of ancestors was performed to prove to the departed spirits that their descendants were prospering. Although offerings to ancestors continued, the main concern of popular religion was man's earthly condition. The attitude seems to have been that earth is near and its demands are pressing, while heaven is remote and its demands are frequently inscrutable. Furthermore, during this period, the Chinese began to attend to the problems of the spirit in which one maintained ancestral piety. Sacrifices generated by an innocent heart out of genuine respect and love were thought to be more efficacious than other offerings. Man must now attend to the state of his conscience, or soul, when he performs ancestral rites, for the only valid religious form must be a natural expression of man's internal nature. Sacrifices were no longer considered right and proper simply because they were performed.

The refocusing of attention in ancestor worship away from the formal rite to the spirit in which it was performed gave rise to a new vision of moral order and proper conduct. Man was no longer a mere shadow of his ancestors, but was now thought to possess those same qualities of mind and spirit which were respected and honored in the spirits of the dead. The principle dawned upon the Chinese mind that no merely formal system of worship could perfect human society if the individuals composing that society were not themselves perfected. If the archaic system was founded upon the principle of "nourishing the dead," then the new attitudes were based upon the idea of "nourishing the living." Without relinquishing their profound concern for their primal ancestors and the continuity of the clan, the Chinese began more and more to grapple with the problem of how one proceeded to care for and about the living. Each of the three major religions of China contributes its own unique answer to this question.

CONFUCIANISM

A full understanding of Confucius' moral and political teachings requires a comprehension of the world in which he lived. Confucius (Kong-fu-tse, i.e., "Kong, the Master") was born at a time when the feudal system, founded near the beginning of the Chou dynasty (ca. 1150 B.C.), was disintegrating. China of Confucius' day (551–479 B.C.) was governed by the descendants of the early Chou dynasty who had overthrown the Shang dynasty during the twelfth century B.C., and hence had acquired power themselves. Under Chou dominion, the greater portion of China was divided into small states, governed by vassals of the Chou royalty who were usually relatives or chieftains of allied tribes. There was no strong central government, so kings of the smaller feudal states were relatively independent. The principalities on the perimeter of this feudal agglomerate were constantly threatened by invasion, pillage and annexation from hostile tribes of barbarians bordering their lands. No feudal state could depend upon assistance from the central government, for this loose federation of states was bound only by common tradition, ancestor worship, and a hereditary ruling aristocracy.

For two centuries preceding the birth of Confucius, the Chou dynasty had shown signs of decay and disunity. Internally, a constant state of conflict existed among the Chou vassals, while externally, the peripheral states of the kingdom were racked by continuous invasion and pillaging raids by barbarian tribes, tribes which were eventually to be assimilated into the Chinese culture. Moreover, the smaller central states of the federation were caught in the vortex of continuous struggle. Vassals of the more powerful states in the Chou kingdom dreamed of usurping the royal prerogatives and sought alliances with other states. But no allegiance could survive the pressures of the age, although covenants binding state to state in loyal fealty and support were made with great ceremony and with invocations to the ancestral spirits to enforce such treaties. Mainly, these covenants were made during a time of such extensive stress that there were no grounds for a stable political or moral order. So the covenants were continuously being broken despite their sacred traditional undergirdings. The agencies which had previously guaranteed order and authority were no longer viable in the society. Traditional order and rule gave way to brute force, and covenants crumbled, having no intrinsic power to bind the moral and political actions of men.

It was, indeed, a lawless world in which might made right and the principle of expediency ruled political affairs. Sacred promises were merely words. Human life was cheap. The aristocracy were engaged in such base forms of social behavior as murder, bribery, cheating, power-mongering, breaking trusts, and so on. The common people, mostly farmers and serfs, were subjected to repeated exploitation, excessive taxation, impossible labor conditions, and other indecencies. Confucius believed that it was his duty to bring some moral and political order out of this insanity and chaos.

Basically, Confucius was a moral and political philosopher and not a prophet or founder of a religious sect. He claimed for himself no special religious authority or revelation; in fact, he insisted that he was not the originator or creator of his teachings, but only a transmitter of received tradition. In his teachings he recommended the traditional "way of heaven," and urged the maintenance of sacrifices to ancestors. However, with Confucius the traditional ancestor worship was clearly relegated to a secondary position, for the more pressing demands of the present age required immediate attention if society were to survive its nihilistic, normless state. Thus, he brought forward a stringent moral code and political theory which could serve as a basis for individual and collective harmony.

The most reliable source of information on Confucius' life and teachings is the *Analects,* a collection of teachings, biographical information, aphorisms, and anecdotes which was made by his disciples. This collection contains much authentic material from Confucius, but it also includes sayings of his disciples and later editorial glosses. Most Confucian scholars maintain that the first ten chapters contain the largest amount of original, authentic material and that the remaining chapters are a mixture of original material and later additions. It is generally conceded that the *Analects* is the oldest text in the Confucian tradition. In it, in contrast to later Confucian texts, Confucius is treated as a normal human being and no extravagant claims are made concerning his origin or his success in life. In later Confucian texts, Confucius is represented as a superhuman teacher and exalted in numerous ways so as to suggest his innate superiority to common people.

Although later Confucian tradition created an illustrious pedigree for Confucius, he was actually born of an aristocratic family whose fortunes had been rather unlucky. His father died when he was very young, and his mother devoted herself to his upbringing and to his education. Evidently from an early age Confucius displayed an extraordinary love for learning and venerated the ancient traditions of his country. At the age of seventeen he entered government service in the province of Lu and held various positions until he was fifty-five. Tradition informs us that he rose from Inspector of Grain to Minister of Justice during the years of his government service. At the age of twenty-three, his administrative duties were interrupted for a time as a result of the death of his mother. Apparently, this was a great personal tragedy for Confucius, and he observed the ancient funeral custom of retiring into isolation for almost three years. During these years passed in solitude, he reflected deeply upon the foundations of political and moral order in society. At the conclusion of his period of mourning, Confucius initiated his teaching career, gathering around him an increasing number of disciples whom he instructed in the arts of history, government, poetry, music, and moral rectitude.

Confucius was probably the first person in Chinese history to teach any significant number of students in a private capacity. Conditions of the age, however, made the concern for learning and the contemplative life a compelling option for younger members of aristocratic families. Because of the disruption and disintegration of the feudal system at that time, there was a large number of aristocrats "at loose ends." They were either refugees from states in conflict, or they were part of a growing number of aristocrats for whom there were no available positions in government. Although the reins of power in the kingdoms were in the hands of the Chou dynasty and their vassals, there were also many relatives of aristocratic families who were without position or influence. Many of these men turned to classical learning and to teaching as a career. Moreover, aristocratic families in power sent their children to Confucius and other tutors to be trained in the classics of the Chinese tradition and the arts of individual deportment and civic government. Confucius was probably only one of a number of literati (ju) who wandered from royal court to royal court acting as tutors in the ancient traditions of ritual, poetry, ceremony, sacrifice, and so on. This class of people might be likened to the Sophists of the Greek civilization, who lived at about the same time. Confucius was not only the most prominent of these literati, but he added something new to those traditions that he interpreted and transmitted. He added a moral fervor and thrust for order and stability that had a charismatic effect upon his disciples and the developing culture of China.

By the age of fifty, Confucius was once again actively engaged in governmental affairs in the state of Lu, acting probably as Minister of Justice. In assuming the full responsibilities of high official rank, he practiced what he unceasingly taught his students, that they should willingly assume public office and practice the moral and political principles with which they had been inculcated. Apparently, some form of political intrigue forced Confucius to resign his official position when he was fifty-five. In the thirteen years following, he moved from state to state seeking another government post and teaching the principles of harmonious government and sound living. He returned to the province of Lu in 484 B.C. and died five years later (479 B.C.), convinced that his career had been a failure.

Throughout his teachings, Confucius showed a great concern for the problem of how man could order his individual and social life so as to produce the greatest possible harmony and power. In attempting to reintroduce sound principles of collective and personal order into the society of his day, Confucius focused upon two problem areas which deserved some attention. Obviously, the most pressing need of his society was the need for social order and stability. Toward this end, Confucius taught the necessity for what he called "the rectification of names." According to Confucius, there ought to be an agreement between what a thing is called or named and what it is in actuality. For example, in his day, men who were named princes or rulers were acting like wolves of prey. A name, said Confucius, identifies and defines a person's social position and the duties attendant thereto. Social virtue requires that men understand what their station is in society and what duties and responsibilities they are expected to assume and exercise. A name defines what a person ought to be, and men need to attend to the gap between what is and what ought to be. Only when one lives in accordance with his name (whether it be father, son, ruler, teacher, farmer, etc.) can social order be achieved and peace and prosperity attained.

Social virtue rests finally upon the virtue of the individual. Confucius was aware of this fact and knew that the best state is one composed of the most superior individuals. Individuals, taught Confucius, should live according to that objective moral order which confronts them in the norms of their society and which is reflected in their own consciences. Men ought to act out of a sense of moral duty and not from calculations of consequences or effects. Confucius taught a form of righteousness which was devotional and sacramental, that had much in common with the teaching of the *Bhagavad-Gita*. He cast the commands of his stringent morality in concrete terms, enjoining the practice of "human-heartedness" (jen), i.e., benevolence for others. Confucius believed that a man ought to do his duties out of a spirit of love for others. This principle of "human-heartedness" was to be the instrument whereby individuals and society were to be harmonized and reformed.

Although in his day Confucius was only one among many teachers, in the succeeding centuries he was alternately viewed as *the* teacher and as a superhuman founder of a dynasty from heaven. Between 206 B.C. and A.D. 220, the period of the Han dynasty, Confucius was elevated to the rank of divinity. A state cult of Confucianism developed during this age, and this government-supported cult underwent elaborate growth throughout the next two thousand years of Chinese history. Temples were erected as centers of Confucian worship and study, sacrifices were performed, festivals and religious holidays associated with Confucius became a vital part of the national life. Interest in Confucianism has waxed and waned throughout Chinese history, usually in response to dramatic internal crises or religious developments, such as the rise of Taoism or the development of Chinese Buddhism.

The appeal of Confucianism was primarily to the official and learned classes. As such, it enjoyed much success in aristocratic circles and flourished under the protection and sponsorship of the ruling powers. It fostered education and learning and became the acknowledged guardian of the classical traditions. In contrast, Taoist and Buddhist scholarship has been viewed as of secondary importance throughout Chinese history. Confucian sages were thought of as repositories of learning and law, but Taoist saints and Buddhist monks were not. The latter may have attained a private wisdom, but it never ranked as high as the official learning of the Confucian.

The governing elite in China are no longer guided by Confucian principles, but rather conform to the ideology of Marx and Lenin. Since the success of the Communist revolution after World War II, the Chinese culture has undergone a series of radical changes and internal strains. Confucianism, whose principles had informed the aristocratic ruling class for many centuries, should have been a natural target for Communist repression. Mao Tse-tung has repeatedly emphasized that the ideals of Confucius and the advocacy of the ancient rules of conduct and education were vestiges of a semifeudal stage in China's historical development and must be overthrown and entirely reformed. In other words, according to Mao, China's traditional culture must be entirely revolutionized on Marxist-Leninist grounds.

In a Communist version of the history of Chinese philosophy, Confucius is portrayed as an idealist seeking to preserve and advance the interests of a declining feudal aristocracy. The Communists are much too clever, however, to abandon entirely China's cultural tradition. After all, Confucius can be appealed to as support for revolutionary and reforming action, and he can be pictured as a champion of the rights of the common people. Recent efforts on the part of Communist propagandists to picture Mao as a sage, a superior teacher, and father of the Chinese people are blatant attempts to play upon the latent Chinese respect for Confucius and the Confucian ideal man. Obviously, a massive effort is being made by the Chinese Communists to reeducate (communize) the Chinese people. What shall become of Confucius and the residual effect of Confucianism in China as a result of the Communist effort is not yet clear. The Confucian element in the Chinese tradition has been a strikingly ineradicable element for over two thousand years. On the other hand, Communism has exhibited itself as one of the most powerful revolutionary forces in human history.

TAOISM

In the primitive Chinese's worship of his ancestors, the only requirement at all resembling a moral principle was that the external forms of sacrifice be scrupulously maintained. Confucius taught that both individual and social order depended upon a system of moral laws and obligations far more elaborate and essential than the barren traditionalism of ancestral offerings. When the Chinese first began to trouble themselves about the problem of the spirit or manner in which sacrifice was undertaken, Confucius had already been teaching his ethic of "humanheartedness" and social duty. If a man questioned his worthiness to sacrifice to his ancestors, let him consult his social conscience, said Confucius, in order to discover whether he has fulfilled the duties concomitant with his place in society.

But if one was interested in preparing oneself for the ritual of communion with ancestors, there was another means of cleansing one's heart. In seeking ways to render themselves fit to engage in the traditional ancestor rites, the Chinese struck upon the way of quietism. They became preoccupied with the inner depths of the self and its relation to actuality. Rather than "turning outward" as Confucius had recommended, measuring themselves against an external social norm, they began to turn inward to create, or to reach, a state of purity or innocence. With a view to purifying themselves for ancestor rites, the Chinese learned to discipline their emotions, desires, thoughts, and actions, so as to bring about that tranquillity and peace which signify inner harmony. The problem was to suppress or still those myriad forces of the self which overlay and threaten to disturb the quiet center of man's being. It was seen as necessary that man break through the layers of disposition and habit built up through everyday living and get to the unsullied innocence of the self. To achieve such stillness or vacuity, one had to bring about a cessation of all those psychic activities which disturb the mind.

In the third and fourth centuries B.C., an extensive quest was initiated to discover disciplines that could assist in bringing about a peaceful spirit and an equanimity of mind. The disciplines that were created or learned during this period were quite similar to the yoga discipline of Hinduism and the dhyana discipline of the Buddhism of the sixth century A.D. in China. By employing these disciplines, men not only achieved states of extraordinary consciousness, but they claimed also to have harnessed a kind of power over themselves and their relations with the world. Their visions in trances were always accompanied by feelings of authoritativeness and finality. A philosophical and mystical Taoism most naturally grew out of this movement, emphasizing the way of internal meditation, spontaneity, nature mysticism, harmony of self and world, simplicity, and, at times, asceticism.

The oldest texts of Taoism are the *Lao Tzu,* or the *Tao Te Ching,* and the *Chuang Tzu.* The *Tao Te Ching* was supposed to have been written by Lao Tzu, a minor official of the state of Lu and an early teacher of Confucius. Few scholars credit this version of the genesis of the *Tao Te Ching,* for internal evidence of the text indicates a later date for the book. But if uncertainty exists regarding the authorship of this Taoist masterpiece, there is no debate regarding the effect that this work has had upon the development of Taoist religion and philosophy. It is the "Book of the Power (Virtue) of the Way," and it is composed in such a way as to contain several layers of meaning. On the surface it offers practical advice for moral action and conduct, but as one presses beyond this level, one begins to encounter its more mystical and metaphysical levels with their doctrines of inaction, vacuity, spontaneity, the immanence of Tao in everything, and the relativity of opposites.

The *Chuang Tzu* also presents a problem of authorship. We do know that Chuang Tzu (369–286 B.C.), a minor government official in the state of Meng, wrote part of it. One tradition tells us that Chuang Tzu spent most of his life as a hermit, writing and meditating. Characteristic of the *Chuang Tzu* is its style, marked by humor, satire, and fantasy. Deeply concerned with individual spirituality, it explores the mysteries of the eternal Tao with a grace and appeal that has made it a favorite Taoist work. Of particular importance is its striking portrayal of the unceasing metamorphoses of all things in nature.

The primary source of religious Taoism is the Taoist Canon, a bible of 1,120 volumes. The textual material of this canon includes such different sorts of material as the books of Lao Tzu and Chuang Tzu, books of alchemy, treatises on magic and longevity, ramblings by saints in states of trance, tracts on the elixir of life, volumes of purported revelations, and so on.

Taoism is probably the oldest popular religion of China, and the philosophical-mystical schools that flourished in the third and fourth centuries B.C. were significant currents of thought and practice within the greater stream that constituted Taoism. Like Confucianism, Taoism is a cultural phenomenon in China that has a strong religious component but is not reducible to its religiosity. As a cultural force, Taoism has included many sorts of activity; e.g., maritime expeditions in search of the "blessed Isles"; sexual orgies; philosophical Taoism; worship of a pantheon of gods; monasteries for meditation and yogic discipline; secret political cults; and so forth. As a religious phenomenon, Taoism, through the centuries, has developed an enormous plethora of deities representing such disparate things as abstract concepts, persons, and vocations. It has given its approval to almost every sort of religious extravagance that the imagination could conjure, manifesting the free play of moribund superstition and fantasy. In its rivalry with Buddhism for the masses of the Chinese population, it made every effort to develop a consistent doctrine and discipline, but like Buddhism in China, it responded to every pressure from the laity to provide whatever succor or spiritual comfort was required by the people.

To trace the proliferation of doctrine and practice in the Taoist religion is beyond the scope of our present task. Its degeneration into magic, superstition, and fantasy was a result of its attempts to be all things to all men, and curiously, it parallels the history of Buddhism in China in this respect. Philosophical and mystical Taoism of the *Lao Tzu* and the *Chuang Tzu,* however, had a dramatic impact upon the development of Buddhism in China and upon later revivals of Confucian doctrine. Philosophical Taoism had an immense effect upon the development of the most prominent school of Buddhism in China, Ch'an Buddhism (Zen Buddhism to Japan); whereas Neo-Confucianism is frequently referred to as philosophical Taoism in disguise.

CHINESE BUDDHISM

Chinese Buddhism is a form of Buddhism produced by the fruitful interaction of the Indian Buddhist tradition with the Chinese cultural and philosophical traditions. The Buddhist movement had its origin in India in the fifth century B.C. Founded by a young aristocrat of the Sakya clan named Gautama (later known as the Buddha), it spread throughout India and eventually into China. The Buddha (560–480 B.C.) was a contemporary of Confucius. As a young man, he gave up a leisurely existence in his father's palace to set out upon a quest for spiritual illumination. After wandering in the forest for several years, meditating upon the limiting conditions of human life—suffering, death, and rebirth—he finally achieved absolute enlightenment. He discovered that desire was the architect of recurring life and that man could be liberated from misery and rebirth only by bringing about a cessation of desire. He taught a "middle path" between unthinking, uncontrolled involvement in life and a radical asceticism and isolationism. Man must achieve equanimity of mind and spirit by exploding the illusions of samsara (the circle of life, suffering, and rebirth).

During the Buddha's lifetime, he founded an order of monks dedicated to Buddhist ideals and practicing vows of poverty, chastity, and noninjury. Following his death, Buddhism in India grew sparsely until the time of the Emperor Asoka (273–232 B.C.), when it became the state religion and underwent tremendous growth both in popularity and influence. It was following the period of Asoka's reign that Buddhism split into two main divisions, Mahayana, the "larger vehicle" or "career," and Hinayana, the "smaller vehicle" or "career," a division emphasized by the advocates of Mahayana who felt that the earlier forms of Buddhism represented a "lesser career" for the ideal Buddhist. Early Buddhism had as its hero the Arhat, a solitary monk seeking liberation or Nirvana by his own strenuous discipline and meditation. In contrast, the Mahayana cherished a different kind of hero, the Bodhisattva, a being qualified to enter Nirvana or enlightenment, but who renounces his final liberation until every sentient being in the universe has been saved. The Bodhisattva displays infinite compassion for the plight of other beings and will sacrifice his own release until that moment when all creatures may be released.

The Mahayanists and Hinayanists disagreed on many matters relating to doctrine, rules for the monastic order, and what constituted authoritative Buddhist scripture. But Mahayana was the wave of the future for Buddhism. Its emotional fervor and compassionate concern made it attractive and compelling to the mass of humanity seeking liberation from an oppressive and hateful existence. The concept of a "larger vehicle" in which all could ride to the farther shores of liberation and enlightenment appealed to a generation of men grown weary of the world. Moreover, Mahayana was tolerant, evolutionary, and accommodating. It achieved prominence in India because it transformed the early, austere practices of Buddhism into warm, charitable, living concerns. In its popular forms, it provided a profusion of sacred beings who were readily accessible to the worshiper and who assisted the faithful in achieving salvation. Superstition, magic, and mythological beings were entirely absent from early Buddhism, but Mahayana, in catering to popular taste, introduced all of these elements into the Buddhist tradition.

The traditional date given for the introduction of Buddhism

into China is A.D. 67, but it is probable that Buddhist communities existed in western China prior to this time. Although the Hinayana form of Buddhism was first carried into China by Buddhist missionaries and Chinese scholars returning from study in India, it was Mahayana Buddhism that struck root and flourished in Chinese soil. In the Tartar states in northwestern China, Buddhism made rapid advances so that by A.D. 381 almost everyone in that section of China was considered to be a Buddhist. It was during the three centuries spanning A.D. 220–589 that Buddhism enjoyed its most extensive period of growth in China, and we know that by the fifth and sixth centuries A.D. Buddhism was a dynamic movement in China, because Confucian literature of that era protests vigorously against the proliferation of Buddhist monasteries, and raises charges of conspiracy against the Buddhist monastic order. China was at this time being swept by barbarian invasions and was subject to political disunity and internal chaos, while the masses were crushed between oppressive rulers and inhuman landowners. Under such circumstances it is not surprising that a religious movement advocating an ethic of love and compassion and giving the promise of salvation would meet with a warm response from the Chinese masses.

However, viewed from another perspective, it is truly remarkable that Buddhism enjoyed the success it did in China, given the ancient traditions of the Chinese. Certain characteristics of Buddhism militated against its success in China, as, for example, its ideal of celibacy, which must have been repugnant to the popular Chinese belief that it was man's sacred duty to guarantee the perpetuation of the family. Buddhism's asceticism must also have been offensive to the Confucian sentiments of the ruling class whose ideal of the "gentleman sage" was in sharp contrast to the ideal of the mendicant in Buddhism. But the early Buddhists in China were exceptionally clever in finding ways to ingratiate themselves with the Chinese masses and the power elite. For example, Buddhist monks willingly took charge of funeral and memorial ceremonies in Chinese communities. In so doing, they played a part in the most significant religious traditions of the family, the maintenance of sacrifices to ancestral spirits. More importantly, Buddhism offered solace and hope to the common man who could not hope to comprehend the high scholarship of the Confucian teachings. The Mahayana forms of Buddhism that achieved widespread popularity in China offered salvation to all people from a world that was oppressive and hellish. In the divine figures and heroic saints (Bodhisattvas), Buddhism made available powerful forces ready to assist the common man.

Chinese Buddhism may roughly be divided into four schools or sects. Most of these schools developed between the fourth and eighth centuries A.D., and no significant new current of Buddhist thought has arisen in China since that time. All the major sects of Chinese Buddhism are Mahayana. Although we cannot enter into a thorough analysis of their diverse doctrines, practices, and history, we can consider briefly their origin and distinguishing doctrines.

1. *The Pure Land School.* Ching-t'u, or the Pure Land School, dates from the fourth century A.D. and was founded by Hui-Yuan. Sometimes called the "white lotus creed," it teaches salvation by faith in Amitabha, who, according to legend, was once a monk living such a perfect existence that he brought into being a Buddhist paradise, a land of bliss. Elevated to Buddhahood by those who worshiped him, he saved all those who invoked his name or meditated upon him. Such a doctrine had extensive popular appeal since it offered emancipation without the necessity for strenuous acts of moral discipline and intellectual endeavor. Some form of this doctrine is found in every school of Chinese Buddhism.

2. *The Intuitive or Meditation School.* Ch'an, or the Meditation School, dates from the visit of Bodhidharma to China in A.D. 520. This Indian saint is reckoned as the founder of the Ch'an School and the twenty-eighth patriarch of Buddhism. His teachings are summed up in four lines:

> A special tradition outside the scriptures:
> Not to depend on books or letters:

To point direct to the heart of man:
To see one's own nature and become Buddha.

The Ch'an sect emphasized the realization of Nirvana by a sudden illumination (satori in Japanese Zen). The basic commitment of the school was to the principle of dhyana (meditation) by which one achieved complete enlightenment. The Ch'an sect eventually split into two schools, Northern and Southern. The Northern School of Ch'an taught that the achievement of enlightenment was a gradual process involving scriptural study, meditative disciplines, and observance of traditional moral duties. It passed out of existence before the tenth century A.D. The Southern School of Ch'an advocated the doctrines of sudden illumination, nonreliance upon scriptures and the traditional methods for achieving enlightenment. One important branch of the Southern School of Ch'an was the sect called Lin-chi. It was founded by I-Hsuan in about A.D. 867 and concentrated on the doctrine of sudden illumination. I-Hsuan insisted that a teacher was essential to maturation toward enlightenment and that most teaching was nonverbal. He placed little emphasis upon prayer, meditation, and study. The Lin-chi School of Ch'an regards knowledge of the Buddha-nature as an end to be pursued for itself alone. This school achieved tremendous success, so that most monasteries in China at the turn of the twentieth century professed allegiance to the Lin-chi School.

3. *The Syncretist School.* T'ien-t'ai, the Syncretist School, was founded in the sixth century by Chih-I (A.D. 531–597). Rejecting the view that contemplation or meditation was sufficient for enlightenment, this school taught that there were a variety of paths to illumination. It accepted the premise that the Buddha-nature was present in all living beings, but insisted that humans required the assistance of teachers, scriptures, and disciplines in order to achieve or realize that nature. Chih-I believed that the Lotus Sutra, a profound Mahayanist text, contained the quintessence of Buddhist truth. However, he also maintained that all scripture and all forms of Buddhist discipline were revelatory in

their own ways to certain people at certain times. Every effort was made by this school to unite the divergent forces of Buddhism, particularly to heal the breach between Hinayana and Mahayana. To achieve this reunification, Chih-I developed an elaborate theory of the different stages of a religion's development and of degrees of religious truth in an attempt to provide a theological foundation for Buddhist cooperation and unity. He sought to find a meaningful place for every form of religious exercise in the Buddhist faith. This movement produced a great monastic establishment and a series of famous Buddhist scholars.

4. *The Mystery or True Word School.* Chen-yen, the True Word School, was founded in the eighth century. It taught an elaborate, symbolic pantheism, emphasizing the worship of Vairocana, a solar Buddha. In many ways, the Chen-yen School of Buddhism parallels the development of Tantrism in Hinduism. It displays the same preoccupation with spells, magic, and fetishism which characterized the Tantric movement in both Hinduism and Buddhism. While this school does not deny the efficacy of asceticism, moral discipline, and intellectual study in achieving emancipation, it indicates that the same results can be achieved by magical formulas and ceremony. The Chen-yen School played a major role in reshaping the traditional funeral rites of the Chinese. An interesting teaching of the school regarding funeral ceremonies was that the ritual could symbolically represent and literally control the fate of the departed soul. If, for example, the ceremony included the withdrawal of a graven image (a doll) from a burning fire, then what was *symbolically represented* and *actually accomplished* was the rescue of a departed soul from the burning fires of a Buddhist hell. The Chen-yen School in its popular aspects achieved great success because it played upon the superstitions of the Chinese people.

CHAPTER II

The Spirit
of Chinese Philosophy

FUNG YU-LAN

There are all kinds and conditions of men. With regard to any one of these kinds, there is the highest form of achievement of which the members of that kind are capable. Take, for example, the men engaged in the practical administration of political affairs. The highest form of achievement in that class is that of the great statesman. So also in the field of art, the highest form of achievement of which artists are capable is that of the great artist. Although there are all these different classes of men, yet all the members of them also belong to the class *homo*. Of the members of this all-embracing class, the men who achieve the highest of which man is capable reach the stature of being sages. This amounts to saying that the highest achievement of man *qua* man is in what we call the transcendent sphere.

If men wish to attain to the transcendent sphere do they necessarily have to leave that general life in society which men enjoy in common, or even to divorce themselves from life? This is a problem. For the philosopher who deals with the transcendent sphere, the easiest tendency is to say "This is necessary." The Buddha said that life itself is the root and fountain-head of the misery of life. Plato also said that the body is the prison of the soul. And some of the Taoists have said, "Life is an excrescence, a tumour, and death is to be taken as the breaking of the tumour."

Reprinted from Fung Yu-Lan, *The Spirit of Chinese Philosophy,* translated by E. R. Hughes (London: Kegan Paul, Trench, Trubner & Co., 1947), pages 1–4. Copyright © 1962 by E. R. Hughes. Used by permission of Harold Ober Associates Incorporated and Routledge & Kegan Paul Ltd.

Here is a view which entails separation from what may be said to be the net of the matter-corrupted world. If the highest sphere is to be reached, that entails separation from the manner of living common to our fellows in general. Indeed, separation from life entirely is entailed. Only so can the final liberation be obtained. This kind of philosophy is what is generally known as "other-worldly philosophy." The life of which this other-worldly philosophy speaks is a sublime one, but it is incompatible with the manner of life maintained in common among men. This manner of life in society is what the Chinese philosophical tradition calls men's relations in their daily functioning, and this is incompatible with the other-worldly philosophical theory as to the highest life of all. We speak of the other-worldly philosophy as sublime but not concerned with the mean of common activity.

There are some philosophies which emphasize men's relations in their daily functioning. They speak about this and about morality but they either are unable to—or at any rate do not—speak of the highest life of all. These philosophies are what are generally described as "this-worldly"; and in truth they are not worthy to be called philosophies. We may describe them as concerned with performing the common task, but not attaining to the sublime. From the point of view of a this-worldly philosophy, an other-worldly philosophy is too idealistic, of no practical use, negative; it is what is known as steeped in emptiness. From the point of view of an other-worldly philosophy, a this-worldly philosophy is too empirical, too superficial: it may be positive, but it is like the quick walking of a man who has taken the wrong road; the quicker he walks the more he deviates from the right road.

There are many people who say that Chinese philosophy is a this-worldly philosophy. This opinion cannot be said to be either wholly right or wholly wrong.

On a superficial view these words are not wholly wrong, because on that view Chinese philosophy, irrespective of its different schools of thought, directly or indirectly concerns itself with government and ethics. It appears to emphasize society not the universe, the daily functioning of human relations and not hell and heaven, man's present life and not his life in a world to come. Mencius said, "The sage is the acme in human relations," and the sentence taken literally means that the sage is the morally perfect man in society. This ideal man being of this world, it seems that what Chinese philosophy calls a sage is a very different order of person from the Buddha in Buddhism and the saint in the Christian religion.

This, however, is only the superficial view of the question. Chinese philosophy cannot be understood in this over-simple way. So far as the main tenets of its tradition are concerned, if we understand them, they cannot be said to be wholly this-worldly, just as, of course, they cannot be said to be wholly other-worldly. We may use a newly coined expression and say that this philosophy is world-transcending. The meaning of this is that it is both of this world and of the other world.

Chinese philosophy has one main tradition, one main stream of thought. This tradition is that it aims at a particular kind of highest life. But this kind of highest life, high though it is, is not divorced from the daily functioning of human relations. Thus it is both of this world and of the other world, and we maintain that it "both attains to the sublime and yet performs the common tasks." What Chinese philosophy aims at is the highest of realms, one which transcends the daily functioning of human relations, although it also comes within the scope of this daily functioning. That is: "It is not divorced from daily regular activity, yet it goes straight to what was before the heavens." The first of these two expressions represents the this-worldly side, the second the other-worldly side. That is to say that, both sides being present, Chinese philosophy is what we describe it to be, namely world-transcending. Because it is of this world it is concerned with common activity: because it is other-worldly it reaches up to the sublime: its attention is directed to both worlds, its concern is with both worlds.

Having this kind of spirit, it is at one and the same time both extremely idealistic and extremely realistic, extremely practical, though not in a shallow way. So also it is positive, but not in the sense of a man taking the wrong road and the faster he walks the more he deviates from the right road.

This-worldliness and other-worldliness stand in contrast to each other as do idealism and realism; and this is the antithesis between what we describe as the sublime and common activity. In ancient Chinese philosophy the antithesis was made between what was called "the inner" and "the outer," "the root," and "the branches" and "the fine" and "the coarse"; and after the Han era there was the contrast between what was called "the abstruse" and "the daily task," the contrast between abandoning the world and being in the world, between the active and the contemplative, between the essence and its functioning. All these contrasts are perhaps the same as the contrast between the sublime and the common, or (at any rate) these contrasts are of the same kind. In a world-transcending philosophy and its accompanying manner of life all these contrasts do not continue to be antithetical. This does not mean that, to put it shortly, they are abolished, but that according to the world-transcending viewpoint they are made to become a whole. The sublime and the common still exist with all their differences, but they are synthesized into one whole. How can this be done? This is one problem which Chinese philosophy attempts to solve, and herein lies the spirit of that philosophy, whilst in the solution it gives lies the contribution which it makes to the study of philosophy.

The philosophers of China hold that the highest life of all, that at which philosophy aims, is both this-worldly and other-worldly; and that the men who are in possession of this highest life are the sages. The life of the sage is a transcendent one, and the spiritual achievement of the Chinese sages corresponds to the saint's achievement in Buddhism and the West. They all come under the same head. But to transcend the world does not mean to be divorced from the world, and therefore the Chinese sage is not the kind of sage who is so sublime that he is not concerned about the business of the world. His character is described as one of sageness in its essence and kingliness in its manifestation. That is to say that in his inner sageness he accomplishes spiritual cultivation, in his outward kingliness he functions in society. It is not necessary that a sage should be the actual head of the government in his society. With regard to practical politics, for the most part the sage certainly has no opportunity to be such; and when the statement is made "sage within and king without" it only means that he who has the noblest spirit should theoretically be king. As to whether he actually had or had not the opportunity to be king, that is immaterial.

Since the character of the sage is one of sageness within and kingliness without, philosophy, according to the Chinese tradition, is a branch of learning which exists to enable men to possess this kind of character. Therefore what philosophy discusses is what the philosophers of China describe as the Tao (Way) of "sageness within and kingliness without."

In China, whatever the school of thought, all Chinese philosophy maintains this Tao in one way or another. But not every school satisfies the criterion of both attaining to the sublime and performing the common task. There are some schools which over-emphasize the sublime, some which over-emphasize the common. This means that some of the philosophies in China are near to being other-worldly, others near to being this-worldly. In the history of Chinese philosophy, from first to last, the more influential philosophers have been those who have attempted to synthesize the two sides, the sublime and the common.

CHAPTER III

Confucianism

Confucius, the Philosopher

H. G. Creel

The number of books that have been written about the ideas of Confucius is staggering. Probably no other philosopher has been the subject of more discussion. Yet our reliable knowledge of his philosophy remains regrettably meager. For this there are several reasons. Very important is the fact that his type of thinking was an extremely evanescent phenomenon. Indeed, it was almost necessarily so.

What happened in Confucius' day has occurred more than once. Old religious beliefs and old social, economic, and political patterns had persisted for many centuries. But then, as the political pattern of early Chou feudalism gradually broke down, every one of the other spheres was affected. The ties that had long held men together failed, bringing relative freedom to the individual and near chaos to society. A very similar crisis occurred in Egypt, around 2100 B.C. Something comparable happened in ancient Greece. As Windelband describes it: "The more the luxuriant

Reprinted from H. G. Creel, *Confucius: The Man and the Myth* (New York: The John Day Company, Inc., 1949; London: Routledge & Kegan Paul Ltd., 1951), pages 109–141. Copyright © 1949 by Herrlee Glessner Creel. Used by permission of The John Day Company, Inc., and Routledge & Kegan Paul Ltd.

development of individualism loosened the old bonds of the common consciousness, of faith, and of morals, and threatened the youthful civilization of Greece with the danger of anarchy, the more pressing did individual men, prominent by their position in life, their insight, and their character, find the duty of recovering in their own reflection the measure that was becoming lost." In Greece, such conditions gave us the philosophy of Socrates. In China, they gave us that of Confucius.

In times of such moral and political crisis, men are thrown back upon their essential humanity. It is no longer enough merely to conjure by the old gods and quote the old authorities, for they command but a dubious respect. It is necessary to get down to fundamentals, to deal with things that all men can understand. Those who dare to pioneer in such times do not win easy acceptance of their ideas. The need constantly to contend with sceptical criticism keeps their philosophy lean and hard.

Such philosophies have a universal quality. They may employ some terms that have little meaning for us. Confucius may speak of "Heaven" as the guarantor of his mission; Socrates may talk of "beauty" as a thing existing in itself apart from any beautiful object; and we may not agree with them. Yet despite the difference in time and culture they seem to speak our language. We feel that they are dealing with real problems and that what they say may make some contribution toward a solution.

Such philosophies cannot last. If they are successful, their very success leads to their perversion. Those who inherit them elaborate their concepts far beyond their original forms. The crisis passes, and society is stabilized. New institutions replace the old, and philosophy conforms to the existing order. In Egypt, according to John A. Wilson, the crisis attending the collapse of the Old Kingdom brought "social-moral advances" under the Middle Kingdom, which were gradually lost under the Empire; thus the earlier individualism was replaced by a sense of man's helplessness, and the pattern became "conforming and formalistic." The philosophical ideas of Socrates, elaborated by Plato, eventuated in the complex mystical Neo-Platonism of Plotinus and Porphyry. Similarly, the predominantly ethical and rational teachings of

Confucius were so altered within three hundred years that the famous Han Confucianist, Tung Chung-shu, preached to his emperor a doctrine in which morality was inextricably mingled with an elaborate technique for the reading of omens and the practice of magic on a cosmic scale. In each of these cases, the later philosophy flourished centuries nearer to our own day, yet intellectually they seem incomparably more remote from us than the earlier.

For the philosophy of Confucius we have two principal kinds of sources. On the one hand there is the *Analects,* not written by him but in the main composed near his own time and on the basis of traditions preserved by his disciples. On the other, we have a variety of later works (some falsely attributed to his authorship) that interpret his thought in terms of the later Confucianism. For the Socratic tradition the case is in some degree comparable since there are on the one hand the works of Plato and Xenophon, who knew him, while on the other we have the elaborations of the philosophy he founded in Neo-Platonism. Yet few would try to work back from the Neo-Platonists to reconstruct the philosophy of Socrates; the usual practice is rather to study such testimony as that of Plato and Xenophon, to determine how much of it may be believed. For Confucius, however, the common practice has been the opposite, and the most prodigious efforts have been directed toward bringing his thought into line with the later Confucian metaphysics. In reversing this approach and limiting our study to the early sources alone, we must resign ourselves in advance to a relatively meager harvest. But though what we learn may not be extensive it will (if we interpret our materials correctly) be true.

Our first problem concerns the source of Confucius' ideas. He has often been represented as one who was merely attempting to revive the glories of a real or fancied golden age of antiquity. The disciple Tzǔ-kung declared that Confucius needed no teacher in the ordinary sense since he was able to learn of the doctrines of the early Chou rulers, King Wên and King Wu. Mencius said that Confucius transmitted a teaching handed down from the mythical early emperors, Yao and Shun. One contemporary Chinese scholar has asserted that Confucius was not merely a reactionary but in fact a "counter-revolutionary" since (in this scholar's opinion) his whole desire was to undo the changes that had taken place in Chinese life and restore the past.

We shall defer until the following chapter a thorough investigation of the degree of Confucius' dependence upon antiquity. Here it may be predicted, however, that when we have examined the evidence we shall conclude that, on the one hand, Confucius did indeed talk about antiquity and derive some of his important ideas from that source, but on the other he did not even pretend that he was trying to revive antiquity, and he could not well have found some of his most basic conceptions there. In important respects he was, in fact, a revolutionary, albeit a discreet one.

We have already seen that Confucius was born in a period of great political and social change. This is a phenomenon of which we still know altogether too little, despite the excellent work that various Chinese scholars have done on it in recent years. Even in art this was a time of change, and it was a time in which art (like Confucius) looked to the great days of the past for some of its inspiration. Bernhard Karlgren has pointed out that "during the 7th–3rd centuries B.C. the Chinese world was already advanced enough to allow of a conscious artistic renaissance movement, which incorporated elements now already ancient and venerated. . . ." In art, however, as in thought, the old was so transmuted that the result was altogether new in character.

What, we must ask, was the particular role of Confucius in this cultural revolution? He was not its instigator, since it was an upheaval caused by forces beyond his control and was already under way before he was born. Some students have suggested that Confucius somehow happened to get the credit for ideas that were in fact developed by far more capable men before his time. In various works, especially the *Tso Chuan*, there appear several statesmen who, living shortly before Confucius, are quoted as having expressed ideas remarkably like his; in fact, their language is sometimes virtually identical with what we find in the *Analects*. This fact has long been noted by Chinese scholars; one has praised these statesmen as being far more advanced in their thinking than was Confucius. He noted admiringly that they figure in the *Tso Chuan* as veritable walking encyclopedias, informed on every subject. He failed to add, however, that the knowledge of such men was so extensive that they were able (according to the *Tso Chuan*) to predict political events even as much as a century in the future, with the most uncanny accuracy.

It is obvious that most if not all of such prophecies were written long after the event, rather than having been spoken by the men to whom they are attributed. It also seems quite certain that many, if not all, of the fine "Confucian" speeches that the *Tso Chuan* puts into the mouths of its various characters were written, when the *Tso Chuan* itself was written, long after the death of Confucius, at a time when such ideas had become common currency.

This does not mean that the men themselves did not exist. They did, and they were undoubtedly able and wise. They may have had ideas very like those of Confucius, and have greatly influenced his thinking; this is quite possible. But we cannot tell whether it is true because we do not have expositions of their ideas in early and unimpeachable works. Yet one point is clear: if Confucius did take over, in significant degree, the ideas of some recent predecessor, that fact is never revealed in the *Analects* nor even in the writings of his enemies. On the contrary, tradition emphasizes his uniqueness. It seems clear that his role, in the changing world in which he found himself, was that of one who articulated and rationalized those changes which he found desirable, tried to suppress those of which he disapproved, and attempted to guide the course of Chinese culture in the way he believed it should go.

As background for our inquiry into his philosophy, let us consider the views of Confucius on religion. Religion is usually conservative, and in so far as we can tell there had been no major change in religion for centuries. In the Shang period, before 1122 B.C., the kings and presumably others had sacrificed elaborately to their ancestors and to other spirits; especially important was a powerful spirit called Ti. They believed that the spirits, and especially their ancestors, supervised human destinies; if pleased they bestowed success, if displeased they scourged mankind with various ills, from defeat in war to toothaches. The Shang people sacrificed to avert disaster and obtain felicity, and they constantly consulted the wishes of their gods through divination.

The Chou, who conquered the Shang, took over some phases of Shang religion and combined them with their own. The principal deity of the Chou was called T'ien; the early form of this character was simply a drawing of a large and therefore important man. From a variety of evidence, we can reconstruct its probable history. It came to refer to the most important men of all, the former kings who had died and taken up their abode in the heavens. As a sort of "council of the gods" they controlled human destinies. Then, because Chinese does not distinguish singular and plural, T'ien came to be thought of as singular, an overruling Providence located in the sky. The same word also came to be used for the material heavens. Thus there was derived the concept of Heaven as a rather impersonal intelligence. When the Chou conquered the Shang, they equated their Heaven with Ti, the Shang deity, as the Romans identified some of their gods with those of the Greeks.

Religion occupied a central place in the culture. The king was called the "Son of Heaven," and ruled by virtue of the help of his great ancestors. Lesser aristocrats were what they were because they had powerful ancestors. Sacrifices to these and other powerful deities were state ceremonies, more important for a good harvest than weeding, for victory than drilling troops. With increased sophistication, however, the rise of scepticism was inevitable. Improved communications brought men into contact with varying beliefs and customs. Treaties were constantly made which were supposed to be guaranteed by the spirits, and as constantly broken; but he who suffered was usually not the breaker but he who had the weaker army. Noble families fell into disgrace and penury, casting doubt on the power of their ancestral spirits. We know little of the details of the rise of scepticism since we have virtually no literature that stems from the period immediately preceding the time of Confucius, but that it did arise is clear. Mo Tzŭ, who was born about the time Confucius died, charged that the Confucians considered "Heaven to be without intelligence, and the spirits of the dead to be without consciousness."

The attitude of Confucius himself toward religion was complex. Some aspects of the traditional religion he approved and emphasized. Others he disapproved and tried either to transform or suppress. In general, however, he refrained from raising fundamental religious issues. This may be interpreted either as cowardice or as wisdom. The fact is that he was attempting to make what he considered vital reforms, of a political and social nature, on bases which were for the most part not metaphysical. It would not have served and might have hindered his purpose to argue metaphysics. He did not do so, and we are sometimes left in doubt as to what he did believe.

Quite clearly, Confucius took an almost childlike pleasure in religious ritual as such. Yet this tells us little about his belief; many sceptical intellectuals delight in "High Church" ceremonial. Confucius also emphasized the duty of children to spend three years in mourning for their parents. To Western minds this seems an excessive measure of devotion, yet it does not conclusively prove a belief in life after death; Confucius could have insisted upon it merely as an aspect of family solidarity.

We have few statements from Confucius about spirits. In fact, it is said specifically that "the Master did not speak about strange phenomena [such as omens], feats of strength, disorders, or spirits." He is quoted, it is true, as having praised the mythical ruler, Yü, for being "extremely filial toward the spirits." However, when Tzŭ-lu asked him how to serve the spirits he replied, "You are not yet able to serve men; how can you serve spirits?" Tzŭ-lu then asked about death, and was told, "You do not yet understand life; how can you understand death?" The disciple Fan

Ch'ih asked about wisdom; Confucius told him, "It is to attend diligently to those concerns which are proper to the people; and to respect the spirits and maintain the proper distance from them." This last passage has been translated as "while respecting spiritual beings, to keep aloof from them," and considered to be clear evidence of agnosticism. But this does not accord with the understanding of most Chinese commentators, and its usefulness as evidence is doubtful. Immanuel Kant has pointed out that men are directed by the principle of respect "to preserve a certain distance from each other," and we can scarcely hold that less is due to spirits. Confucius' view seems to have been that one should do for them all that was proper but should not fawn upon them with excessive attentions, any more than one should upon a ruler or an official superior.

Although there are several passages on sacrifice in the *Analects,* they do not (with one exception, which we shall discuss later) tell us clearly whether Confucius believed there was actual efficacy in the ceremony, or valued it merely as a social act. It is significant, however, that among the activities which he positively advocated for remedying the world's ills, neither sacrifice nor any other religious activity seems to have been included. As for prayer, we have already seen that he declined to have it made in his behalf even though he was very ill, declaring that he had "done his praying long ago," presumably with deeds rather than words.

If we look for a firm and frankly stated conviction on the part of Confucius as to things religious, we shall find it most clearly in connection with T'ien, Heaven. It is an interesting fact that nowhere in the *Analects* does he mention the name of the more personally conceived aspect of the same deity, Ti. He looked upon Heaven, however, as the author of his power, which had entrusted him with a sacred mission as the champion of China's culture. In danger, he dismissed his enemies as powerless against him in the face of Heaven. In despondency, he took comfort in the fact that Heaven, at least, understood him. When accused of wrongdoing, he called upon Heaven to witness his innocence. Upon the death of his favorite disciple, Yen Hui, he declared, "Heaven is destroying me!"

This last passage is best understood as a simple cry of anguish, not as meaning that Confucius considered Heaven to be taking special and malevolent action against him. For we have no indication that Confucius conceived of Heaven in this manner. Anciently it had been so conceived. Thus we read repeatedly in the *Book of History* and the *Book of Poetry*, and in inscriptions on early bronzes, that Heaven supervised the change of dynasties, punishing vice by extinguishing the line of the oppressive ruler and rewarding virtue by setting up the good as his successor. Such works spoke of Heaven as "waiting for five years" to see whether an evil king would change his ways, and as "sending down destruction" and becoming "angry." King Ch'êng, the son of the founder of the Chou dynasty, was quoted as saying, on his deathbed, "Heaven has sent down illness upon me."

All of this seems to hark back to the origin of "Heaven" as a collective name for the great ancestors, who lived above and constantly watched the conduct of their descendants, rewarding or punishing as they pleased. For Confucius, however, Heaven was far less personal. He tells us little of how he did conceive it; the disciple Tzŭ-kung said that the Master did not talk about "the way of Heaven." Yet it seems clear that Confucius thought of Heaven as an impersonal ethical force, a cosmic counterpart of the ethical sense in man, a guarantee that somehow there is sympathy with man's sense of right in the very nature of the universe.

This did not mean, however, that justice must triumph or that virtue must certainly lead to success. If Confucius had ever supposed that this were true his own career, as well as history, must have disillusioned him. We never find him promising success as the reward for virtue. He does say that it tends toward success, just as oppressive conduct on the part of a ruler tends to bring about his downfall, but there is no simple and certain correlation between these things. Rather, the greatest rewards of virtue are the peace of mind it brings, and the satisfaction which comes from helping others. One's reasons for acting as one ought have nothing directly to do with prosperity or its reverse. "The Master said, 'A gentleman, in making his plans, thinks of the Way; he does not think of making a living. Even if one tills the soil, he may sometimes suffer hunger; and if one studies, he may be able to earn a high salary. But the concern of the gentleman is about the progress of the Way; he does not worry about poverty.' "

This is very different from what we commonly find in the earlier literature and bronze inscriptions. There, religious observances and especially sacrifice are regarded as something almost resembling a barter transaction. In the *Book of Poetry* a king, whose realm is devastated by drought, asks why Heaven and his ancestors are thus afflicting him, saying, "There is no spirit to whom I have not sacrificed and no victim that I have grudged. ... Why am I not heard?" Time after time we read in this work and in the *Book of History* that the purpose of sacrifice is to secure blessings. The inscriptions on scores if not hundreds of bronze sacrificial vessels tell us quite frankly that they were made for the purpose of seeking blessings such as long life, long enjoyment of office, many sons and grandsons, and so on. A bronze bell cast in the state of Ch'i, at about the time when Confucius was born, recounts at particular length and in special detail the benefits its maker expected from his ancestors in return for his piety. Mo Tzŭ, who lived just after Confucius, condemned the practice of "offering one pig and asking for a hundred blessings"; but he seems to have been bothered chiefly by the inequity of this bargain, for he clearly believed that the spirits were influenced, in their bestowal of blessings, by the quantity and quality of the offerings they received.

From all such thinking Confucius stood wholly apart. It is quite true that one can also find, in literature from a time much earlier than his, occasional statements to the effect that virtue as well as sacrifice is pleasing to Heaven. But if Confucius derived his ideas from these works, he must have selected only this aspect, for his emphasis was almost exclusively ethical.

He also rejected certain elements of the traditional religion that had been very important, such as, for instance, human sacrifice. In the Shang period great numbers of human beings were sacrificed. The practice continued under the Chou and is referred to at least twice in the *Book of Poetry* and some eleven times in the *Tso Chuan.* Of the instances of human sacrifice mentioned in the latter work, three took place during Confucius' lifetime, one in the state of Lu itself. Mo Tzŭ, just after Confucius, declared that those who advocated elaborate burial wanted large numbers of men, as many as hundreds in the case of an emperor, killed to attend important persons in death. When the "First Emperor" of the Ch'in dynasty was buried in 210 B.C., a large number of the women of his harem are reported to have been killed to follow him in death. As late as the first century B.C. a prince of the house of Han ordered that his slave musicians should follow him in death, and sixteen of them were forced to commit suicide when he died.

In the *Analects,* however, there is no mention of human sacrifice. Mencius quotes Confucius as having condemned even the burying of images of men with the dead, presumably because this might tend to suggest the burial of actual men. The *Records on Ceremonial* recounts an incident in which Confucius' disciple Tzŭ-ch'in is supposed to have prevented the killing of some persons at the funeral of his brother. Confucians in general opposed human sacrifice, ultimately with great success. Thus the last instance of human sacrifice mentioned in the preceding paragraph was severely punished. Even though the prince whose slaves were killed was descended from a Han emperor, his son was not allowed to succeed him, and his fief was abolished. The language of the criminal charge against him shows clearly that it was made on Confucian grounds. The Confucians not only reduced the practice of human sacrifice; they all but abolished the mention of it in the literature. Thus when it is mentioned in the *Tso Chuan* it is commonly censured, and several times is said not to have been practiced "in antiquity," which is far from true. Even in the twentieth century a number of archeologists refused to believe that the Shang had practiced human sacrifice, until the discovery of the skeletons of hundreds of decapitated victims proved it. The Confucians were so successful that they almost destroyed the traces of their own success.

Another important Confucian innovation in religion has gone

almost unnoticed. Before Confucius the most important possession of a ruler was his ancestors. They not only gave him legiti-
mate title to rule but provided the powerful help of the gods that
he must have for success in peace and victory in war. The *Book
of Poetry* tells us that the house of Chou had "three rulers in
Heaven, and the king is their counterpart in the capital." A lesser
ruler boasted, in an inscription on a bronze vessel, that his illustrious ancestors above "grandly open up a path for their descendant below."

Confucius ignored all this. He went further and declared that
it was not heredity but the qualities of the man himself that were
important. Something, it is not clear what, seems to have been
wrong with the heredity of the disciple Jan Yung. Confucius
declared, however, that this should in no way be held against
him. Furthermore, he said of Jan Yung alone among the disciples
that he might properly occupy the place of a ruler. This statement, concerning a man who seems to have been without eminent ancestors, is revolutionary; it quietly abolishes much that
had been central in the earlier religion.

This was, in effect, to say that a man's fitness to rule depended
on his own virtue and ability, which greatly reinforced the in-
centive to ethical conduct. This transition from ritual to ethical
thinking has occurred, of course, in many religions. It has been
remarked in ancient Egypt and in Mesopotamia; the instance
that comes most readily to mind is that of the Hebrew prophets.
The factor that makes Confucius unusual, if not unique, is the
degree to which he divorced ethics from dependence upon anything outside of the ordinary understanding of all intelligent
men. Max Weber has said, "In the absence of all metaphysics and
almost all residues of religious anchorage, Confucianism is rationalist to such a far-going extent that it stands at the extreme
boundary of what one might possibly call a 'religious' ethic. At
the same time, Confucianism is more rationalist and sober, in
the sense of the absence and the rejection of all non-utilitarian
yardsticks, than any other ethical system, with the possible exception of J. Bentham's."

It should be noted that Weber was speaking of Confucianism, not of Confucius. Nevertheless, these remarks will apply to Confucius himself if we note that Weber speaks of the absence of *"almost* all residues of religious anchorage." We have already seen that Confucius did retain, in the idea of Heaven, a sense of an impersonal ethical Providence. He seems also to have had a sense of an ideal cosmic harmony. This is probably the purport of the following passage: "Someone asked the meaning of the *ti* sacrifice. The Master replied, 'I do not know. He who knew its meaning would be able to deal with all things under heaven as easily as I show you this'—pointing to his palm." In this, and in some other passages, it is possible to see reference to a vaguely conceived universal order having some connection with religion. Yet even this is not stressed. It is there, but it is (to use Weber's term) a residue, a pale surviving counterpart of the ancient dominion of the all-powerful spirits.

Closely allied with this conception is that of *ming,* "decree," often translated as "fate." Used in this way, "decree" is an abbreviation of "decree of Heaven," although Confucius seldom used the latter expression. The book of *Mo Tzŭ* accuses the Confucians of saying that all things are determined by a fate that human effort cannot change. For some later Confucians this may have been true, but it was not the doctrine of Confucius. He used the term "decree" as a synonym for "life" or "life span"; but it is perfectly clear that he did not think that this was fixed and beyond any control by the individual, for he speaks of one who "in view of danger is prepared to give up his life" (literally "decree") rather than his principles. This would be nonsense if the span of life were fixed, so that the individual could do nothing about it.

There is one (and only one) passage that at first glance makes Confucius seem a fatalist. At one time while Tzŭ-lu held office with the Chi, a friend and colleague of Tzŭ-lu told Confucius that another of his colleagues was slandering Tzŭ-lu to the head of the Chi family. The friend offered to use his influence to have the slanderer put to death. But Confucius told him, "If the Way is to prevail, it is so decreed. If the Way is to be rejected, it is so decreed." What, he asked, could the slanderer have to do with this decree (*ming*)?

Why did Confucius answer in this way? Let us consider the possibilities. He could have agreed to have the enemy executed, but this would have been opposed to his principles, for he did not believe that forming cliques and fomenting intrigue were even good policy in the long run. In refusing he could have said, "The course that you propose is unworthy," but this would have been gratuitously to insult and alienate a well-meaning friend. Instead, he fell back on reference to the common concept of what was "decreed," and handled the situation without injuring any feelings.

It is quite clear, however, that Confucius did not himself rely on destiny nor advise others to do so. On the contrary, he repeatedly insisted upon the importance of effort by the individual, the moral responsibility to do one's best, and the efficacy of striving. There is, nevertheless, still another passage in the *Analects* that has undoubtedly contributed to the development of fatalism in some circles within Confucianism. It begins, "Tzŭ-hsia said, 'There is a saying which I have heard . . .' "; from this it is commonly supposed that Tzŭ-hsia was quoting Confucius himself. The passage reads, "Death and life are as decreed, wealth and rank depend upon Heaven; the gentleman is serious and does not fail in his duties, he behaves courteously to others and accords with *li*." Those who quote this passage commonly stop with "Heaven," but this is to miss its point. Life and death are matters about which one can do relatively little; he does his best, but when death comes after all one must simply resign himself and say, "It is fate." That is what Confucius did, and we today can do no better. About wealth and rank one *could* do something, but a gentleman *would* not. As ends to be striven for, they were beneath his notice. "The concern of the gentleman is about the progress of the Way; he does not worry about poverty." About such matters, then, one did nothing, but dismissed them as "depending on Heaven." What one did do (and this is the importance of the second half of the quotation) was to attend to his own character and his relations with his fellow men. Here is the key, then, to Confucius' attitude toward religion. He believed in it, apparently, but he was not much interested in it. It had to do with the realm of forces beyond man's control. But Confucius was interested in making over an intolerable world into a good world; what nothing could be done about did not concern him very much. He was occupied with the very practical problem of how best to utilize such ability as we have to act effectively.

The central conception in the philosophy of Confucius is that of the Way, to which we have often referred without describing it. This has come to be, in much of Chinese thinking, a metaphysical conception, but it was not so for Confucius.

The character commonly translated as "Way" is *tao*. It does not seem to occur on the oracle bones of the Shang period. In bronze inscriptions from a time earlier than that of Confucius it seems to be used seldom, and only in two ways: in its original sense of "road," and as a proper name. In all of the pre-Confucian literature put together it is used only some forty-four times, which is only half as many times as it appears in the *Analects*. In this earlier literature its most frequent meaning is "road"; rarely it has the related meanings of "to conduct" and "to tell" (developed from "to guide"); six times it has the sense of "a course of action."

In the *Analects, tao* occurs with all of these meanings. Almost always, however, it refers to a "way of action"; in any other sense it is rare. We find it used of ways that are bad as well as those that are good; Confucius speaks of a way which is inadequate. Thus far, we have nothing new. But what does appear to have no precedent in the pre-Confucian literature is the use of *tao* to mean "*the* way" above all other ways; what we may conveniently write as "the Way." It is only with this sense in mind that Confucius could have said that "a great minister is one who serves his ruler in accord with the Way." It is with this new significance that the character *tao* is used most frequently in the *Analects*.

The Way is the way in which Confucius thought that individuals, states, and the world should conduct themselves and be conducted. If "all under heaven [*i.e.,* the Chinese world] has the Way," or a particular state "has the Way," this means that they are governed as they should be and that moral principles prevail. If an individual "has the Way" he acts as he should act, and is a person of high moral character. The conception is not, however, as colorless as this description might suggest.

Confucius once said, "My Way is pervaded by [literally, "is strung upon"] a single principle." What the principle was we are never told. But if we study the *Analects* closely, in its historical setting, we can see it plainly enough. It was a vision of a cooperative world. It was the conviction that antagonism and suspicion, strife and suffering, were largely unnecessary. It was a profound faith that men's true interests did not conflict but complemented each other, that war and injustice and exploitation injured those who profited by them as well as those they caused to suffer. This was, indeed, a thread which "ran through" all of Confucius' thinking, and from which much of his philosophy can be derived by logical deduction. The conception of the Way, as *the* way in which this vision of a better world could be made into reality was thus no sterile moral code of not doing wrong, but a body of principle that demanded positive and sometimes dangerous action.

In a recent study Lorraine Creel has analyzed the significance of the idea of the Way (*tao*), from the sociological point of view, as follows:

Tao . . . is what Confucius considered to be the ideal way of life for the individual and the state. It is a way of life which includes all the virtues, sincerity, respectfulness, justice, kindness, and the like. It pays full attention to the rules of propriety [*li*] and to music. Like the human body however, it is more than the sum of its parts; for by a kind of "emergent synthesis" it attains a character and a power of its own. . . .

While law provides a standard of action more constant and enduring than a virtuous ruler, *tao* provides a standard of action more constant and enduring than law. Law is dependent on the vagaries of a governing body and derives its authority from that body. *Tao,* on the other hand is completely independent of any government; it derives its authority from itself. It is, therefore, of especial value in periods of such disorganization and chaos as were the Ch'un Ch'iu (722–481 B.C.) and the Chan Kuo (468–221 B.C.). For it could provide a common standard and bond for men, over whom there was no central authority. The *chün tzŭ* [gentleman] in Ch'i and the *chün tzŭ* in Lu could both look to *tao* for their standard.

Tao is also superior to law in that it calls for more than a minimum standard of conduct . . . *tao* not only prohibits one from killing or injuring a neighbor, it also requires that one have a friendly and helpful attitude toward him. This is probably connected with the fact that *tao* does not operate by the use of sanctions. If punishments are invoked as a result of failure to conform to a standard, it is not possible to have such a high standard that the mass of the people are unable to conform to it. . . . Also related to the fact that *tao* has no sanctions is the fact that its stimulus to virtue is not based on an appeal to self-interest. Because it does not encourage the individual to be good by the promise of reward or punishment, it does not turn the attention of the individual back on himself and on what is profitable or unprofitable for himself. This is important because once the individual comes to assume that his own interest and profit are the ultimate end of action, he will do what is morally right only so long as the advantages outweigh the disadvantages.

If the individual strives to follow *tao,* the self and its interests cease to be the focus of attention. His criterion of action becomes conformity to *tao* rather than profit to himself. At the same time, his actions cease to be separate and meaningful only in themselves, for they are now related through a common focusing on *tao.* Likewise, the individual is able to place himself in a historical perspective, for he is able to view himself as a member of a group of men who may be distant in time and space, but who are all interested in the progress of the *tao.*

When Confucius speaks of a man or a state as "having" the Way, this sounds as if he conceived of it as a thing, perhaps as a metaphysical entity. Clearly, the idea was well adapted to being so conceived, and in later Chinese thought this was done. For Confucius, however, it remained a way, or better *the* way, of conduct. This is evident when he says, "Who can go out of a house except by the door? Why are there none who follow this Way?" Yet it is clear that he considered it of the highest importance, as shown by the famous passage, "The Master said, 'If one hear the Way in the morning, he may die in the evening without regret.'"

Precisely because the Way summed up the totality of his philosophy, Confucius never clearly defined it; to understand it we must look at his philosophy as a whole. We can, however, learn something of the source of its central conception, the idea of a cooperative world. It is probable that it was essentially based on the relationship which existed between the members of a family.

The family has been important in many cultures, but it is doubtful that it has anywhere been more important, for a longer time, than in China. Certain aspects of its importance, especially nepotism, have been deplorable, yet it has probably done more than any other institution to make possible the remarkable survival of Chinese culture. It has dealt with many social problems in their nascent stages. By virtue of it, China has consisted of a vast number of almost self-contained social cells, whose functioning has been little affected even by national catastrophe. It has been the incubator of morality and a microcosm of the state. From one point of view, Confucianism might be defined as the philosophy of the Chinese family system.

As regards the family, Confucius seems to have added little that was new. From what light the oracle bones give us (which is not very much), it seems to have been important even in Shang times. In Chou literature the basic importance of the family is constantly emphasized. It must be borne in mind, however, that from the early literature we learn very little about the common people. For the aristocrats the family was essential; their status depended upon their ancestors. Furthermore the Chou empire, won in battle, was cemented by a network of feudal and familial ties, which were inextricably mingled through intermarriage and the enfeoffment of royal relatives. The early Chou rulers were fully aware of the basic role of the family in the maintenance of order in their dominions. One of the sections of the *Book of History* is a charge given to his brother by the Duke of Chou (to whom Confucius looked as an early precursor in the Way). The Duke instructs his brother in the way in which he should govern the territory he is to rule and adjures him to be especially cautious in the regulation of his own family. He further declares that if his subjects do not respect family ties, "the principles [of morality] given to the people by Heaven will be thrown into disorder." The unfilial and unbrotherly are, the Duke declares, worse than thieves and murderers and must be punished without leniency. But—and this is of the first importance—not only the unfilial son but also the hard-hearted father, not only the unruly younger brother but also the overbearing elder brother, are condemned as deserving punishment.

The duty of filial piety was constantly urged in the early literature. Its importance was obvious when the dead ancestors controlled one's destiny. Confucius interpreted filial piety as a social duty, but he still emphasized it. There was a potential conflict, of course, between the idea that one should obey his father and the idea that one should act in accordance with the Way; what if they disagreed? Confucius says very little about this. In one case, however, he does say that one may "remonstrate with his father and mother, but gently."

In another passage the conflict between the state and the family appears sharply. "The Duke of Shê said to Confucius, 'Among us there are those who are upright; if his father steals a sheep, the son will testify against him.' Confucius replied, 'Among us the upright act quite differently. The son shields the father, and the father shields the son; we see this as uprightness.' " This conflict still exists, even in the Occident; if you knew that your father had committed a murder, would you inform the authorities? Confucius was not unaware of the claims of society, but he put the family first. It seems doubtful, however, that he enjoined the taking of "blood revenge" against the slayer of one's relatives, as later books have claimed. He did not believe that the interests of family and state were fundamentally opposed; quite the reverse. It was in the family, as he saw it, that the individual learned those attitudes of obedience and cooperation, and gained the experience in socialized activity, which made it possible for him to be a useful citizen or official.

Confucius was not the first person in China to see some analogy between the family and the state; two early poems refer to rulers as "the father and mother of the people." Such expressions are common enough in many lands, but the important question is, what do they mean in attitudes and actions? Too often paternalism is a near synonym for despotism. There is little evidence that such ideas ever greatly mitigated the lot of the Chinese common people in the early period. In the Confucian application of this conception, however, it became a potent force for reform.

It is undoubtedly true that Confucius was attracted, in the analogy of the family with the state, by the fact that it was a pattern of orderly subordination to authority. But it is probable that another aspect attracted him still more strongly. The Chinese family was an organization in which every member was inherently "as good as" every other member. This does not mean that there was no subordination. The children were subject to the authority of their parents, but in time they would come in their turn to be parents. A younger son would never, under normal circumstances, be head of the family, but no stigma attached to this fact. He would have his voice in the family councils. Economic advantages were shared with considerable equity. If any member of the family were treated unfairly he could protest, with a considerable chance of success. In theory, the head of the family could be a despot; in practice it was difficult for him long to resist the disapproval of a majority of those with whom he lived every day. The Chinese family seems always to have been monarchic in theory, and largely democratic in practice. The result was that its members were, as some sociologists would put it, members of the "we group"; they were treated as ends, not as means. There was subordination among them, but each had his place, his functions, and his dignity.

It was into such status, and to such a community, that Confucius wished to welcome all men everywhere. This is the significance of the statement by Tzŭ-hsia that he had heard (almost certainly from the Master) that "within the four seas, all men are brothers." It is worthy of note that Confucius betrays no chauvinistic bias against the non-Chinese "barbarians"; Waley even attributes to him "a certain idealization of the 'noble savage.' " Certainly Confucius would have liked them to become "civilized" according to Chinese standards. His ideal state, however, was the world. It is of interest that, at the time when the League of Nations was being projected, K'ang Yu-wei submitted his understanding of Confucius' views on the world state, at the request of President Wilson.

Even more revolutionary, in his day, was Confucius' insistence that men of all classes possessed worth in themselves, and must be treated not merely as the means *by* which the state accomplished its purposes, but as the ends *for* which the state existed. That he held this is clear, for instance, from the fact that he said that the end of government was that it should make the people happy. The idea that the state was a mutual enterprise, in the good or bad fortunes of which all, high and low, should share, was stated by the disciple Yu Jo. Duke Ai of Lu declared that since the harvest was poor he did not know how he was to raise sufficient revenues, and asked what Yu Jo advised. Yu suggested that he levy a tax of one tenth. "With two tenths I have not enough," the duke replied. "How could I possibly get along with one tenth?" Confucius' disciple answered, "When the people have plenty, with whom will you be obliged to share want? But when your people are in want, with whom can their ruler share abundance?"

In a cooperative world made up of agents who are (within limits) free, as opposed to a world dominated by coercion, the individual is paramount. The world can be no better than the sum of the individuals who compose it, and if a significant proportion of them are wanting in morality, the world is in danger. Thus Confucius begins with the individual. He emphasizes the necessity of self-examination, of the cultivation of virtue, and of education. He himself concentrated on the education of men who were, he hoped, to govern; there was a tremendous job of education to do, and this seemed the most important place to begin. But it has not been sufficiently noted that several passages in the *Analects* make it clear that his goal included at least some education for all the people. This was logically necessary; the totally ignorant may blindly obey, but they cannot cooperate for they do not know how. Thus Confucius said, "When the common people study the Way, they are easily directed." They are easily caused, that is, to do what is for the common good, since they have some understanding of the orders issued to them, their purpose, and how to carry them out. Recent discussions of military training have emphasized the importance of political indoctrination, the theory being that soldiers who know what they are fighting for will fight better. Confucius expressed the same idea in this way: "To lead an uneducated people to war is to throw them away."

He conceived education, as we have noted, as being largely directed toward the cultivation of character. It was designed to develop such virtues as loyalty, sincerity, good faith, justice, kindness, accord with *li,* and so forth. Concerning loyalty it should be noted, however, that this was not mere loyalty to an individual. Confucius specifically denounced blind personal loyalty, of the feudal variety. His ideal retainer served his lord with all his strength as long as he could do so in accord with the Way, but when he had to choose between them he held to the Way and left the ruler's service.

This allegiance to principle rather than to persons is essential to democracy; without it, the state is constantly at the mercy of any general or politician who may accumulate a following. By providing such allegiance, Confucianism established one of the essential conditions for democratic government. It was this loyalty to principle which later made possible the Censorate, that body in the Chinese government which has been charged, during the past two thousand years, with the function of criticizing derelictions of duty by any official or even by the emperor himself. It was this loyalty which caused some members of that body to do their duty fearlessly even when they knew that exile or death would reward their temerity. It may be that legend has exaggerated the frequency with which censors opposed the emperor, but the very existence of the legend is significant. What reward did Confucius promise those who should be loyal to principle and cleave to duty, forsaking all others? Wealth, rank, and power? Not at all. Not only are they uncertain, but he considered it beneath the dignity of a gentleman to make such private gain his controlling object. Immortality, happiness after death? Confucius never mentions them. Then what in the world is it that men can want so much that they will be willing, "seeing danger, to sacrifice their lives"?

It is this: The man who cultivates and *practices* virtue, who loves the Way and does his best to *try* to realize it in the world, has fulfilled the whole duty of man. Poverty cannot touch him; Confucius declared, "With coarse food to eat, water to drink, and my bended arm for a pillow, I still have joy in the midst of these things." If one who practices the Way fails to gain high office, that is unfortunate since he might otherwise have been able to do much good; but it is cause for reproach, not to the virtuous individual, but only to the government that fails to employ him. "The Master said, 'Do not be concerned that you are not in office, but only about making yourself fit for one. Do not be concerned if you win no recognition; only seek to make yourself worthy of it.' " It was in this sense that it could truly be said of Confucius that he was "one who knows that what he is trying to do is impossible, and yet goes on trying." A nice calculation of one's chances of success was irrelevant. "If upon looking into my heart I find that I am right," Confucius is quoted as having said, "I will go forward though those that oppose me number thousands and tens of thousands." It was only necessary that one determine what he *ought* to do and then do his best.

Thus Confucius offered that most priceless possession, peace of mind. "If, looking within his own heart, one finds no cause for self-reproach, why should he worry, what shall he fear?" He put peace of mind within the reach of each individual, without regard to the vagaries of the external world. "Is virtue a distant thing?" he asked. "If I really want virtue, then it is here." Thus the individual possessed a kind of majestic autonomy; his heart was his castle. "Even the general of a great army may be kidnaped, but no force can steal the determination of even the humblest man." Historically this was very important. It enabled the Confucian "when the state had the Way, to take office; when the state lacked the Way, to roll up his principles and preserve them in his bosom." It made possible the continuance of Confucianism as a doctrine of the private scholar, biding its time, with little public recognition, until the Han dynasty.

Self-sufficiency for the individual is, within reason, good. But if it goes too far it cuts him off from all contact with his fellows. Shall one then relax his principles, become one of the crowd, and be a "good fellow"? No! says Confucius. "Do not choose your friends among those who are not your [moral] equals." This raises the familiar problem of whether equality is to be achieved by reducing everyone to a common level, or rather by raising the level of the masses. Confucius stood firmly for the latter course. Yet this did not mean that he held himself entirely aloof; we have seen that he was freer in his associations than some of the disciples would have liked. Confucius and Kant expressed themselves on this matter very similarly. Kant wrote that "it is the duty of man . . . to construct for himself an impregnable center of principle, yet to regard this circle which he draws around himself as also being one part of an all-inclusive circle of cosmopolitan sympathy." Confucius said that one should "feel kindly toward everyone, but be intimate only with the virtuous."

Yet mere kindly feeling is not enough; we must do something for others if we are truly virtuous. The disciple Tsêng Shên once declared that his Master's doctrine consisted of nothing more than "integrity and reciprocity." Legge translates this more freely, but with a fine sense of its true meaning, as "to be true to the principles of our nature and the benevolent exercise of them to others." Confucius said that "reciprocity" was a principle which should be practiced always, and explained it as meaning that "what one does not want done to himself, he should not do to others." This has sometimes been criticized as being merely a negative conception. Whether that is true or not, Confucius certainly did not conceive of duty as merely negative. "The truly virtuous man," he said, "desiring to be established himself, seeks to establish others; desiring success for himself, he strives to help others succeed. To find in the wishes of one's own heart the principle for his conduct toward others is the method of true virtue."

The reader will at once have been reminded of Kant's famous categorical imperative: "Act as if by your will the maxim of your act were about to be made into a universal law of nature." This dictum is, as one would expect, much more sophisticated, yet its principle is similar. Both Kant and Confucius, being individualists, saw the world as consisting, from the individual's point of view, of two great aspects: one's self and the world. As regards himself, one's control and thus his responsibility are virtually unlimited. He must therefore, with unremitting diligence, cultivate his character. Having done so, and attained a knowledge of what is good, he must then do his utmost to realize this good for all other men. Thus Kant asserts that there are two ends toward which we are morally obliged to strive: "our own perfection—the happiness of others." This might serve to summarize the moral lessons of the *Analects*.

This is an austere and rational doctrine, yet it implies considerable optimism concerning human nature. If it is one's duty to act toward others with reciprocity, there should be that in them which can respond. Indeed, this is the necessary condition for a cooperative world. That Confucius did believe in this capacity for response is very clear. He declared that the influence of the example of a true gentleman was so powerful that even if he went among the barbarians he would find no rudeness, for it would disappear upon his advent. He told the head of the Chi family in Lu that he should not employ capital punishment since if his own desires were as they should be the people would be good.

We need not, however, take these fine phrases too seriously. The last statement was very much in order, as addressed to a despot who had just proposed the policy of killing off all those with the "wrong" ideas. But Confucius knew that perfection could not be attained overnight, and elsewhere we find him agreeing that if good men were to govern the state it would require a century before capital punishment could be eliminated. Likewise we cannot lay too much stress on such a statement as the following: "The Master said, 'Man's very life is uprightness; without it, he is lucky to escape with his life.'" If this be true, the world was full of lucky people in his own day, as Confucius well knew.

Clearly enough, Confucius thought that men have certain tendencies toward good and tremendous capacity to be influenced by education. "It is only the wisest and the most stupid," he said, "who cannot be changed." He also thought that there were some so perverse that it was futile to waste one's time with them. But he seems to have taken no stand on the question of whether men are naturally good or bad, though he did say that "men are by nature very similar, but by practice come to be very different." It is highly improbable that, as has often been supposed, he believed that some men were "born wise," endowed with knowledge from birth.

How then do men acquire knowledge? More important, when they have acquired it how can they evaluate it; how does one distinguish the true from the false? And what is virtue? It is said that one should practice the Way, but how does one find out what the Way is? What is the great standard by which all things are to be measured? This is perhaps the most searching question that can be asked of any philosophy. And when we ask it of Confucius, we receive our greatest surprise.

He has no such standard.

He did not say that one need only imitate the ancients, such as the mythical emperors Yao and Shun. Mencius said this, and it has been supposed that Confucius believed it, but there is no such statement in the *Analects*. Nor did he say that the standard of truth was to be found in any book, or any set of books. We have seen that he himself did not depend on books as the sole source of his ideas, and there is no indication that he advised others to do so. Although Confucianism did in time come to regard certain books (the Classics) with the utmost veneration, there are indications that this tendency arose late, as part of what was in reality a reaction against the essence of Confucius' own teachings. Finally, he did not set up his own words as an ultimate authority; on the contrary, as we have seen, he made no claim to infallibility and permitted his disciples to differ with him unrebuked.

Nevertheless, the mere fact that he never states in the *Analects* that antiquity or certain books provide the ultimate basis of truth, does not prove that he did not think they did. Such proof comes, rather, from the fact that even when tightly pressed in argument he makes no appeal to them.

That he had no such standard is stated in the *Analects* again and again. "There were four qualities from which the Master was entirely free: he had no foregone conclusions, he was not over-positive, not obstinate, and never saw things from his own point of view alone." He himself said that he hated obstinacy. His reputation for flexibility, acting always in accord with a careful consideration of all the circumstances, was so great that Mencius discussed it in detail a century later and called Confucius "the timely sage." Confucius' own best statement of this principle is the following: "The true gentleman, in the world, is neither predisposed for anything nor against anything; he will side with whatever is right."

What is here translated as "right" is *i*. This is another conception that is very important. Its sense is not simply that of what is "right" or "righteous" in the ordinary meaning of these words. It means rather that which is fitting and suitable. Thus when the disciple Yu Jo said, "If in making promises one stays close to *i*, his words can be fulfilled," he meant that before one agrees to do something one should consider all the circumstances and promise only what is proper and suitable. It was with a similar intent that Confucius approved the conduct of one who "seeing an opportunity for gain, thinks of *i*." Such a man reflects upon whether, by taking the profit which is possible, he will violate a trust, wrong another person, or in any respect act in a way which is unsuitable under the given circumstances.

Obviously this concept of *i* is an extremely important moral force. It is a regulator of conduct similar to *li* and the Way; and one that constantly places his own responsibility squarely before the individual. For whereas the Way is general, and one may look to others for some guidance concerning it, the question of what is suitable in each given situation is one that the individual must decide for himself. We have already seen instances in which Confucius was guided by this criterion of suitability.

Yet the question still pursues us: how is one to determine what is suitable? By meditation? "The Master said, 'I once spent a whole day without food and a whole night without sleep, in order to meditate. It was no use. It is better to study.'" But study alone is not the answer. "The Master said, 'Study without thought is labor lost; thought without study is dangerous.'"

There are several statements in the *Analects* that describe the way in which Confucius thought that truth might be attained. "The Master said, 'I am not one who was born with knowledge; rather, I love the past, and am diligent in investigating it.'" Investigation of the past is still one of our chief sources of knowledge. But it must be done methodically. "The Master said, 'I can say something about the *li* of the Hsia dynasty, but the state of Ch'i [a small state supposed to be ruled by the descendants of the Hsia kings] has no adequate evidence concerning it. I can say something about the *li* of the Yin [Shang] dynasty, but the state of Sung likewise lacks such evidence. . . . If the evidence were sufficient, I could then give descriptions for which there would be real proof.'"

Not everything is equally reliable as evidence, however. To a student who wanted to know how to conduct himself in practical politics Confucius said, "Hear much, but leave to one side that which is doubtful, and speak with due caution concerning the remainder; in this way you will seldom incur blame. See much, but leave to one side that of which the meaning is not clear, and act carefully with regard to the rest; thus you will have few occasions for regret." We must always keep our eyes open, learning all we can from experience. Yet we cannot expect to understand everything; we must understand what we can, and concerning the rest maintain suspended judgment. Thus he commended the practice of copyists who, instead of guessing when a word is illegible, "leave a blank in the text." He described his own way of acquiring knowledge in these words: "To hear much, select what is good, and follow it; to see much and remember it; these are the steps by which knowledge [or, wisdom] is attained."

So far Confucius sounds very much like what philosophers call an empiricist, relying wholly on experience for his knowledge. Another time, however, he asked the disciple Tzŭ-kung, "Do you think that my way of acquiring knowledge is simply to study many things and remember them?" "Yes," Tzŭ-kung replied, "Isn't that the case?" "No," was the reply, "I have one principle which I use like a thread, upon which to string them all." Here he sounds like a rationalist, seeking to arrange the world's phenomena according to the principle of his own mind. In fact, as we have already seen, he was partly the one and partly the other.

Yet we still have not found the answer to our question: what is the standard for truth? And we will get no answer to this question from Confucius. If we could put it to him, he would undoubtedly reply that every man must find it for himself. *That is the only answer possible in a truly cooperative world.* A machine is operated, but it cannot cooperate. And in a world in which there is a fixed standard of truth and authority, the role of the individual is no more creative than that of a machine. He may refuse to conform, or he may conform, but he cannot truly contribute. If men have responsibility for the achievements of society, they must also have the opportunity to help in the choice of its ends, which means in the discovery (not merely the unveiling) of truth. Thus Kant saw clearly that it is impossible for anyone to achieve a fully developed personality unless "he has the power to determine his own ends for himself, according to his own ideas of duty."

Here again we are back to the individual. Are we to conclude, then, that one man is just as capable of judging what is right and true as any other? In one sense, yes. We are dealing here with a type of thinking which is similar to that of science. The scientist, like Confucius, looks to experience for his data and tries to link it all with one pervasive hypothesis, or series of hypotheses. The scientist also believes that essentially one normal man is *potentially* as good a judge of truth as another; royal birth or the possession of a billion dollars will not increase the respect accorded to a man's opinions as a scientist. The only things that will increase that respect are education, experience, and demonstrated competence.

Confucius judged similarly. He believed that all men were potentially equal; he was not awed by rank nor contemptuous of poverty. But those whose opinions were entitled to respect were those who realized their potentialities by study and by the cultivation of virtue. Thus the opinions of one enlightened man might count for more than those of a multitude of the unthinking crowd.

To prevent misunderstanding, let it be stated clearly that there is no intention to claim here that Confucius "anticipated the methods of modern science." In some respects his thinking fell far short of the scientific ideal; that is in no way surprising. But his thinking was characterized by an absence of dogma, a clear realization of the necessity of suspended judgment, and an espousal of intellectual democracy that, in its forthright acceptance of the minimal philosophic conditions of scientific thinking, is altogether remarkable. It may be asked whether, if this be true, the Chinese should not then have developed scientific method long ago. This may or may not be the case, but as we shall see these aspects of Confucius' thinking were soon lost, in large degree, from Confucianism.

Science, like Confucius, has no unalterable standard for truth; it is searching for truth, not deducing it from a prearranged formula. Yet this is not to say that it gives us no help toward finding the truth. It does not tell us *what* truth is, but it gives us a great deal of advice as to *how* to look for it. So does Confucius.

Surely few philosophers, or at any rate few prescientific philosophers, have laid such emphasis on flexibility as did Confucius. In the Occident we have tended to think of truth as being immutable, and to think that a god or a very wise man must partake of the unbending character of absolute truth. The ancient Mesopotamians (who are, through the Hebrews, among our intellectual ancestors) considered inflexibility to be an attribute of godliness; "The king's word is right; his utterance, like that of a god, cannot be changed!" We have commonly felt that it infringes the dignity of a man of position to change his mind and admit himself at fault; this shows that he was not, as he should have been, in possession of the immutable truth.

Confucius argued differently: "To be mistaken, and yet not to change; this is indeed to be in error." "If you have made a mistake, do not be afraid to admit the fact and amend your ways." He stressed this theme repeatedly. The disciple Tzŭ-kung said, "The mistakes of a gentleman may be compared to the eclipses of the sun or the moon. When he makes a mistake, all men see it; when he corrects it, all men look up to him."

This readiness at all times to change is, of course, merely one necessary aspect of living in a state of suspended judgment. However noble such a state may be, it is not wholly comfortable. One walks on the sidewalk in front of one's dwelling every day and expects it to be there. Yet if one morning a gaping hole appears in it, one will (let us hope!) respond to the new situation and stay out of trouble. The fact is, however, that some circumstance *could* undermine that sidewalk so that, although it still appeared solid, it would in fact be a trap, only waiting for one to put his weight on it to collapse. Is one therefore to walk in the street—where the danger will probably be still greater? If one carried such fears far enough he would have, of course, to stop eating. No one (except a few of the mentally deranged) does any such thing. What we do is to estimate the probabilities of success or failure, safety or danger, in any given situation, and act in the light of this judgment. We do this all the time; it is the way we live. These judgments are personal, conditioned by all our previous training and experience, and they are *practical*. One may bring to them all the theory that he knows, but in the end there comes a time when he has to make a choice between two or more possible courses and hope it is correct.

Similarly one must draw a practical line in the matter of suspended judgment. To say, for instance, that since I know nothing with absolute certainty, I do not know that it is my duty to feed my neighbor when he is starving, is not true. Confucius recognized the need for drawing a practical line in the matter of knowledge; he defined wisdom as "when you know a thing, to recognize that you know it, and when you do not know a thing, to recognize that you do not know it." From what has gone before it is clear, of course, that Confucius was not using the word know in an absolute sense. Rather he was insisting upon the necessity of striking a reasonable and proper balance between unwarrantable scepticism and all-embracing dogmatic certainty.

This idea of striking a balance, of keeping to the middle path, was very important for Confucius. Mencius tells us that "Confucius did not go to extremes." In the *Analects* we read that "the Master said, 'Since I cannot get men who pursue the middle course with whom to practice my principles, I must take the impetuous and the over-cautious.'" He considered one kind of failing as bad as the other; "to go too far is as bad as to fall short." "The Master said, 'The middle course is indeed the way of the highest virtue; but its practice has long been rare among the people.'"

We have here essentially a philosophy of compromise. In Western thought there has been some tendency to look upon compromise with disfavor. This stems from our idea that truth and virtue are somehow fixed and absolute things with which the wise and good man has established communion; this being so, he should hold to the strict path of rectitude. Confucius, too, believed that one must draw a line beyond which he would not compromise his principles though death be the cost. But while he never expressed himself as to whether truth may or may not change, he quite clearly believed that our understanding of it must always be changing, just as long as we continue to be thinking and moral beings. Furthermore, no person has the right to regard himself as the sole anointed guardian of the truth. If your opinion differs from mine, we must discuss the matter; perhaps there is some truth in both our views, and something nearer the truth *may* lie between them. The necessity for such compromise follows logically, of course, from the conception of the world as cooperative, and it is essential to democracy.

Furthermore, even if I did know the truth, this would not tell me how to apply it in a concrete situation. We saw, for instance, that when rebellious vassals invited Confucius to direct their governments he was tempted to do so. He did not wholly approve of their actions; but did the desire to maintain his personal purity justify him in refusing an opportunity that might have led to alleviating the sufferings of the people? This was a real problem. Max Weber has pointed out that "no ethics in the world can dodge the fact that in numerous instances the attainment of 'good' ends is bound to the fact that one must be willing to pay the price of using morally dubious means or at least dangerous ones—and facing the possibility or even the probability of evil ramifications. From no ethics in the world can it be concluded when and to what extent the ethically good purpose 'justifies' the ethically dangerous means and ramifications."

Confucius recognized that the individual is constantly faced with such problems, which are in each case to some degree unique, for the circumstances are never twice the same. This recognition persists in Chinese law, to our own day. The French jurist, Jean Escarra, has pointed out in his book *Le Droit Chinois* that Chinese legal procedure remains basically Confucian. Thus the Chinese authorities "are preoccupied," he says, "with tempering the nominal severity of [the legally prescribed] punishments by an application which we may describe as rather humane, rather 'individualized.' And this explains the veritable genius of Chinese writers on criminal law for creating, with the utmost sublety and refinement, all varieties of penal theory, from the casuistic analysis of the intent to . . . complicity, excuses, extenuating circumstances, recidivism, the accumulation of offences, etc." In China, even the courts know that morality is not, for the individual, a simple matter of keeping his conduct in accord with a set of hard and fast rules.

Since, in Confucius' philosophy, so much responsibility is left to the individual, little can be done for him except to educate his mind and strengthen his character for his tasks. In the training of character, the ideal of the mean has an important function. Like *li*, the Way, and *i*, it is another principle which can assist one in his self-discipline. One who is moderate may err, but he is unlikely to go so far wrong as the man who goes to extremes. Even in cultivation, Confucius held, one should not become so over-refined as to obscure one's basic manhood, which is the true foundation of character.

Even one's benevolence should be tempered with reason. The recalcitrant disciple Tsai Yü once said to Confucius, "If a man is really virtuous, I suppose that even if you told him that there was a man in the well he would go right in after him." "Why do you think so?" Confucius replied. "You could, in that way, get a gentleman to go to the well, but not to jump in; he can be deceived, but not made an utter fool."

Thus virtue and truth are not, for Confucius, snug havens in which we may rest in complacent security. Rather they are goals toward which we must continually make our way. "Study," he said, "as if you were following someone you could not overtake, and were afraid of losing." This does not mean that life must always be hectic and one's mind harassed. On the contrary, the race is not always to the swift, nor does the most impatient seeker always find the object of his search. Through education and self-discipline, and by keeping to the middle path, we may achieve poise and freedom from confusion. But so long as we live, our very possession of moral faculties imposes a corresponding obligation to exercise them, and to choose in each new situation between the various courses of action open to us. Confucius made this very clear; "If a man does not constantly ask himself, 'What is the right thing to do?' I really don't know what is to be done about him."

Selections from the *Analects*

Reprinted from The Harvard Classics

THE SAYINGS OF CONFUCIUS

II

[1] The Master said: "In governing, cleave to good; as the north star holds his place, and the multitude of stars revolve upon him."

[2] The Master said: "To sum up the three hundred songs in a word, they are free from evil thought."

[3] The Master said: "Guide the people by law, subdue them by punishment; they may shun crime, but will be void of shame. Guide them by example, subdue them by courtesy; they will learn shame, and come to be good."

[4] The Master said: "At fifteen, I was bent on study; at thirty, I could stand; at forty, doubts ceased; at fifty, I understood the

Reprinted from *The Harvard Classics,* edited by Charles W. Eliot, Vol. 44 (P. F. Collier & Son Company, 1910).

laws of Heaven; at sixty, my ears obeyed me; at seventy, I could do as my heart lusted, and never swerve from right."

[5] Meng Yi asked the duty of a son.

The Master said: "Obedience."

As Fan Ch'ih was driving him, the Master said: "Mengsun asked me the duty of a son; I answered 'Obedience.' "

"What did ye mean?" said Fan Ch'ih.

"To serve our parents with courtesy whilst they live," said the Master; "to bury them with all courtesy when they die; and to worship them with all courtesy."

. . .

[15] The Master said: "Study without thought is vain: thought without study is dangerous."

[16] The Master said: "Work on strange doctrines does harm."

[17] The Master said: "Yu, shall I teach thee what is understanding? To know what we know, and know what we do not know, that is understanding."

[18] Tzu-chang studied with an eye to pay.

The Master said: "Listen much, keep silent when in doubt, and always take heed of the tongue; thou wilt make few mistakes. See much, beware of pitfalls, and always give heed to thy walk; thou wilt have little to rue. If thy words are seldom wrong, thy deeds leave little to rue, pay will follow."

. . .

IV

[1] The Master said: "Love makes a spot beautiful: who chooses not to dwell in love, has he got wisdom?"

[2] The Master said: "Loveless men cannot bear need long, they cannot bear fortune long. Loving hearts find peace in love; clever heads find profit in it."

[3] The Master said: "Love can alone love others, or hate others."

[4] The Master said: "A heart set on love will do no wrong."

[5] The Master said: "Wealth and honours are what men desire; but abide not in them by help of wrong. Lowliness and want are hated of men; but forsake them not by help of wrong.

"Shorn of love, is a gentleman worthy the name? Not for one moment may a gentleman sin against love; not in flurry and haste, nor yet in utter overthrow."

[6] The Master said: "A friend to love, a foe to evil, I have yet to meet. A friend to love will set nothing higher. In love's service, a foe to evil will let no evil touch him. Were a man to give himself to love, but for one day, I have seen no one whose strength would fail him. Such men there may be, but I have not seen one."

[7] The Master said: "A man and his faults are of a piece. By watching his faults we learn whether love be his."

[8] The Master said: "To learn the truth at daybreak and die at eve were enough."

[9] The Master said: "A scholar in search of truth who is ashamed of poor clothes and poor food it is idle talking to."

[10] The Master said: "A gentleman has no likes and no dislikes below heaven. He follows right."

[11] The Master said: "Gentlemen cherish worth; the vulgar cherish dirt. Gentlemen trust in justice; the vulgar trust in favour."

[12] The Master said: "The chase of gain is rich in hate."

[13] The Master said: "What is it to sway a kingdom by courteous yielding? Who cannot by courteous yielding sway a kingdom, what can he know of courtesy?"

[14] The Master said: "Be not concerned at want of place; be concerned that thou stand thyself. Sorrow not at being unknown, but seek to be worthy of note."

[15] The Master said: "One thread, Shen, runs through all my teaching."

"Yes," said Tseng-tzu.

After the Master had left, the disciples asked what was meant.

Tseng-tzu said: "The Master's teaching all hangs on faithfulness and fellow-feeling."

[16] The Master said: "A gentleman considers what is right; the vulgar consider what will pay."

[17] The Master said: "At sight of worth, think to grow like it. When evil meets thee, search thine own heart."

[18] The Master said: "A father or mother may be gently

chidden. If they will not bend, be the more lowly, but persevere; nor murmur if trouble follow."

[19] The Master said: "Whilst thy father and mother live, do not wander afar. If thou must travel, hold a set course."

[20] The Master said: "If for three years a son do not forsake his father's ways, he may be called dutiful."

[21] The Master said: "A father's and a mother's age must be borne in mind; with joy on the one hand, fear on the other."

[22] The Master said: "Men of old were loth to speak; lest a word that they could not make good should shame them."

[23] The Master said: "Who contains himself goes seldom wrong."

[24] The Master said: "A gentleman wishes to be slow to speak and quick to act."

[25] The Master said: "Good is no hermit. It has ever neighbours."

[26] Tzu-yu said: "Preaching to princes brings disgrace, nagging at friends estrangement."

. . .

VI

[1] The Master said: "Yung might fill the seat of a prince."
"And might Tzu-sang Po-tzu?" asked Chung-kung.

"Yes," said the Master, "but he is lax."

"To be lax in his claims on the people might be right," said Chung-kung, "were he stern to self; but to be lax to self and lax to others must surely be over-lax."

The Master said: "What Yung says is true."

[2] Duke Ai asked which disciples were fond of learning.

Confucius answered: "Yen Hui loved learning. His anger fell not astray; he made no mistake twice. By ill-luck his life was cut short. Now that he is gone, I hear of no one who is fond of learning."

[3] Tzu-hua having been sent to Ch'i, the disciple Jan asked for grain to give to his mother.

The Master said: "Give her a bushel."
He asked for more.
The Master said: "Give her half a quarter."
Jan gave her twenty-five quarters.
The Master said: "On his way to Ch'i, Ch'ih was drawn by sleek horses, clad in fine furs. A gentleman, I have heard, helps the needy: he does not swell riches."

. . .

[16] The Master said: "Nature outweighing art begets roughness; art outweighing nature begets pedantry. Art and nature well blent make a gentleman."

[17] The Master said: "Man is born upright. If he cease to be so and live, he is lucky to escape!"

[18] The Master said: "Who knows does not rank with him who likes, nor he who likes with him who is glad therein."

[19] The Master said: "To men above the common we may speak of things above the common. To men below the common we must not speak of things above the common."

[20] Fan Ch'ih asked, What is wisdom?

The Master said: "To foster right amongst the people; to honour the ghosts of the dead, whilst keeping aloof from them, may be called wisdom."

He asked, What is love?

The Master said: "To rank the effort above the prize may be called love."

[21] The Master said: "Wisdom delights in water; love delights in hills. Wisdom is stirring; love is quiet. Wisdom enjoys life; love grows old."

. . .

VII

[1] The Master said: "A teller and not a maker, one who trusts and loves the past; I may be likened to our old P'eng."

[2] The Master said: "A silent communer, an ever hungry learner, a still unflagging teacher; am I any of these?"

[3] The Master said: "Neglect of what is good in me; want of thoroughness in study; failure to do the right when told me; lack of strength to overcome faults, these are my sorrows."

[4] In his free moments the Master was easy and cheerful.

[5] The Master said: "How deep is my decay! It is long since I saw the Duke of Chou in a dream."

[6] The Master said: "Will the right; hold to good won; rest in love; move in art."

[7] The Master said: "From the man who paid in dried meat upwards, I have withheld teaching from no one."

[8] The Master said: "Only to those fumbling do I open, only for those stammering do I find the word. From him who cannot turn the whole when I lift a corner I desist."

. . .

[19] The Master said: "I was not born to understanding. I loved the past, and questioned it earnestly."

[20] The Master never spake of ghosts or strength, crime or spirits.

[21] The Master said: "Walking three together I am sure of teachers. I pick out the good and follow it; I see the bad and shun it."

[22] The Master said: "Heaven planted worth in me; what harm can come of Huan T'ui?"

[23] The Master said: "My boys, do ye think that I hide things from you? I hide nothing. One who keeps from his boys nought that he does, such is Ch'iu."

[24] The four things the Master taught were culture, conduct, faithfulness, and truth.

[25] The Master said: "A holy man I shall not live to see; enough could I find a gentleman! A good man I shall not live to see; enough could I find a steadfast one! But when nothing poses as something, cloud as substance, want as riches, steadfastness must be rare."

[26] The Master angled, but did not fish with a net; he shot, but not at birds sitting.

[27] The Master said: "There may be men who act without

understanding why. I do not. To listen much, pick out the good and follow it; to see much and ponder it: this comes next to understanding."

[28] It was ill talking to the Hu villagers. A lad having been admitted, the disciples wondered.

The Master said: "I allow his coming, not what is to come. Why be so harsh? If a man cleanse himself to gain admission, I admit his cleanness, but go not bail for his past."

. . .

[32] The Master said: "I have no more culture than others: to live as a gentleman is not yet mine."

[33] The Master said: "How dare I lay claim to holiness or love? A man of endless craving I might be called, an unflagging teacher; but nothing more."

"That is just what we disciples cannot learn," said Kung-hsi Hua.

. . .

[35] The Master said: "Waste begets self-will; thrift begets meanness: but better be mean than self-willed."

[36] The Master said: "A gentleman is calm and spacious: the vulgar are always fretting."

[37] The Master was friendly, yet dignified; he inspired awe, but not fear; he was respectful, yet easy.

VIII

[1] The Master said: "T'ai-po might indeed be called a man of highest worth. Thrice he gave up the throne. Men were at a loss how to praise him."

[2] The Master said: "Without a sense of courtesy, attentions grow into fussiness, heed turns to fearfulness, courage becomes unruliness, uprightness turns to harshness. When the gentry are true to kinsmen, love will thrive among the people. If they do not forsake old friends, the people will not be selfish."

. . .

[4] When Tseng-tzu lay sick Meng Ching came to ask after him.

Tseng-tzu said: "When a bird is to die, his note is sad; when a man is to die, his words are true. There are three duties that a gentleman prizes: to banish from his bearing violence and levity; to sort his face to the truth; to purge his speech of the low and unfair. As for temple matters there are officers to mind them."

[5] Tseng-tzu said: "Out of knowledge to learn from ignorance, out of wealth to learn from penury; having to seem wanting, real to seem shadow; when gainsaid never answering back: I had once a friend who would act thus."

[6] Tseng-tzu said: "A man to whom an orphan stripling or the fate of an hundred townships may be entrusted, and whom no crisis can corrupt, is he not a gentleman, a gentleman indeed?"

[7] Tseng-tzu said: "The scholar had need be strong and bold; for his burden is heavy, the road is far. His burden is love, is it not a heavy one? Death is the goal, is that not far?"

[8] The Master said: "Poetry rouses, courtesy upholds us, music is our crown."

[9] The Master said: "The people may be made to follow: they cannot be made to understand."

[10] The Master said: "Love of daring, inflamed by poverty, leads to crime: a man without love, if deeply ill-treated, will turn to crime."

[11] The Master said: "All the glorious gifts of the Duke of Chou, if coupled with pride and meanness, would not be worth one glance."

[12] The Master said: "A man to whom three years of study have borne no fruit would be hard to find."

[13] The Master said: "A man who loves learning with simple faith, who to mend his life is content to die, will not enter a tottering kingdom, nor stay in a land distraught. When right prevails below heaven, he is seen; when wrong prevails, he is unseen. When right prevails, he would blush to be poor and lowly; when wrong prevails, wealth and honours would shame him."

[14] The Master said: "When not in office, discuss not policy."

[15] The Master said: "In the first days of the music master Chih how grand was the ending of the Kuan-chü! How it filled the ear!"

[16] The Master said: "Of such as are eager, but not straight; shallow, but not simple; dull, but not truthful, I will know nothing."

[17] The Master said: "Study as though the time were short, as one who fears to lose."

[18] The Master said: "It was sublime how Shun and Yü swayed the world and made light of it!"

[19] The Master said: "How great was Yao in kingship! Sublime! Heaven alone is great; Yao alone was patterned on it! Boundless! Men's words failed them. Sublime the work he did, dazzling the wealth of his culture!"

[20] Shun had five ministers, and order reigned below heaven. King Wu said: "Ten in number are my able ministers." Confucius said: " 'The dearth of talent,' is not that the truth? The days when Yü succeeded T'ang were rich in talent; yet there were but nine men in all, and one of these was a woman. The utmost worth was the worth of Chou! Lord of two-thirds of the earth, he submitted all to Yin."

[21] The Master said: "I find no flaw in Yü. Frugal in eating and drinking, he was lavish to the ghosts of the dead: ill-clad, he was gorgeous in cap and gown: his home a hovel, he poured out his strength upon dikes and ditches. No kind of flaw can I find in Yü."

IX

[1] The Master seldom spake of gain, doom, or love.

[2] A man from the Ta-hsiang village said: "The great Confucius, with his vast learning, has made no name in anything." When the Master heard it, he said to his disciples: "What shall I take up? Shall I take up charioteering? Shall I take up bowmanship? I must take up charioteering."

[3] The Master said: "A linen cap is correct: to-day silk is worn. It is cheap, and I follow the many. To bow below is correct: to-day it is done above. This is overweening, and, despite the many, I bow below."

[4] From four things the Master was quite free. He had no by-views; he knew not "must," or "shall," or "I."

[5] When the Master was affrighted in K'uang, he said: "Since the death of King Wen, is not this the home of culture? Had Heaven condemned culture, later mortals had missed their share in it. If Heaven uphold culture, what can the men of K'uang do to me?"

[6] A high minister said to Tzu-kung: "The Master must be a holy man, he can do so many things!"

Tzu-kung said: "Heaven has indeed well-nigh endowed him with holiness, and he is many-sided too."

When the Master heard it, he said: "Does the minister know me? Being lowly born, I learned many an humble trade in my youth. But has a gentleman skill in many things? No, in few things."

Lao said that the Master would say: "Having no post, I learned a craft."

[7] The Master said: "Have I in truth understanding? I have no understanding. But if a yokel ask me aught in an empty way, I tap it on this side and that, and sift it to the bottom."

[8] The Master said: "The phoenix comes not, nor does the river give forth a sign. All is over with me!"

[9] When the Master saw folk clad in mourning, or in robes of state, or else a blind man, he made a point of rising—even for the young—or, if he were passing by, of quickening his step.

[10] Yen Yüan heaved a sigh and said: "As I gaze it grows higher, more remote as I dig! I sight it in front, next moment astern! The Master tempts men forward deftly bit by bit. He widened me with culture, he bound me with courtesy. Until my strength was spent I had no power to stop. The goal seemed at hand: I longed to reach it, but the way was closed."

[11] When the Master was very ill, Tzu-lu moved the disciples to act as ministers.

During a better spell the Master said: "Yu has long been feigning. This show of ministers, when I have no ministers, whom can it deceive? Will it deceive Heaven? Moreover, is it not better to die in your arms, my boys, than to die in the arms of ministers? And if I lack a grand burial, shall I die by the roadside?"

[12] Tzu-kung said: "Were a beauteous jadestone mine, ought I to hide it away in a case, or seek a good price and sell it?"

The Master said: "Sell it, sell it! I tarry for my price."

[13] The Master wished to make his home among the nine tribes.

One said: "They are low, how could ye?"

The Master said: "Where a gentleman has his home, can aught live that is low?"

[14] The Master said: "After I came back from Wei to Lu the music was set straight and each song found its place."

[15] The Master said: "To serve men of high rank when abroad, and father and brothers when at home; to dread slackness in graveside duties, and be no thrall to wine: to which of these have I won?"

[16] As he stood by a stream, the Master said: "Hasting away like this, day and night without stop!"

[17] The Master said: "I have found none who love good as they love women."

[18] The Master said: "In making a mound, if I stop when one basketful more would end it, it is I that stop. In levelling ground, if I go on after throwing down one basketful, it is I that proceed."

[19] The Master said: "Never listless when spoken to, such was Hui!"

[20] Speaking of Yen Yüan, the Master said: "The pity of it! I have seen him go on, but never have I seen him stop."

[21] The Master said: "Some sprouts do not blossom, some blossoms bear no fruit."

[22] The Master said: "Awe is due to youth. May not to-morrow be bright as to-day? To men of forty or fifty, who are unknown still, no awe is due."

[23] The Master said: "Who would not give ear to a down-

right word? But to mend is of price. Who would not be pleased by a guiding word? But to ponder the word is of price. With such as give ear, but will not mend; who are pleased, but will not ponder, I can do nothing."

[24] The Master said: "Make faithfulness and truth thy masters: have no friends unlike thyself: be not ashamed to mend thy faults."

[25] The Master said: "Three armies may be robbed of their leader, no wretch can be robbed of his will."

[26] The Master said: "Clad in a tattered, quilted cloak, Yu will stand unabashed amidst robes of fox and badger.

" 'Void of hatred and greed,
What but good does he do?' "

But when Tzu-lu was ever humming these words, the Master said: "This is the way: but is it the whole of goodness?"

[27] The Master said: "Erst the cold days show how fir and cypress are last to fade."

[28] The Master said: "The wise are free from doubt; love is never vexed; the bold have no fears."

[29] The Master said: "With some we can join in learning, but not in aims; with others we can join in aims, but not in standpoint; and with others again in standpoint, but not in measures."

. . .

XII

[1] Yen Yüan asked, What is love?

The Master said: "Love is to conquer self and turn to courtesy. Could we conquer self and turn to courtesy for but one day, all mankind would turn to love. Does love flow from within, or does it flow from others?"

Yen Yüan said: "May I ask what are its signs?"

The Master said: "To be ever courteous of eye and ever courteous of ear; to be ever courteous in word and ever courteous in deed."

Yen Yüan said: "Dull as I am, I hope to live by these words."

[2] Chung-kung asked, What is love?

The Master said: "Without the door to behave as though a great guest were come; to treat the people as though we tendered the high sacrifice; not to do unto others what we would not they should do unto us; to breed no wrongs in the state and breed no wrongs in the home."

Chung-kung said: "Dull as I am, I hope to live by these words."

[3] Ssu-ma Niu asked, What is love?

The Master said: "Love is slow to speak."

"To be slow to speak! Can that be called love?"

The Master said: "That which is hard to do, can it be lightly spoken?"

[4] Ssu-ma Niu asked, What is a gentleman?

The Master said: "A gentleman knows neither sorrow nor fear."

"No sorrow and no fear! Can that be called a gentleman?"

The Master said: "He finds no sin in his heart, so why should he sorrow, what should he fear?"

[5] Ssu-ma Niu cried sadly: "All men have brothers, I alone have none!"

Tzu-hsia said: "I have heard that life and death are allotted, that wealth and honours are in Heaven's hand. A gentleman is careful and does not trip; he is humble towards others and courteous. All within the four seas are brethren; how can a gentleman mourn his lack of them?"

[6] Tzu-chang asked, What is insight?

The Master said: "To be unmoved by lap and wash of slander, or by plaints that pierce to the quick, may be called insight. Yea, whom lap and wash of slander, or plaints that pierce to the quick cannot move may be called far-sighted."

[7] Tzu-kung asked, What is kingcraft?

The Master said: "Food enough, troops enough, and a trusting people."

Tzu-kung said: "Were there no help for it, which could best be spared of the three?"

"Troops," said the Master.

"And were there no help for it, which could better be spared of the other two?"

"Food," said the Master. "From of old all men die, but without trust a people cannot stand."

. . .

[20] Tzu-chang asked, When may a scholar be called eminent?

The Master said: "What dost thou mean by eminence?"

Tzu-chang answered: "To be famous in the state, and famous in his home."

The Master said: "That is fame, not eminence. The eminent man is plain and straight. He loves right, weighs men's words, and scans their looks. At pains to step down to them, he will be eminent in the state, and eminent in his home. The famous man wears a mask of love, but his deeds belie it. He knows no misgivings, and fame will be his in the state and fame be his in his home."

[21] Whilst wandering through the Rain God's glade with the Master, Fan Ch'ih said to him: "May I ask how to raise the mind, amend evil, and scatter errors?"

The Master said: "A good question! Rate the task above the prize; will not the mind be raised? Fight thine own faults, not the faults of others; will not evil be mended? One angry morning to forget both self and kin, is that no error?"

[22] Fan Ch'ih asked, What is love?

The Master said: "To love mankind."

He asked, What is wisdom?

The Master said: "To know mankind."

Fan Ch'ih did not understand.

The Master said: "Exalt the straight, put aside the crooked; the crooked will grow straight."

. . .

XIV

[1] Hsien asked, What is shame?

The Master said: "Hire when right prevails, hire when wrong prevails, hire is always shame."

[2] "To eschew strife and boasting, spite and greed, can that be called love?"

The Master said: "I call that hard to do: I do not know that it is love."

[3] The Master said: "A scholar who loves comfort is not worthy the name."

[4] The Master said: "When right prevails, be fearless of speech and fearless in deed: when wrong prevails, be fearless in deed but soft of speech."

[5] The Master said: "A man of worth can always talk, but talkers are not always men of worth. Love is always bold, though boldness is found without love."

[6] Nan-kung Kuo said to Confucius: "Yi was good at archery, Ao could push a boat overland; each died before his time. Yü and Chi toiled at their crops, and won the world."

The Master did not answer.

But when Nan-kung Kuo had left, the Master said: "What a gentleman he is! How he prizes worth!"

[7] The Master said: "Gentlemen without love there may be, but the vulgar must ever be strangers to love."

[8] The Master said: "Can one love, yet take no pains? Can he be faithful who gives no counsel?"

. . .

[44] The Master said: "When those above love courtesy, the people are easy to lead."

[45] Tzu-lu asked, What is a gentleman?

The Master said: "A man bent on shaping his mind."

"Is that all?" said Tzu-lu.

"On shaping his mind to give happiness to others."

"And is that all?"

"On shaping his mind to give happiness to the people," said the Master. "To shape the mind and give happiness to the people, for this both Yao and Shun still pined."

. . .

XV

[1] Ling, Duke of Wei, asked Confucius about the line of battle.

Confucius answered: "Of temple ware I have learned: arms I have not studied."

On the morrow he went his way.

In Ch'en grain ran out. His followers grew too ill to rise. Tzu-lu could not hide his vexation.

"Must gentlemen also face misery?" he said.

"Of course a gentleman must face misery," said the Master. "It goads the vulgar to violence."

[2] The Master said: "Dost thou not think, Tz'u, that I am a man who learns much, and bears it in mind?"

"Yes," he answered, "is it not so?"

"No," said the Master. "I string all into one."

[3] The Master said: "Yu, how few know what is worthy!"

[4] The Master said: "To rule doing nothing, that was Shun's way. What need to be doing? Self-respect and a kingly look are all."

[5] Tzu-chang asked how to get on.

The Master said: "Be faithful and true of word; let thy walk be plain and lowly: thou wilt get on, though in savage land. If thy words be not faithful and true, thy walk plain and lowly, wilt thou get on, though in thine own home? Standing, see these words ranged before thee; driving, see them written upon the yoke. Then thou wilt get on."

Tzu-chang wrote them upon his girdle.

[6] The Master said: "Straight indeed was the historian Yü! Straight as an arrow when right prevailed, and straight as an arrow when wrong prevailed! What a gentleman was Ch'ü Po-yü! When right prevailed he took office: when wrong prevailed he rolled himself up in thought."

[7] The Master said: "To keep silence to him who has ears to hear is to spill the man. To speak to a man without ears to hear is to spill thy words. Wisdom spills neither man nor word."

[8] The Master said: "A high will, or a loving heart, will not seek life at cost of love. To fulfil love they will kill the body."

[9] Tzu-kung asked how to practise love. The Master said: "A workman bent on good work will first sharpen his tools. In the land that is thy home, serve the best men in power, and get thee friends who love."

[10] Yen Yüan asked how to rule a kingdom. The Master said: "Follow the Hsia seasons; drive in the chariot of Yin; wear the head-dress of Chou; choose for music the Shao and its dance. Banish the strains of Cheng, and shun men of glib tongue; for wanton are the strains of Cheng; there is danger in a glib tongue."

[11] The Master said: "Without thought for far off things, there will be troubles near at hand."

[12] The Master said: "It is finished! I have met no one who loves good as he loves women!"

. . .

[14] The Master said: "By asking much of self, and throwing little on others, ill feeling is put to flight."

[15] The Master said: "Unless a man ask, 'Will this help? will that help?' I know not how to help him."

[16] The Master said: "When all day long there is no talk of right, and sharp moves find favour, the company is in hard case."

[17] The Master said: "A gentleman makes right his base. Done with courtesy, spoken with deference, rounded with truth, right makes a gentleman."

[18] The Master said: "His unworthiness vexes a gentleman: to live unknown cannot vex him."

[19] The Master said: "A gentleman fears lest his name should die when life is done."

[20] The Master said: "A gentleman looks within: the vulgar look unto others."

[21] The Master said: "A gentleman is firm, not quarrelsome; a friend, not a partisan."

[22] The Master said: "A gentleman does not raise a man for his words, nor scorn what is said for the speaker."

[23] Tzu-kung asked: "Can one word cover the whole duty of man?"

The Master said: "Fellow-feeling, perhaps. Do not do unto others what thou wouldst not they should do unto thee."

[24] The Master said: "Of the men that I meet, whom do I decry? whom do I flatter? Or if I flatter, it is after trial. Because of this people three lines of kings followed the straight road."

[25] The Master said: "Even in my time an historian would leave a blank in his text, an owner of a horse would lend him to others to ride. To-day it is so no more."

[26] The Master said: "Honeyed words confound goodness: impatience of trifles confounds great projects."

[27] The Master said: "The hatred of the many calls for search: the favour of the many calls for search."

[28] The Master said: "The man can exalt the truth: truth cannot exalt the man."

[29] The Master said: "The fault is to cleave to a fault."

[30] The Master said: "In vain have I spent in thought whole days without food, whole nights without sleep! Study is better."

[31] The Master said: "A gentleman aims at truth; he does not aim at food. Ploughing may end in famine; study may end in pay. But a gentleman pines for truth: he is not pined with poverty."

[32] The Master said: "What the mind has won will be lost again, unless love hold it fast. A mind to understand and love to hold fast, without dignity of bearing, will go unhonoured. A mind to understand, love to hold fast and dignity of bearing are incomplete, without courteous ways."

[33] The Master said: "A gentleman has no skill in trifles, but has strength for big tasks: the vulgar are skilled in trifles, but have no strength for big tasks."

[34] The Master said: "Love is more to the people than fire and water. I have known men come to their death by fire and water: I have met no man whom love brought unto death."

[35] The Master said: "When love is at stake yield not to an army."

[36] The Master said: "A gentleman is consistent, not change-less."

[37] The Master said: "A servant of the king honours work and rates pay last."

[38] The Master said: "All educated men are peers."

. . .

XVI

. . .

[4] Confucius said: "There are three friends that do good, and three friends that do harm. The friends that do good are a straight friend, a sincere friend, and a friend who has heard much. The friends that do harm are a smooth friend, a fawning friend, and a friend with a glib tongue."

[5] Confucius said: "There are three joys that do good, and three joys that do harm. The joys that do good are joy in dissecting courtesy and music, joy in speaking of the good in men, and joy in a number of worthy friends. The joys that do harm are joy in pomp, joy in roving, and joy in the joys of the feast."

[6] Confucius said: "Men who wait upon princes fall into three mistakes. To speak before the time has come is rashness. Not to speak when the time has come is secrecy. To speak heedless of looks is blindness."

[7] Confucius said: "A gentleman has three things to guard against. In the days of thy youth, ere thy strength is steady, beware of lust. When manhood is reached, in the fulness of strength, beware of strife. In old age, when thy strength is broken, beware of greed."

[8] Confucius said: "A gentleman holds three things in awe. He is in awe of Heaven's doom: he is in awe of great men: he is awed by the speech of the holy.

"The vulgar are blind to doom, and hold it not in awe. They are saucy towards the great, and of the speech of the holy they make their game."

[9] Confucius said: "The best men are born wise. Next come

those who grow wise by learning: then, learned, narrow minds. Narrow minds, without learning, are the lowest of the people."

[10] Confucius said: "A gentleman has nine aims. To see clearly; to understand what he hears; to be warm in manner, dignified in bearing, faithful of speech, painstaking at work; to ask when in doubt; in anger to think of difficulties; in sight of gain to remember right."

[11] Confucius said: "In sight of good to be filled with longing; to regard evil as scalding to the touch: I have met such men, I have heard such words.

"To dwell apart and search the will; to unriddle truth by righteous life: I have heard these words, but met no such men."
. . .

XVII

[1] Yang Huo wished to see Confucius. Confucius did not visit him. He sent Confucius a suckling pig. Confucius chose a time when he was out, and went to thank him. They met on the road.

He said to Confucius: "Come, let us speak together. To cherish a gem and undo the kingdom, is that love?"

"It is not," said Confucius.

"To be fond of power and let each chance of office slip, is that wisdom?"

"It is not," said Confucius.

"The days and months glide by; the years do not tarry for us."

"True," said Confucius; "I must take office."

[2] The Master said: "Men are near to each other at birth: the lives they lead sunder them."

[3] The Master said: "Only the wisest and the stupidest of men never change."
. . .

[23] Tzu-lu said: "Does a gentleman honour courage?"

The Master said: "Right comes first for a gentleman. Courage, without sense of right, makes rebels of the great, and robbers of the poor."

[24] Tzu-kung said: "Does a gentleman also hate?"

"He does," said the Master. "He hates the sounding of evil deeds; he hates men of low estate who slander their betters; he hates courage without courtesy; he hates daring matched with blindness."

"And Tz'u," he added, "dost thou hate too?"

"I hate those who mistake spying for wisdom. I hate those who take want of deference for courage. I hate evil speaking, cloaked as honesty."

CHAPTER IV

Taoism

Lao Tzu

Fung Yu-Lan

According to tradition, Lao Tzu (a name which literally means the "Old Master") was a native of the state of Ch'u in the southern part of the present Honan province, and was an older contemporary of Confucius, whom he is reputed to have instructed in ceremonies. The book bearing his name, the *Lao-tzu,* and in later times also known as the *Tao Te Ching* (*Classic of the Way and Power*), has therefore been traditionally regarded as the first philosophical work in Chinese history. Modern scholarship, however, has forced us drastically to change this view and to date it to a time considerably after Confucius.

LAO TZU THE MAN AND *Lao-tzu* THE BOOK

Two questions arise in this connection. One is about the date of the man, Lao Tzu (whose family name is said to have been Li, and personal name, Tan), and another about the date of the book itself. There is no necessary connection between the two, for it is quite possible that there actually lived a man known

Reprinted from Fung Yu-Lan, *A Short History of Chinese Philosophy,* edited by Derk Bodde (The Macmillan Company, 1948), pages 93–103. Copyright 1948 by The Macmillan Company. Used by permission of the publisher.

as Lao Tan who was senior to Confucius, but that the book titled the *Lao-tzu* is a later production. This is the view I take, and it does not necessarily contradict the traditional accounts of Lao Tzu the man, because in these accounts there is no statement that the man, Lao Tzu, actually wrote the book by that name. Hence I am willing to accept the traditional stories about Lao Tzu the man, while at the same time placing the book, *Lao-tzu,* in a later period. In fact, I now believe the date of the book to be later than I assumed when I wrote my *History of Chinese Philosophy.* I now believe it was written or composed after Hui Shih and Kung-sun Lung, and not before, as I there indicated. This is because the *Lao-tzu* contains considerable discussion about the Nameless, and in order to do this it would seem that men should first have become conscious of the existence of names themselves.

My position does not require me to insist that there is absolutely no connection between Lao Tzu the man and *Lao-tzu* the book, for the book may indeed contain a few sayings of the original Lao Tzu. What I maintain, however, is that the system of thought in the book as a whole cannot be the product of a time either before or contemporary with that of Confucius. In the pages following, however, to avoid pedantry, I shall refer to Lao Tzu as having said so and so, instead of stating that the book *Lao-tzu* says so and so, just as we today still speak of sunrise and sunset, even though we know very well that the sun itself actually neither rises nor sets.

Tao, THE UNNAMABLE

In the last chapter, we have seen that the philosophers of the School of Names, through the study of names, succeeded in discovering "that which lies beyond shapes and features." Most people, however, think only in terms of "what lies within shapes and features," that is, the actual world. Seeing the actual, they have no difficulty in expressing it, and though they use names for it, they are not conscious that they are names. So when the phi-

losophers of the School of Names started to think about the
names themselves, this thought represented a great advance. To
think about names is to think about thinking. It is thought about
thought and therefore is thought on a higher level.

All things that "lie within shapes and features" have names,
or, at least, possess the possibility of having names. They are
namable. But in contrast with what is namable, Lao Tzu speaks
about the unnamable. Not everything that lies beyond shapes
and features is unnamable. Universals, for instance, lie beyond
shapes and features, yet they are not unnamable. But on the other
hand, what is unnamable most certainly does lie beyond shapes
and features. The *Tao* or Way of the Taoists is a concept of this
sort.

In the first chapter of the *Lao-tzu* we find the statement: "The
Tao that can be comprised in words is not the eternal *Tao;* the
name that can be named is not the abiding name. The Unnamable is the beginning of Heaven and Earth; the namable is
the mother of all things." And in chapter thirty-two: "The *Tao*
is eternal, nameless, the Uncarved Block. . . . Once the block is
carved, there are names." Or in chapter forty-one: "The *Tao*,
lying hid, is nameless." In the Taoist system, there is a distinction
between *yu* (being) and *wu* (non-being), and between *yu-ming*
(having-name, namable) and *wu-ming* (having-no-name, unnamable). These two distinctions are in reality only one, for *yu*
and *wu* are actually simply abbreviated terms for *yu-ming* and
wu-ming. Heaven and Earth and all things are namables. Thus
Heaven has the name of Heaven, Earth the name Earth, and
each kind of thing has the name of that kind. There being
Heaven, Earth and all things, it follows that there are the names
of Heaven, Earth, and all things. Or as Lao Tzu says: "Once the
Block is carved, there are names." The *Tao*, however, is unnamable; at the same time it is that by which all namables come
to be. This is why Lao Tzu says: "The Unnamable is the beginning of Heaven and Earth; the namable is the mother of all
things."

Since the *Tao* is unnamable, it therefore cannot be comprised in words. But since we wish to speak about it, we are forced to give it some kind of designation. We therefore call it *Tao*, which is really not a name at all. That is to say, to call the *Tao Tao*, is not the same as to call a table table. When we call a table table, we mean that it has some attributes by which it can be named. But when we call the *Tao Tao*, we do not mean that it has any such namable attributes. It is simply a designation, or to use an expression common in Chinese philosophy, *Tao* is a name which is not a name. In chapter twenty-one of the *Lao-tzu* it is said: "From the past to the present, its [*Tao's*] name has not ceased to be, and has seen the beginning [of all things]." The *Tao* is that by which anything and everything comes to be. Since there are always things, *Tao* never ceases to be and the name of *Tao* also never ceases to be. It is the beginning of all beginnings, and therefore it has seen the beginning of all things. A name that never ceases to be is an abiding name, and such a name is in reality not a name at all. Therefore it is said: "The name that can be named is not the abiding name."

"The Unnamable is the beginning of Heaven and Earth." This proposition is only a formal and not a positive one. That is to say, it fails to give any information about matters of fact. The Taoists thought that since there are things, there must be that by which all these things come to be. This "that" is designated by them as *Tao*, which, however, is really not a name. The concept of *Tao*, too, is a formal and not a positive one. That is to say, it does not describe anything about what it is through which all things come to be. All we can say is that *Tao*, since it is that through which all things come to be, is necessarily not a mere thing among these other things. For if it were such a thing, it could not at the same time be that through which *all* things whatsoever come to be. Every kind of thing has a name, but *Tao* is not itself a thing. Therefore it is "nameless, the Uncarved Block."

Anything that comes to be is a being, and there are many beings. The coming to be of beings implies that first of all there is Being. These words, "first of all," here do not mean first in point of time, but first in a logical sense. For instance, if we say there was first a certain kind of animal, then man, the word "first" in this case means first in point of time. But if we say that first there must be animals before there are men, the word "first" in this case means first in a logical sense. The statement about "the origin of the species" makes an assertion about matters of fact, and required many years' observation and study by Charles Darwin before it could be made. But the second of our sayings makes no assertion about matters of fact. It simply says that the existence of men logically implies the existence of animals. In the same way, the being of all things implies the being of Being. This is the meaning of Lao Tzu's saying: "All things in the world come into being from Being (*Yu*); and Being comes into being from Non-being (*Wu*)." (Ch. 40.)

This saying of Lao Tzu does not mean that there was a time when there was only Non-being, and that then there came a time when Being came into being from Non-being. It simply means that if we analyze the existence of things, we see there must first be Being before there can be any things. *Tao* is the unnamable, is Non-being, and is that by which all things come to be. Therefore, before the being of Being, there must be Non-being, from which Being comes into being. What is here said belongs to ontology, not to cosmology. It has nothing to do with time and actuality. For in time and actuality, there is no Being; there are only beings.

There are many beings, but there is only one Being. In the *Lao-tzu* it is said: "From *Tao* there comes one. From one there comes two. From two there comes three. From three there comes all things." (Ch. 42.) The "one" here spoken of refers to Being. To say that "from *Tao* comes one," is the same as that from Non-being comes Being. As for "two" and "three," there are many interpretations. But this saying, that "from one there comes two. From two there comes three. From three there comes all things," may simply be the same as saying that from Being come all things. Being is one, and two and three are the beginning of the many.

The Invariable Law of Nature

In the final chapter of the *Chuang-tzu*, "The World," it is said that the leading ideas of Lao Tzu are those of the *T'ai Yi* or "Super One," and of Being, Non-being, and the invariable. The "Super One" is the *Tao*. From the *Tao* comes one, and therefore *Tao* itself is the "Super One." The "invariable" is a translation of the Chinese word *ch'ang*, which may also be translated as eternal or abiding. Though things are ever changeable and changing, the laws that govern this change of things are not themselves changeable. Hence in the *Lao-tzu* the word *ch'ang* is used to show what is always so, or in other words, what can be considered as a rule. For instance, Lao Tzu tells us: "The conquest of the world comes invariably from doing nothing." (Ch. 48.) Or again: "The way of Heaven has no favorites, it is invariably on the side of the good man." (Ch. 79.)

Among the laws that govern the changes of things, the most fundamental is that "when a thing reaches one extreme, it reverts from it." These are not the actual words of Lao Tzu, but a common Chinese saying, the idea of which no doubt comes from Lao Tzu. Lao Tzu's actual words are: "Reversing is the movement of the *Tao*" (ch. 40), and: "To go further and further means to revert again." (Ch. 25.) The idea is that if anything develops certain extreme qualities, those qualities invariably revert to become their opposites.

This constitutes a law of nature. Therefore: "It is upon calamity that blessing leans, upon blessing that calamity rests." (Ch. 58.) "Those with little will acquire, those with much will be led astray." (Ch. 22.) "A hurricane never lasts the whole morning, nor a rainstorm the whole day." (Ch. 23.) "The most yielding things in the world master the most unyielding." (Ch. 43.) "Diminish a thing and it will increase. Increase a thing and it will diminish." (Ch. 42.) All these paradoxical theories are no longer paradoxical, if one understands the fundamental law of nature. But to the ordinary people who have no idea of this law, they seem paradoxical indeed. Therefore Lao Tzu says:

"The gentleman of the low type, on hearing the Truth, laughs loudly at it. If he had not laughed, it would not suffice to be the Truth." (Ch. 41.)

It may be asked: Granted that a thing, on reaching an extreme, then reverts, what is meant by the word "extreme"? Is there any absolute limit for the development of anything, going beyond which would mean going to the extreme? In the *Lao-tzu* no such question is asked and therefore no answer is given. But if there had been such a question, I think Lao Tzu would have answered that no absolute limit can be prescribed for all things under all circumstances. So far as human activities are concerned, the limit for the advancement of a man remains relative to his subjective feelings and objective circumstances. Isaac Newton, for example, felt that compared with the total universe, his knowledge of it was no more than the knowledge of the sea possessed by a boy who is playing at the seashore. With such a feeling as this, Newton, despite his already great achievements in physics, was still far from reaching the limits of advancement in his learning. If, however, a student, having just finished his textbook on physics, thinks that he then knows all there is to know about science, he certainly cannot make further advancement in his learning, and will as certainly "revert back." Lao Tzu tells us: "If people of wealth and exalted position are arrogant, they abandon themselves to unavoidable ruin." (Ch. 9.) Arrogance is the sign that one's advancement has reached its extreme limit. It is the first thing that one should avoid.

The limit of advancement for a given activity is also relative to objective circumstances. When a man eats too much, he suffers. In overeating, what is ordinarily good for the body becomes something harmful. One should eat only the right amount of food. But this right amount depends on one's age, health, and the quality of food one eats.

These are the laws that govern the changes of things. By Lao Tzu they are called the invariables. He says: "To know the invariables is called enlightenment." (Ch. 16.) Again: "He who knows the invariable is liberal. Being liberal, he is without prejudice. Being without prejudice, he is comprehensive. Being comprehensive, he is vast. Being vast, he is with the Truth. Being with the Truth, he lasts forever and will not fail throughout his lifetime." (*Ibid.*)

HUMAN CONDUCT

Lao Tzu warns us: "Not to know the invariable and to act blindly is to go to disaster." (*Ibid.*) One should know the laws of nature and conduct one's activities in accordance with them. This, by Lao Tzu, is called "practicing enlightenment." The general rule for the man "practicing enlightenment" is that if he wants to achieve anything, he starts with its opposite, and if he wants to retain anything, he admits in it something of its opposite. If one wants to be strong, one must start with a feeling that one is weak, and if one wants to preserve capitalism, one must admit in it some elements of socialism.

Therefore Lao Tzu tells us: "The sage, putting himself in the background, is always to the fore. Remaining outside, he is always there. Is it not just because he does not strive for any personal end, that all his personal ends are fulfilled?" (Ch. 7.) Again: "He does not show himself; therefore he is seen everywhere. He does not define himself; therefore he is distinct. He does not assert himself; therefore he succeeds. He does not boast of his work; therefore he endures. He does not contend, and for that very reason no one in the world can contend with him." (Ch. 22.) These sayings illustrate the first point of the general rule.

In the *Lao-tzu* we also find: "What is most perfect seems to have something missing, yet its use is unimpaired. What is most full seems empty, yet its use is inexhaustible. What is most straight seems like crookedness. The greatest skill seems like clumsiness. The greatest eloquence seems like stuttering." (Ch. 45.) Again: "Be twisted and one shall be whole. Be crooked and one shall be straight. Be hollow and one shall be filled. Be tattered and one shall be renewed. Have little and one shall obtain. But have much and one shall be perplexed." (Ch. 22.) This illustrates the second point of the general rule.

Such is the way in which a prudent man can live safely in the world and achieve his aims. This is Lao Tzu's answer and solution to the original problem of the Taoists, which was, how to preserve life and avoid harm and danger in the human world. The man who lives prudently must be meek, humble, and easily content. To be meek is the way to preserve your strength and so be strong. Humility is the direct opposite of arrogance, so that if arrogance is a sign that a man's advancement has reached its extreme limit, humility is a contrary sign that that limit is far from reached. And to be content safeguards one from going too far, and therefore from reaching the extreme. Lao Tzu says: "To know how to be content is to avoid humiliation; to know where to stop is to avoid injury." (Ch. 45.) Again: "The sage, therefore, discards the excessive, the extravagant, the extreme." (Ch. 29.)

All these theories are deducible from the general theory that "reversing is the movement of the *Tao*." The well-known Taoist theory of *wu-wei* is also deducible from this general theory. *Wu-wei* can be translated literally as "having-no-activity" or "non-action." But using this translation, one should remember that the term does not actually mean complete absence of activity, or doing nothing. What it does mean is lesser activity or doing less. It also means acting without artificiality and arbitrariness.

Activities are like many other things. If one has too much of them, they become harmful rather than good. Furthermore, the purpose of doing something is to have something done. But if there is over-doing, this results in something being over-done, which may be worse than not having the thing done at all. A well-known Chinese story describes how two men were once competing in drawing a snake; the one who would finish his drawing first would win. One of them, having indeed finished his drawing, saw that the other man was still far behind, so decided to improve it by adding feet to his snake. Thereupon the other man said: "You have lost the competition, for a snake has no feet." This is an illustration of over-doing which defeats its own purpose. In the *Lao-tzu* we read: "Conquering the world is invariably due to doing nothing; by doing something one cannot conquer the world." (Ch. 48.) The term "doing nothing" here really means "not over-doing."

Artificiality and arbitrariness are the opposite of naturalness and spontaneity. According to Lao Tzu, *Tao* is that by which all things come to be. In this process of coming to be, each individual thing obtains something from the universal *Tao,* and this something is called *Te. Te* is a word that means "power" or "virtue," both in the moral and non-moral sense of the latter term. The *Te* of a thing is what it naturally is. Lao Tzu says: "All things respect *Tao* and value *Te*." (Ch. 51.) This is because *Tao* is that by which they come to be, and *Te* is that by which they are what they are.

According to the theory of "having-no-activity," a man should restrict his activities to what is necessary and what is natural. "Necessary" means necessary to the achievement of a certain purpose, and never over-doing. "Natural" means following one's *Te* with no arbitrary effort. In doing this one should take simplicity as the guiding principle of life. Simplicity (*p'u*) is an important idea of Lao Tzu and the Taoists. *Tao* is the "Uncarved Block" (*p'u*), which is simplicity itself. There is nothing that can be simpler than the unnamable *Tao. Te* is the next simplest, and the man who follows *Te* must lead as simple a life as possible.

The life that follows *Te* lies beyond the distinctions of good and evil. Lao Tzu tells us: "If all people of the world know that beauty is beauty, there is then already ugliness. If all people of the world know that good is good, there is then already evil." (Ch. 2.) Lao Tzu, therefore, despised such Confucian virtues as human-heartedness and righteousness, for according to him these virtues represent a degeneration from *Tao* and *Te*. Therefore he says: "When the *Tao* is lost, there is the *Te*. When the *Te* is lost, there is [the virtue of] human-heartedness. When human-heartedness is lost, there is [the virtue of] righteousness. When righteousness is lost, there are the ceremonials. Ceremonials are the degeneration of loyalty and good faith, and are the beginning of disorder in the world." (Ch. 38.) Here we find the direct conflict between Taoism and Confucianism.

People have lost their original *Te* because they have too many desires and too much knowledge. In satisfying their desires, people are seeking for happiness. But when they try to satisfy too many desires, they obtain an opposite result. Lao Tzu says: "The five colors blind the eye. The five notes dull the ear. The five tastes fatigue the mouth. Riding and hunting madden the mind. Rare treasures hinder right conduct." (Ch. 5.) Therefore, "there is no disaster greater than not knowing contentment with what one has; no greater sin than having desire for acquisition." (Ch. 46.) This is why Lao Tzu emphasizes that people should have few desires.

Likewise Lao Tzu emphasizes that people should have little knowledge. Knowledge is itself an object of desire. It also enables people to know more about the objects of desire and serves as a means to gain these objects. It is both the master and servant of desire. With increasing knowledge people are no longer in a position to know how to be content and where to stop. Therefore, it is said in the *Lao-tzu:* "When knowledge and intelligence appeared, Gross Artifice began." (Ch. 18.)

POLITICAL THEORY

From these theories Lao Tzu deduces his political theory. The Taoists agree with the Confucianists that the ideal state is one which has a sage as its head. It is only the sage who can and should rule. The difference between the two schools, however, is that according to the Confucianists, when a sage becomes the ruler, he should do many things for the people, whereas according to the Taoists, the duty of the sage ruler is not to do things, but rather to undo or not to do at all. The reason for this, according to Lao Tzu, is that the troubles of the world come, not because there are many things not yet done, but because too many things are done. In the *Lao-tzu* we read: "The more restrictions and prohibitions there are in the world, the poorer the people will be. The more sharp weapons the people have, the more troubled will be the country. The more cunning craftsmen there are, the more pernicious contrivances will appear. The more laws are promulgated, the more thieves and bandits there will be." (Ch. 27.)

The first act of a sage ruler, then, is to undo all these. Lao Tzu says: "Banish wisdom, discard knowledge, and the people will be benefited a hundredfold. Banish human-heartedness, discard righteousness, and the people will be dutiful and compassionate. Banish skill, discard profit, and thieves and robbers will disappear." (Ch. 19.) Again: "Do not exalt the worthies, and the people will no longer be contentious. Do not value treasures that are hard to get, and there will be no more thieves. If the people never see such things as excite desire, their minds will not be confused. Therefore the sage rules the people by emptying their minds, filling their bellies, weakening their wills, and toughening their sinews, ever making the people without knowledge and without desire." (Ch. 3.)

The sage ruler would undo all the causes of trouble in the world. After that, he would govern with non-action. With non-action, he does nothing, yet everything is accomplished. The *Lao-tzu* says: "I act not and the people of themselves are transformed. I love quiescence and the people of themselves go straight. I concern myself with nothing, and the people of themselves are prosperous. I am without desire, and the people of themselves are simple." (Ch. 57.)

"Do nothing, and there is nothing that is not done." This is another of the seemingly paradoxical ideas of the Taoists. In the *Lao-tzu* we read: "*Tao* invariably does nothing and yet there is nothing that is not done." (Ch. 37.) *Tao* is that by which all things come to be. It is not itself a thing and therefore it cannot act as do such things. Yet all things come to be. Thus *Tao* does nothing, yet there is nothing that is not done. It allows each thing to do what it itself can do. According to the Taoists, the ruler of a state should model himself on *Tao*. He, too, should do nothing and should let the people do what they can do themselves. Here is another meaning of *wu-wei* (non-action), which later, with certain modifications, becomes one of the important theories of the Legalists (*Fa chia*).

Children have limited knowledge and few desires. They are not far away from the original *Te*. Their simplicity and innocence are characteristics that every man should if possible retain. Lao Tzu says: "Not to part from the invariable *Te* is to return to the state of infancy." (Ch. 28.) Again: "He who holds the *Te* in all its solidity may be likened to an infant." (Ch. 55.) Since the life of the child is nearer to the ideal life, the sage ruler would like all of his people to be like small children. Lao Tzu says: "The sage treats all as children." (Ch. 49.) He "does not make them enlightened, but keeps them ignorant." (Ch. 65.)

"Ignorant" here is a translation of the Chinese *yu,* which means ignorance in the sense of simplicity and innocence. The sage not only wants his people to be *yu,* but wants himself to be so too. Lao Tzu says: "Mine is the mind of the very ignorant." (Ch. 20.) In Taoism *yu* is not a vice, but a great virtue.

But is the *yu* of the sage really the same as the *yu* of the child and the common people? Certainly not. The *yu* of the sage is the result of a conscious process of cultivation. It is something higher than knowledge, something more, not less. There is a common Chinese saying: "Great wisdom is like ignorance." The *yu* of the sage is great wisdom, and not the *yu* of the child or of ordinary people. The latter kind of *yu* is a gift of nature, while that of the sage is an achievement of the spirit. There is a great difference between the two. But in many cases the Taoists seemed to have confused them. We shall see this point more clearly when we discuss the philosophy of Chuang Tzu.

Selections from the *Tao Te Ching*

Translated by James Legge

2. 2. So it is that existence and non-existence give birth each to the idea of the other; that difficulty and ease produce the idea of each other; that length and shortness fashion out the one the figure of the other; that the ideas of height and lowness arise from the contrast of the one with the other; that the musical

Reprinted from James Legge, tr., *The Sacred Books of China,* Part I: The Texts of Taoism, in *The Sacred Books of the East,* edited by F. Max Müller, Vol. XXXIX (1891). Modified.

notes and tones become harmonious through the relation of one with another; and that being before and behind give the idea of one following another.

3. Therefore the sage manages affairs without doing anything, and conveys his instructions without the use of speech.

4. All things spring up, and there is not one which declines to show itself; they grow, and no claim is made for their owner-ship; they go through their processes, and there is no expectation of a reward for the results. The work is accomplished, and there is no resting in it as an achievement.

The work is done, but how no one can see;
'Tis this that makes the power not cease to be.

3. 1. Not to value and employ men of superior ability is the way to keep the people from rivalry among themselves; not to prize articles which are difficult to procure is the way to keep them from becoming thieves; not to show them what is likely to excite their desires is the way to keep their minds from disorder.

2. Therefore the sage, in the exercise of his government, empties their minds, fills their bellies, weakens their wills, and strengthens their bones.

3. He constantly tries to keep them without knowledge and without desire, and where there are those who have knowledge, to keep them from presuming to act on it. When there is this abstinence from action, good order is universal.

4. 1. The Tâo is like the emptiness of a vessel; and in our employment of it we must be on our guard against all fulness. How deep and unfathomable it is, as if it were the Honoured Ancestor of all things!

2. We should blunt our sharp points, and unravel the compli-cations of things; we should moderate our brightness, and bring ourselves into agreement with the obscurity of others. How pure and still the Tâo is, as if it would ever so continue!

3. I do not know whose son it is. It might appear to have been before God.

5. 1. Heaven and earth do not act from the impulse of any wish to be benevolent; they deal with all things as the dogs of grass are dealt with. The sages do not act from any wish to be benevolent; they deal with the people as the dogs of grass are dealt with.

2. May not the space between heaven and earth be compared to a bellows?

'Tis emptied, yet it loses not its power;
'Tis moved again, and sends forth air the more.
Much speech to swift exhaustion lead we see;
Your inner being guard, and keep it free.

7. 1. Heaven is long-enduring and earth continues long. The reason why heaven and earth are able to endure and continue thus long is because they do not live of, or for, themselves. This is how they are able to continue and endure.

2. Therefore the sage puts his own person last, and yet it is found in the foremost place; he treats his person as if it were foreign to him, and yet that person is preserved. Is it not because he has no personal and private ends, that therefore such ends are realised?

8. 1. The highest excellence is like that of water. The excellence of water appears in its benefiting all things, and in its occupying, without striving to the contrary, the low place which all men dislike. Hence its way is near to that of the Tâo.

2. The excellence of a residence is in the suitability of the place; that of the mind is in abysmal stillness; that of associations is in their being with the virtuous; that of government is in its securing good order; that of the conduct of affairs is in its ability; and that of the initiation of any movement is in its timeliness.

3. And when one with the highest excellence does not wrangle about his low position, no one finds fault with him.

9. 1. It is better to leave a vessel unfilled, than to attempt to carry it when it is full. If you keep feeling a point that has been sharpened, the point cannot long preserve its sharpness.

2. When gold and jade fill the hall, their possessor cannot keep them safe. When wealth and honours lead to arrogancy,

this brings its evil on itself. When the work is done, and one's name is becoming distinguished, to withdraw into obscurity is the way of Heaven.

10. 1. When the intelligent and animal souls are held together in one embrace, they can be kept from separating. When one gives undivided attention to the vital breath, and brings it to the utmost degree of pliancy, he can become as a tender babe. When he has cleansed away the most mysterious sights of his imagination, he can become without a flaw.

2. In loving the people and ruling the state, cannot he proceed without any purpose of action? In the opening and shutting of his gates of heaven, cannot he do so as a female bird? While his intelligence reaches in every direction, cannot he appear to be without knowledge?

3. The Tâo produces all things and nourishes them; it produces them and does not claim them as its own; it does all, and yet does not boast of it; it presides over all, and yet does not control them. This is what is called 'The mysterious Quality' of the Tâo.

12. 1. Colour's five hues from th' eyes their sight will take;
Music's five notes the ears as deaf can make;
The flavours five deprive the mouth of taste;
The chariot course, and the wild hunting waste
Make mad the mind; and objects rare and strange,
Sought for, men's conduct will to evil change.

2. Therefore the sage seeks to satisfy the craving of the belly, and not the insatiable longing of the eyes. He puts from him the latter, and prefers to seek the former.

14. 1. We look at it, and we do not see it, and we name it 'the Equable.' We listen to it, and we do not hear it, and we name it 'the Inaudible.' We try to grasp it, and do not get hold of it, and we name it 'the Subtle.' With these three qualities, it cannot be made the subject of description; and hence we blend them together and obtain The One.

2. Its upper part is not bright, and its lower part is not obscure.

Ceaseless in its action, it yet cannot be named, and then it again returns and becomes nothing. This is called the Form of the Formless, and the Semblance of the Invisible; this is called the Fleeting and Indeterminable.

3. We meet it and do not see its Front; we follow it, and do not see its Back. When we can lay hold of the Tâo of old to direct the things of the present day, and are able to know it as it was of old in the beginning, this is called unwinding the clue of Tâo.

15. 1. The skilful masters of the Tâo in old times, with a subtle and exquisite penetration, comprehended its mysteries, and were deep also so as to elude men's knowledge. As they were thus beyond men's knowledge, I will make an effort to describe of what sort they appeared to be.

2. Shrinking looked they like those who wade through a stream in winter; irresolute like those who are afraid of all around them; grave like a guest in awe of his host; evanescent like ice that is melting away; unpretentious like wood that has not been fashioned into anything; vacant like a valley, and dull like muddy water.

3. Who can make the muddy water clear? Let it be still, and it will gradually become clear. Who can secure the condition of rest? Let movement go on, and the condition of rest will gradually arise.

4. They who preserve this method of the Tâo do not wish to be full of themselves. It is through their not being full of themselves that they can afford to seem worn and not appear new and complete.

16. 1. The state of vacancy should be brought to the utmost degree, and that of stillness guarded with unwearying vigour. All things alike go through their processes of activity, and then we see them return to their original state. When things in the vegetable world have displayed their luxuriant growth, we see each of them return to its root. This returning to their root is what we call the state of stillness; and that stillness may be called a reporting that they have fulfilled their appointed end.

2. The report of that fulfilment is the regular, unchanging rule. To know that unchanging rule is to be intelligent; not to know it leads to wild movements and evil issues. The knowledge of that unchanging rule produces a grand capacity and forbearance, and that capacity and forbearance lead to a community of feeling with all things. From this community of feeling comes a kingliness of character; and he who is king-like goes on to be heaven-like. In that likeness to heaven he possesses the Tâo. Possessed of the Tâo, he endures long; and to the end of his bodily life, is exempt from all danger of decay.

17. 1. In the highest antiquity, the people did not know that there were their rulers. In the next age they loved them and praised them. In the next they feared them; in the next they despised them. Thus it was that when faith in the Tâo was deficient in the rulers a want of faith in them ensued in the people.

19. 1. If we could renounce our sageness and discard our wisdom, it would be better for the people a hundredfold. If we could renounce our benevolence and discard our righteousness, the people would again become filial and kindly. If we could renounce our artful contrivances and discard our scheming for gain, there would be no thieves nor robbers.
2. Those three methods of government
Though olden ways in elegance did fail
And made these names their want of worth to veil;
But simple views, and courses plain and true
Would selfish ends and many lusts eschew.

21. The grandest forms of active force
From Tâo come, their only source.
Who can of Tâo the nature tell?
Our sight it flies, our touch as well.
Eluding sight, eluding touch,
The forms of things all in it crouch;
Eluding touch, eluding sight,
There are their semblances, all right.
Profound it is, dark and obscure;

Things' essences all there endure.
Those essences the truth enfold
Of what, when seen, shall then be told.
Now it is so; 'twas so of old.
Its name—what passes not away;
So, in their beautiful array,
Things form and never know decay.

How know I that it is so with all the beauties of existing things?
By this nature of the Tâo.

22. 1. The partial becomes complete; the crooked, straight; the empty, full; the worn out, new. He whose desires are few gets them; he whose desires are many goes astray.

2. Therefore the sage holds in his embrace the one thing of humility, and manifests it to all the world. He is free from self-display, and therefore he shines; from self-assertion, and therefore he is distinguished; from self-boasting, and therefore his merit is acknowledged; from self-complacency, and therefore he acquires superiority. It is because he is thus free from striving that therefore no one in the world is able to strive with him.

3. That saying of the ancients that 'the partial becomes complete' was not vainly spoken:—all real completion is comprehended under it.

23. 1. Abstaining from speech marks him who is obeying the spontaneity of his nature. A violent wind does not last for a whole morning; a sudden rain does not last for the whole day. To whom is it that these two things are owing? To Heaven and Earth. If Heaven and Earth cannot make such spasmodic actings last long, how much less can man!

2. Therefore when one is making the Tâo his business, those who are also pursuing it, agree with him in it, and those who are making the manifestation of its course their object agree with him in that; while even those who are failing in both these things agree with him where they fail.

3. Hence, those with whom he agrees as to the Tâo have the happiness of attaining to it; those with whom he agrees as to its manifestation have the happiness of attaining to it; and those

with whom he agrees in their failure have also the happiness of attaining to the Tâo. But when there is not faith sufficient on his part, a want of faith in him ensues on the part of the others.

25. 1. There was something undefined and complete, coming into existence before Heaven and Earth. How still it was and formless, standing alone, and undergoing no change, reaching everywhere and in no danger of being exhausted! It may be regarded as the Mother of all things.

2. I do not know its name, and I give it the designation of the Tâo the Way or Course. Making an effort further to give it a name I call it The Great.

3. Great, it passes on in constant flow. Passing on, it becomes remote. Having become remote, it returns. Therefore the Tâo is great; Heaven is great; Earth is great; and the sage king is also great. In the universe there are four that are great, and the sage king is one of them.

4. Man takes his law from the Earth; the Earth takes its law from Heaven; Heaven takes its law from the Tâo. The law of the Tâo is its being what it is.

27. 1. The skilful traveller leaves no traces of his wheels or footsteps; the skilful speaker says nothing that can be found fault with or blamed; the skilful reckoner uses no tallies; the skilful closer needs no bolts or bars, while to open what he has shut will be impossible; the skilful binder uses no strings or knots, while to unloose what he has bound will be impossible. In the same way the sage is always skilful at saving men, and so he does not cast away any man; he is always skilful at saving things, and so he does not cast away anything. This is called 'Hiding the light of his procedure.'

2. Therefore the man of skill is a master to be looked up to by him who has not the skill; and he who has not the skill is the helper of the reputation of him who has the skill. If the one did not honour his master, and the other did not rejoice in his helper, an observer, though intelligent, might greatly err about them. This is called 'The utmost degree of mystery.'

29. 1. If any one should wish to get the kingdom for himself, and to effect this by what he does, I see that he will not succeed. The kingdom is a spiritlike thing, and cannot be got by active doing. He who would so win it destroys it; he who would hold it in his grasp loses it.

2. The course and nature of things is such that

What was in front is now behind;
What warmed anon we freezing find.
Strength is of weakness oft the spoil;
The store in ruins mocks our toil.

Hence the sage puts away excessive effort, extravagance, and easy indulgence.

30. 1. He who would assist a lord of men in harmony with the Tâo will not assert his mastery in the kingdom by force of arms. Such a course is sure to meet with its proper return.

2. Wherever a host is stationed, briars and thorns spring up. In the sequence of great armies there are sure to be bad years.

3. A skilful commander strikes a decisive blow, and stops. He does not dare by continuing his operations to assert and complete his mastery. He will strike the blow, but will be on his guard against being vain or boastful or arrogant in consequence of it. He strikes it as a matter of necessity; he strikes it, but not from a wish for mastery.

4. When things have attained their strong maturity they become old. This may be said to be not in accordance with the Tâo: and what is not in accordance with it soon comes to an end.

31. 1. Now arms, however beautiful, are instruments of evil omen, hateful, it may be said, to all creatures. Therefore they who have the Tâo do not like to employ them.

2. The superior man ordinarily considers the left hand the most honourable place, but in time of war the right hand. Those sharp weapons are instruments of evil omen, and not the instruments of the superior man;—he uses them only on the compulsion of necessity. Calm and repose are what he prizes; victory by force of arms is to him undesirable. To consider this desirable

would be to delight in the slaughter of men; and he who delights in the slaughter of men cannot get his will in the kingdom.

3. On occasions of festivity to be on the left hand is the prized position; on occasions of mourning, the right hand. The second in command of the army has his place on the left; the general commanding in chief has his on the right;—his place, that is, is assigned to him as in the rites of mourning. He who has killed multitudes of men should weep for them with the bitterest grief; and the victor in battle has his place rightly according to those rites.

32. 1. The Tâo, considered as unchanging, has no name.

2. Though in its primordial simplicity it may be small, the whole world dares not deal with one embodying it as a minister. If a feudal prince or the king could guard and hold it, all would spontaneously submit themselves to him.

3. Heaven and Earth under its guidance unite together and send down the sweet dew, which, without the directions of men, reaches equally everywhere as of its own accord.

4. As soon as it proceeds to action, it has a name. When it once has that name, men can know to rest in it. When they know to rest in it, they can be free from all risk of failure and error.

5. The relation of the Tâo to all the world is like that of the great rivers and seas to the streams from the valleys.

34. 1. All-pervading is the Great Tâo! It may be found on the left hand and on the right.

2. All things depend on it for their production, which it gives to them, not one refusing obedience to it. When its work is accomplished, it does not claim the name of having done it. It clothes all things as with a garment, and makes no assumption of being their lord;—it may be named in the smallest things. All things return to their root and disappear, and do not know that it is it which presides over their doing so;—it may be named in the greatest things.

3. Hence the sage is able in the same way to accomplish his great achievements. It is through his not making himself great that he can accomplish them.

35. 1. To him who holds in his hands the Great Image of the invisible Tâo, the whole world repairs. Men resort to him, and receive no hurt, but find rest, peace, and the feeling of ease.

2. Music and dainties will make the passing guest stop for a time. But though the Tâo as it comes from the mouth, seems insipid and has no flavour, though it seems not worth being looked at or listened to, the use of it is inexhaustible.

37. 1. The Tâo in its regular course does nothing for the sake of doing it, and so there is nothing which it does not do.

2. If princes and kings were able to maintain it, all things would of themselves be transformed by them.

3. If this transformation became to me an object of desire, I would express the desire by the nameless simplicity.

> Simplicity without a name
> Is free from all external aim.
> With no desire, at rest and still,
> All things go right as of their will.

38. 1. Those who possessed in highest degree the attributes of the Tâo did not seek to show them, and therefore they possessed them in fullest measure. Those who possessed in a lower degree those attributes sought how not to lose them, and therefore they did not possess them in fullest measure.

2. Those who possessed in the highest degree those attributes did nothing with a purpose, and had no need to do anything. Those who possessed them in a lower degree were always doing, and had need to be so doing.

3. Those who possessed the highest benevolence were always seeking to carry it out, and had no need to be doing so. Those who possessed the highest righteousness were always seeking to carry it out, and had need to be so doing.

4. Those who possessed the highest sense of propriety were always seeking to show it, and when men did not respond to it, they bared the arm and marched up to them.

5. Thus it was that when the Tâo was lost, its attributes appeared; when its attributes were lost, benevolence appeared;

when benevolence was lost, righteousness appeared; and when righteousness was lost, the proprieties appeared.

6. Now propriety is the attenuated form of leal-heartedness and good faith, and is also the commencement of disorder; swift apprehension is only a flower of the Tâo, and is the beginning of stupidity.

7. Thus it is that the Great man abides by what is solid, and eschews what is flimsy; dwells with the fruit and not with the flower. It is thus that he puts away the one and makes choice of the other.

39. 1. The things which from of old have got the One the Tâo are—

> Heaven which by it is bright and pure;
> Earth rendered thereby firm and sure;
> Spirits with powers by it supplied;
> Valleys kept full throughout their void;
> All creatures which through it do live;
> Princes and kings who from it get
> The model which to all they give.

All these are the results of the One Tâo.

2. If heaven were not thus pure, it soon would rend;
If earth were not thus sure, 'twould break and bend;
Without these powers, the spirits soon would fail;
If not so filled, the drought would parch each vale;
Without that life, creatures would pass away;
Princes and kings, without that moral sway,
However grand and high, would all decay.

3. Thus it is that dignity finds its firm root in its previous meanness, and what is lofty finds its stability in the lowness from which it rises. Hence princes and kings call themselves 'Orphans,' 'Men of small virtue,' and as 'Carriages without a nave.' Is not this an acknowledgment that in their considering themselves mean they see the foundation of their dignity? So it is that in the enumeration of the different parts of a carriage we do not

come on what makes it answer the ends of a carriage. They do not wish to show themselves elegant-looking as jade, but prefer to be coarse-looking as an ordinary stone.

40. 1. The movement of the Tâo
      By contraries proceeds;
      And weakness marks the course
      Of Tâo's mighty deeds.

2. All things under heaven sprang from It as existing and named; that existence sprang from It as non-existent and not named.

41. 1. Scholars of the highest class, when they hear about the Tâo, earnestly carry it into practice. Scholars of the middle class, when they have heard about it, seem now to keep it and now to lose it. Scholars of the lowest class, when they have heard about it, laugh greatly at it. If it were not thus laughed at, it would not be fit to be the Tâo.

2. Therefore the sentence-makers have thus expressed themselves:—

    'The Tâo, when brightest seen, seems light to lack;
    Who progress in it makes, seems drawing back;
    Its even way is like a rugged track.
    Its highest virtue from the vale doth rise;
    Its greatest beauty seems to offend the eyes;
    And he has most whose lot the least supplies.
    Its firmest virtue seems but poor and low;
    Its solid truth seems change to undergo;
    Its largest square doth yet no corner show;
    A vessel great, it is the slowest made;
    Loud is its sound, but never word it said;
    A semblance great, the shadow of a shade.'

3. The Tâo is hidden, and has no name; but it is the Tâo which is skilful at imparting to all things what they need and making them complete.

42. 1. The Tâo produced One; One produced Two; Two

produced Three; Three produced All things. All things leave behind them the Obscurity out of which they have come, and go forward to embrace the Brightness into which they have emerged, while they are harmonised by the Breath of Vacancy.

2. What men dislike is to be orphans, to have little virtue, to be as carriages without naves; and yet these are the designations which kings and princes use for themselves. So it is that some things are increased by being diminished, and others are diminished by being increased.

3. What other men thus teach, I also teach. The violent and strong do not die their natural death. I will make this the basis of my teaching.

44. 1. Or fame or life,
          Which do you hold more dear?
      Or life or wealth,
          To which would you adhere?
      Keep life and lose those other things;
      Keep them and lose your life:—which brings
          Sorrow and pain more near?

2. Thus we may see,
       Who cleaves to fame
       Rejects what is more great;
   Who loves large stores
       Gives up the richer state.

3. Who is content
   Needs fear no shame.
   Who knows to stop
   Incurs no blame.
   From danger free
   Long live shall he.

49. 1. The sage has no invariable mind of his own; he makes the mind of the people his mind.

2. To those who are good to me, I am good; and to those who are not good to me, I am also good;—and thus all get to be good. To those who are sincere with me, I am sincere; and to

those who are not sincere with me, I am also sincere;—and thus all get to be sincere.

3. The sage has in the world an appearance of indecision, and keeps his mind in a state of indifference to all. The people all keep their eyes and ears directed to him, and he deals with them all as his children.

50. 1. Men come forth and live; they enter again and die.

2. Of every ten three are ministers of life to themselves; and three are ministers of death.

3. There are also three in every ten whose aim is to live, but whose movements tend to the land or place of death. And for what reason? Because of their excessive endeavours to perpetuate life.

4. But I have heard that he who is skilful in managing the life entrusted to him for a time travels on the land without having to shun rhinoceros or tiger, and enters a host without having to avoid buff coat or sharp weapon. The rhinoceros finds no place in him into which to thrust its horn, nor the tiger a place in which to fix its claws, nor the weapon a place to admit its point. And for what reason? Because there is in him no place of death.

51. 1. All things are produced by the Tâo, and nourished by its outflowing operation. They receive their forms according to the nature of each, and are completed according to the circumstances of their condition. Therefore all things without exception honour the Tâo, and exalt its outflowing operation.

2. This honouring of the Tâo and exalting of its operation is not the result of any ordination, but always a spontaneous tribute.

3. Thus it is that the Tâo produces all things, nourishes them, brings them to their full growth, nurses them, completes them, matures them, maintains them, and overspreads them.

4. It produces them and makes no claim to the possession of them; it carries them through their processes and does not vaunt its ability in doing so; it brings them to maturity and exercises no control over them;—this is called its mysterious operation.

52. 1. The Tâo which originated all under the sky is to be considered as the mother of them all.

2. When the mother is found, we know what her children should be. When one knows that he is his mother's child, and proceeds to guard the qualities of the mother that belong to him, to the end of his life he will be free from all peril.

3. Let him keep his mouth closed, and shut up the portals of his nostrils, and all his life he will be exempt from laborious exertion. Let him keep his mouth open, and spend his breath in the promotion of his affairs, and all his life there will be no safety for him.

4. The perception of what is small is the secret of clearsightedness; the guarding of what is soft and tender is the secret of strength.

5. Who uses well his light,
Reverting to its source so bright,
Will from his body ward all blight,
And hides the unchanging from men's sight.

53. 1. If I were suddenly to become known, and put into a position to conduct a government according to the Great Tâo, what I should be most afraid of would be a boastful display.

2. The great Tâo or way is very level and easy; but people love the by-ways.

3. Their court-yards and buildings shall be well kept, but their fields shall be ill-cultivated, and their granaries very empty. They shall wear elegant and ornamented robes, carry a sharp sword at their girdle, pamper themselves in eating and drinking, and have a superabundance of property and wealth;—such princes may be called robbers and boasters. This is contrary to the Tâo surely!

55. 1. He who has in himself abundantly the attributes of the Tâo is like an infant. Poisonous insects will not sting him; fierce beasts will not seize him; birds of prey will not strike him.

2. The infant's bones are weak and its sinews soft, but yet its grasp is firm. It knows not yet the union of male and female, and yet its virile member may be excited;—showing the perfection of

its physical essence. All day long it will cry without its throat becoming hoarse;—showing the harmony in its constitution.

3. To him by whom this harmony is known,
The secret of the unchanging Tâo is shown,
And in the knowledge wisdom finds its throne.
All life-increasing arts to evil turn;
Where the mind makes the vital breath to burn,
False is the strength, and o'er it we should mourn.

4. When things have become strong, they then become old, which may be said to be contrary to the Tâo. Whatever is contrary to the Tâo soon ends.

56. 1. He who knows the Tâo does not care to speak about it; he who is ever ready to speak about it does not know it.

2. He who knows it will keep his mouth shut and close the portals of his nostrils. He will blunt his sharp points and unravel the complications of things; he will attemper his brightness, and bring himself into agreement with the obscurity of others. This is called 'the Mysterious Agreement.'

3. Such an one cannot be treated familiarly or distantly; he is beyond all consideration of profit or injury; of nobility or meanness:—he is the noblest man under heaven.

57. 1. A state may be ruled by measures of correction; weapons of war may be used with crafty dexterity; but the kingdom is made one's own only by freedom from action and purpose.

2. How do I know that it is so? By these facts:—In the kingdom the multiplication of prohibitive enactments increases the poverty of the people; the more implements to add to their profit that the people have, the greater disorder is there in the state and clan; the more acts of crafty dexterity that men possess, the more do strange contrivances appear; the more display there is of legislation, the more thieves and robbers there are.

3. Therefore a sage has said, 'I will do nothing of purpose, and the people will be transformed of themselves; I will be fond of keeping still, and the people will of themselves become correct. I will take no trouble about it, and the people will of themselves

become rich; I will manifest no ambition, and the people will of themselves attain to the primitive simplicity.'

58. 1. The government that seems the most unwise,
Oft goodness to the people best supplies;
That which is meddling, touching everything,
Will work but ill, and disappointment bring.

Misery!—happiness is to be found by its side! Happiness!—misery lurks beneath it! Who knows what either will come to in the end?

2. Shall we then dispense with correction? The method of correction shall by a turn become distortion, and the good in it shall by a turn become evil. The delusion of the people on this point has indeed subsisted for a long time.

3. Therefore the sage is like a square which cuts no one with its angles; like a corner which injures no one with its sharpness. He is straightforward, but allows himself no license; he is bright, but does not dazzle.

59. 1. For regulating the human in our constitution and rendering the proper service to the heavenly, there is nothing like moderation.

2. It is only by this moderation that there is effected an early return to man's normal state. That early return is what I call the repeated accumulation of the attributes of the Tâo. With that repeated accumulation of those attributes, there comes the subjugation of every obstacle to such return. Of this subjugation we know not what shall be the limit; and when one knows not what the limit shall be, he may be the ruler of a state.

3. He who possesses the mother of the state may continue long. His case is like that of the plant of which we say that its roots are deep and its flower stalks firm:—this is the way to secure that its enduring life shall long be seen.

62. 1. Tâo has of all things the most honoured place.
No treasures give good men so rich a grace;
Bad men it guards, and doth their ill efface.

2. Its admirable words can purchase honour; its admirable

deeds can raise their performer above others. Even men who are not good are not abandoned by it.

3. Therefore when the sovereign occupies his place as the Son of Heaven, and he has appointed his three ducal ministers, though a prince were to send in a round symbol-of-rank large enough to fill both the hands, and that as the precursor of the team of horses in the court-yard, such an offering would not be equal to a lesson of this Tâo, which one might present on his knees.

4. Why was it that the ancients prized this Tâo so much? Was it not because it could be got by seeking for it, and the guilty could escape from the stain of their guilt by it? This is the reason why all under heaven consider it the most valuable thing.

63. 1. It is the way of the Tâo to act without thinking of acting; to conduct affairs without feeling the trouble of them; to taste without discerning any flavour; to consider what is small as great, and a few as many; and to recompense injury with kindness.

2. The master of it anticipates things that are difficult while they are easy, and does things that would become great while they are small. All difficult things in the world are sure to arise from a previous state in which they were easy, and all great things from one in which they were small. Therefore the sage, while he never does what is great, is able on that account to accomplish the greatest things.

3. He who lightly promises is sure to keep but little faith; he who is continually thinking things easy is sure to find them difficult. Therefore the sage sees difficulty even in what seems easy, and so never has any difficulties.

64. 1. That which is at rest is easily kept hold of; before a thing has given indications of its presence, it is easy to take measures against it; that which is brittle is easily broken; that which is very small is easily dispersed. Action should be taken before a thing has made its appearance; order should be secured before disorder has begun.

2. The tree which fills the arms grew from the tiniest sprout; the tower of nine storeys rose from a small heap of earth; the journey of a thousand lî commenced with a single step.

3. He who acts with an ulterior purpose does harm; he who takes hold of a thing in the same way loses his hold. The sage does not act so, and therefore does no harm; he does not lay hold so, and therefore does not lose his hold. But people in their conduct of affairs are constantly ruining them when they are on the eve of success. If they were careful at the end, as they should be at the beginning, they would not so ruin them.

4. Therefore the sage desires what other men do not desire, and does not prize things difficult to get; he learns what other men do not learn, and turns back to what the multitude of men have passed by. Thus he helps the natural development of all things, and does not dare to act with an ulterior purpose of his own.

65. 1. The ancients who showed their skill in practising the Tâo did so, not to enlighten the people, but rather to make them simple and ignorant.

2. The difficulty in governing the people arises from their having much knowledge. He who tries to govern a state by his wisdom is a scourge to it; while he who does not try to do so is a blessing.

3. He who knows these two things finds in them also his model and rule. Ability to know this model and rule constitutes what we call the mysterious excellence of a governor. Deep and far-reaching is such mysterious excellence, showing indeed its possessor as opposite to others, but leading them to a great conformity to him.

66. 1. That whereby the rivers and seas are able to receive the homage and tribute of all the valley streams, is their skill in being lower than they;—it is thus that they are the kings of them all. So it is that the sage ruler, wishing to be above men, puts himself by his words below them, and, wishing to be before them, places his person behind them.

2. In this way though he has his place above them, men do

not feel his weight, nor though he has his place before them, do they feel it an injury to them.

3. Therefore all in the world delight to exalt him and do not weary of him. Because he does not strive, no one finds it possible to strive with him.

67. 1. All the world says that, while my Tâo is great, it yet appears to be inferior to other systems of teaching. Now it is just its greatness that makes it seem to be inferior. If it were like any other system, for long would its smallness have been known!

2. But I have three precious things which I prize and hold fast. The first is gentleness; the second is economy; and the third is shrinking from taking precedence of others.

3. With that gentleness I can be bold; with that economy I can be liberal; shrinking from taking precedence of others, I can become a vessel of the highest honour. Now-a-days they give up gentleness and are all for being bold; economy, and are all for being liberal; the hindmost place, and seek only to be foremost; —of all which the end is death.

4. Gentleness is sure to be victorious even in battle, and firmly to maintain its ground. Heaven will save its possessor, by his very gentleness protecting him.

71. 1. To know and yet think we do not know is the highest attainment; not to know and yet think we do know is a disease.

2. It is simply by being pained at the thought of having this disease that we are preserved from it. The sage has not the disease. He knows the pain that would be inseparable from it, and therefore he does not have it.

74. 1. The people do not fear death; to what purpose is it to try to frighten them with death? If the people were always in awe of death, and I could always seize those who do wrong, and put them to death, who would dare to do wrong?

2. There is always One who presides over the infliction of death. He who would inflict death in the room of him who so presides over it may be described as hewing wood instead of a

great carpenter. Seldom is it that he who undertakes the hewing, instead of the great carpenter, does not cut his own hands!

76. 1. Man at his birth is supple and weak; at his death, firm and strong. So it is with all things. Trees and plants, in their early growth, are soft and brittle; at their death, dry and withered.

2. Thus it is that firmness and strength are the concomitants of death; softness and weakness, the concomitants of life.

3. Hence he who relies on the strength of his forces does not conquer; and a tree which is strong will fill the out-stretched arms, and thereby invites the feller.

4. Therefore the place of what is firm and strong is below, and that of what is soft and weak is above.

77. 1. May not the Way or Tâo of Heaven be compared to the method of bending a bow? The part of the bow which was high is brought low, and what was low is raised up. So Heaven diminishes where there is superabundance, and supplements where there is deficiency.

2. It is the Way of Heaven to diminish superabundance, and to supplement deficiency. It is not so with the way of man. He takes away from those who have not enough to add to his own superabundance.

3. Who can take his own superabundance and therewith serve all under heaven? Only he who is in possession of the Tâo!

4. Therefore the ruling sage acts without claiming the results as his; he achieves his merit and does not rest arrogantly in it:— he does not wish to display his superiority.

80. 1. In a little state with a small population, I would so order it, that, though there were individuals with the abilities of ten or a hundred men, there should be no employment of them; I would make the people, while looking on death as a grievous thing, yet not remove elsewhere to avoid it.

2. Though they had boats and carriages, they should have no occasion to ride in them; though they had buff coats and sharp weapons, they should have no occasion to don or use them.

3. I would make the people return to the use of knotted cords instead of the written characters.

4. They should think their coarse food sweet; their plain clothes beautiful; their poor dwellings places of rest; and their common simple ways sources of enjoyment.

5. There should be a neighbouring state within sight, and the voices of the fowls and dogs should be heard all the way from it to us, but I would make the people to old age, even to death, not have any intercourse with it.

81. 1. Sincere words are not fine; fine words are not sincere. Those who are skilled in the Tâo do not dispute about it; the disputations are not skilled in it. Those who know the Tâo are not extensively learned; the extensively learned do not know it.

2. The sage does not accumulate for himself. The more that he expends for others, the more does he possess of his own; the more that he gives to others, the more does he have himself.

3. With all the sharpness of the Way of Heaven, it injures not; with all the doing in the way of the sage he does not strive.

Chuang Tzu

Fung Yu-Lan

WAY OF ACHIEVING RELATIVE HAPPINESS

The first chapter of the *Chuang-tzu,* titled "The Happy Excursion," is a simple text, full of amusing stories. Their underlying idea is that there are varying degrees in the achievement of happiness. A free development of our natures may lead us to a relative kind of happiness; absolute happiness is achieved through higher understanding of the nature of things.

Reprinted from Fung Yu-Lan, *A Short History of Chinese Philosophy,* edited by Derk Bodde (The Macmillan Company, 1948), pages 105–117. Copyright 1948 by The Macmillan Company. Used by permission of the publisher.

To carry out the first of these requirements, the free development of our nature, we should have a full and free exercise of our natural ability. That ability is our *Te,* which comes directly from the *Tao.* Regarding the *Tao* and *Te,* Chuang Tzu has the same idea as Lao Tzu. For example, he says: "At the great beginning there was Non-being. It had neither being nor name and was that from which came the One. When the One came into existence, there was the One but still no form. When things obtained that by which they came into existence, it was called the *Te.*" (Ch. 12.) Thus our *Te* is what makes us what we are. We are happy when this *Te* or natural ability of ours is fully and freely exercised, that is, when our nature is fully and freely developed.

In connection with this idea of free development, Chuang Tzu makes a contrast between what is of nature and what is of man. "What is of nature," he says, "is internal. What is of man is external. . . . That oxen and horses should have four feet is what is of nature. That a halter should be put on a horse's head, or a string through an ox's nose, is what is of man." (Ch. 17.) Following what is of nature, he maintains, is the source of all happiness and goodness, while following what is of man is the source of all pain and evil.

Things are different in their nature and their natural ability is also not the same. What they share in common, however, is that they are all equally happy when they have a full and free exercise of their natural ability. In "The Happy Excursion" a story is told of a very large and a small bird. The abilities of the two are entirely different. The one can fly thousands of miles, while the other can hardly reach from one tree to the next. Yet they are both happy when they each do what they are able and like to do. Thus there is no absolute uniformity in the natures of things, nor is there any need for such uniformity. Another chapter of the *Chuang-tzu* tells us: "The duck's legs are short, but if we try to lengthen them, the duck will feel pain. The crane's legs are long, but if we try to shorten them, the crane will feel grief. Therefore we are not to amputate what is by nature long, nor to lengthen what is by nature short." (Ch. 8.)

POLITICAL AND SOCIAL PHILOSOPHY

Such, however, is just what artificiality tries to do. The purpose of all laws, morals, institutions, and governments is to establish uniformity and suppress difference. The motivation of the people who try to enforce this uniformity may be wholly admirable. When they find something that is good for them, they may be anxious to see that others have it also. This good intention of theirs, however, only makes the situation more tragic. In the *Chuang-tzu* there is a story which says: "Of old, when a seabird alighted outside the capital of Lu, the Marquis went out to receive it, gave it wine in the temple, and had the Chiu-shao music played to amuse it, and a bullock slaughtered to feed it. But the bird was dazed and too timid to eat or drink anything. In three days it was dead. This was treating the bird as one would treat oneself, not the bird as a bird. . . . Water is life to fish but is death to man. Being differently constituted, their likes and dislikes must necessarily differ. Therefore the early sages did not make abilities and occupations uniform." (Ch. 18.) When the Marquis treated the bird in a way which he considered the most honorable, he certainly had good intentions. Yet the result was just opposite to what he expected. This is what happens when uniform codes of laws and morals are enforced by government and society upon the individual.

This is why Chuang Tzu violently opposes the idea of governing through the formal machinery of government, and maintains instead that the best way of governing is through non-government. He says: "I have heard of letting mankind alone, but not of governing mankind. Letting alone springs from the fear that people will pollute their innate nature and set aside their *Te*. When people do not pollute their innate nature and set aside their *Te*, then is there need for the government of mankind?" (Ch. 11.)

If one fails to leave people alone, and tries instead to rule them with laws and institutions, the process is like putting a halter around a horse's neck or a string through an ox's nose. It is also like lengthening the legs of the duck or shortening those of the crane. What is natural and spontaneous is changed into something artificial, which is called by Chuang Tzu "overcoming what is of nature by what is of man." (Ch. 17.) Its result can only be misery and unhappiness.

Thus Chuang Tzu and Lao Tzu both advocate government through non-government, but for somewhat different reasons. Lao Tzu emphasizes his general principle that "reversing is the movement of the *Tao*." The more one governs, he argues, the less one achieves the desired result. And Chuang Tzu emphasizes the distinction between what is of nature and what is of man. The more the former is overcome by the latter, the more there will be misery and unhappiness.

Thus far we have only seen Chuang Tzu's way of achieving relative happiness. Such relative happiness is achieved when one simply follows what is natural in oneself. This every man can do. The political and social philosophy of Chuang Tzu aims at achieving precisely such relative happiness for every man. This and nothing more is the most that any political and social philosophy can hope to do.

EMOTION AND REASON

Relative happiness is relative because it has to depend upon something. It is true that one is happy when one has a full and free exercise of one's natural ability. But there are many ways in which this exercise is obstructed. For instance, there is death which is the end of all human activities. There are diseases which handicap human activities. There is old age which gives man the same trouble. So it is not without reason that the Buddhists consider these as three of the four human miseries, the fourth, according to them, being life itself. Hence, happiness which depends upon the full and free exercise of one's natural ability is a limited and therefore relative happiness.

In the *Chuang-tzu* there are many discussions about the greatest of all disasters that can befall man, death. Fear of death and anxiety about its coming are among the principal sources of human unhappiness. Such fear and anxiety, however, may be diminished if we have a proper understanding of the nature of things. In the *Chuang-tzu* there is a story about the death of Lao Tzu. When Lao Tzu died, his friend Chin Shih, who had come after the death, criticized the violent lamentations of the other mourners, saying: "This is to violate the principle of nature and to increase the emotion of man, forgetting what we have received [from nature]. These were called by the ancients the penalty of violating the principle of nature. When the Master came, it was because he had the occasion to be born. When he went, he simply followed the natural course. Those who are quiet at the proper occasion and follow the natural course, cannot be affected by sorrow or joy. They were considered by the ancients as the men of the gods, who were released from bondage." (Ch. 3.)

To the extent that the other mourners felt sorrow, to that extent they suffered. Their suffering was the "penalty of violating the principle of nature." The mental torture inflicted upon man by his emotions is sometimes just as severe as any physical punishment. But by the use of understanding, man can reduce his emotions. For example, a man of understanding will not be angry when rain prevents him from going out, but a child often will. The reason is that the man possesses greater understanding, with the result that he suffers less disappointment or exasperation than the child who does get angry. As Spinoza has said: "In so far as the mind understands all things are necessary, so far has it greater power over the effects, or suffers less from them." (*Ethics,* Pt. 5, Prop. VI.) Such, in the words of the Taoists, is "to disperse emotion with reason."

A story about Chuang Tzu himself well illustrates this point. It is said that when Chuang Tzu's wife died, his friend Hui Shih went to condole. To his amazement he found Chuang Tzu sitting on the ground, singing, and on asking him how he could be so unkind to his wife, was told by Chuang Tzu: "When she had just died, I could not help being affected. Soon, however, I examined the matter from the very beginning. At the very beginning, she was not living, having no form, nor even substance. But somehow or other there was then her substance, then her form, and then her life. Now by a further change, she has died. The whole process is like the sequence of the four seasons, spring, summer, autumn, and winter. While she is thus lying in the great mansion of the universe, for me to go about weeping and wailing would be to proclaim myself ignorant of the natural laws. Therefore I stop." (*Chuang-tzu,* ch. 18.) On this passage the great commentator Kuo Hsiang comments: "When ignorant, he felt sorry. When he understood, he was no longer affected. This teaches man to disperse emotion with reason." Emotion can be counteracted with reason and understanding. Such was the view of Spinoza and also of the Taoists.

The Taoists maintained that the sage who has a complete understanding of the nature of things, thereby has no emotions. This, however, does not mean that he lacks sensibility. Rather it means that he is not disturbed by the emotions, and enjoys what may be called "the peace of the soul." As Spinoza says: "The ignorant man is not only agitated by external causes in many ways, and never enjoys true peace in the soul, but lives also ignorant, as it were, both of God and of things, and as soon as he ceases to suffer, ceases also to be. On the other hand, the wise man, in so far as he is considered as such, is scarcely moved in his mind, but, being conscious by a certain eternal necessity of himself, of God, and things, never ceases to be, and always enjoys the peace of the soul." (*Ethics,* Pt. 5, Prop. XLII.)

Thus by his understanding of the nature of things, the sage is no longer affected by the changes of the world. In this way he is not dependent upon external things, and hence his happiness is not limited by them. He may be said to have achieved absolute happiness. Such is one line of Taoist thought, in which there is not a little atmosphere of pessimism and resignation. It is a line which emphasizes the inevitability of natural processes and the fatalistic acquiescence in them by man.

WAY OF ACHIEVING ABSOLUTE HAPPINESS

There is another line of Taoist thought, however, which emphasizes the relativity of the nature of things and the identification of man with the universe. To achieve this identification, man needs knowledge and understanding of still a higher level, and the happiness resulting from this identification is really absolute happiness, as expounded in Chuang Tzu's chapter on "The Happy Excursion."

In this chapter, after describing the happiness of large and small birds, Chuang Tzu adds that among human beings there was a man named Lieh Tzu who could even ride on the wind. "Among those who have attained happiness," he says, "such a man is rare. Yet although he was able to dispense with walking, he still had to depend upon something." This something was the wind, and since he had to depend upon the wind, his happiness was to that extent relative. Then Chuang Tzu asks: "But suppose there is one who chariots on the normality of the universe, rides on the transformation of the six elements, and thus makes excursion into the infinite, what has he to depend upon? Therefore it is said that the perfect man has no self; the spiritual man has no achievement; and the true sage has no name." (Ch. 1.)

What is here said by Chuang Tzu describes the man who has achieved absolute happiness. He is the perfect man, the spiritual man, and the true sage. He is absolutely happy, because he transcends the ordinary distinctions of things. He also transcends the distinction between the self and the world, the "me" and the "non-me." Therefore he has no self. He is one with the *Tao*. The *Tao* does nothing and yet there is nothing that is not done. The *Tao* does nothing, and therefore has no achievements. The sage is one with the *Tao* and therefore also has no achievements. He may rule the whole world, but his rule consists of just leaving mankind alone, and letting everyone exercise his own natural ability fully and freely. The *Tao* is nameless and so the sage who is one with the *Tao* is also nameless.

The Finite Point of View

The question that remains is this: How can a person become such a perfect man? To answer it, we must make an analysis of the second chapter of the *Chuang-tzu*, the *Ch'i Wu Lun*, or "On the Equality of Things." In the "Happy Excursion" Chuang Tzu discusses two levels of happiness, and in "On the Equality of Things" he discusses two levels of knowledge. Let us start our analysis with the first or lower level. In our chapter on the School of Names, we have said that there is some similarity between Hui Shih and Chuang Tzu. Thus in the *Ch'i Wu Lun*, Chuang Tzu discusses knowledge of a lower level which is similar to that found in Hui Shih's ten so-called paradoxes.

The chapter *Ch'i Wu Lun* begins with a description of the wind. When the wind blows, there are different kinds of sound, each with its own peculiarity. These this chapter calls "the sounds of earth." But in addition there are other sounds that are known as "the sounds of man." The sounds of earth and the sounds of man together constitute "the sounds of Heaven."

The sounds of man consist of the words (*yen*) that are spoken in the human world. They differ from such "sounds of earth" as those caused by the wind, inasmuch as when words are said, they represent human ideas. They represent affirmations and denials, and the opinions that are made by each individual from his own particular finite point of view. Being thus finite, these opinions are necessarily one-sided. Yet most men, not knowing that their opinions are based on finite points of view, invariably consider their own opinions as right and those of others as wrong. "The result," as the *Ch'i Wu Lun* says, "is the affirmations and denials of the Confucianists and Mohists, the one regarding as right what the other regards as wrong, and regarding as wrong what the other regards as right."

When people thus argue each according to his own one-sided view, there is no way either to reach a final conclusion, or to determine which side is really right or really wrong. The *Ch'i Wu Lun* says: "Suppose that you argue with me. If you beat me, instead of my beating you, are you necessarily right and am I necessarily wrong? Or, if I beat you, and not you me, am I necessarily right and are you necessarily wrong? Is one of us right and the other wrong? Or are both of us right or both of us wrong? Neither you nor I can know, and others are all the more in the dark. Whom shall we ask to produce the right decision? We may ask someone who agrees with you; but since he agrees with you, how can he make the decision? We may ask someone who agrees with me; but since he agrees with me, how can he make the decision? We may ask someone who agrees with both you and me; but since he agrees with both you and me, how can he make the decision? We may ask someone who differs from both you and me; but since he differs from both you and me, how can he make the decision?"

This passage is reminiscent of the manner of argument followed by the School of Names. But whereas the members of that school argue thus in order to contradict the common sense of ordinary people, the *Ch'i Wu Lun's* purpose is to contradict the followers of the School of Names. For this school did actually believe that argument could decide what is really right and really wrong.

Chuang Tzu, on the other hand, maintains that concepts of right and wrong are built up by each man on the basis of his own finite point of view. All these views are relative. As the *Ch'i Wu Lun* says: "When there is life, there is death, and when there is death, there is life. When there is possibility, there is impossibility, and when there is impossibility, there is possibility. Because there is right, there is wrong. Because there is wrong, there is right." Things are ever subject to change and have many aspects. Therefore many views can be held about one and the same thing. Once we say this, we assume that a higher standpoint exists. If we accept this assumption, there is no need to make a decision ourselves about what is right and what is wrong. The argument explains itself.

THE HIGHER POINT OF VIEW

To accept this premise is to see things from a higher point of view, or, as the *Ch'i Wu Lun* calls it, to see things "in the light of Heaven." "To see things in the light of Heaven" means to see things from the point of view of that which transcends the finite, which is the *Tao*. It is said in the *Ch'i Wu Lun:* "The 'this' is also 'that.' The 'that' is also 'this.' The 'that' has a system of right and wrong. The 'this' also has a system of right and wrong. Is there really a distinction between 'that' and 'this'? Or is there really no distinction between 'that' and 'this'? That the 'that' and the 'this' cease to be opposites is the very essence of *Tao*. Only the essence, an axis as it were, is the center of the circle responding to the endless changes. The right is an endless change. The wrong is also an endless change. Therefore it is said that there is nothing better than to use the 'light.' " In other words, the "that" and the "this," in their mutual opposition of right and wrong, are like an endlessly revolving circle. But the man who sees things from the point of view of the *Tao* stands, as it were, at the center of the circle. He understands all that is going on in the movements of the circle, but does not himself take part in these movements. This is not owing to his inactivity or resignation, but because he has transcended the finite and sees things from a higher point of view. In the *Chuang-tzu,* the finite point of view is compared with the view of the well-frog. The frog in the well can see only a little sky, and so thinks that the sky is only so big.

From the point of view of the *Tao*, everything is just what it is. It is said in the *Ch'i Wu Lun:* "The possible is possible. The impossible is impossible. The *Tao* makes things and they are what they are. What are they? They are what they are. What are they not? They are not what they are not. Everything is something and is good for something. There is nothing which is not something or is not good for something. Thus it is that there are roof-slats and pillars, ugliness and beauty, the peculiar and the extraordinary. All these by means of the *Tao* are united and become one." Although all things differ, they are alike in that they all constitute something and are good for something. They all equally come from the *Tao*. Therefore from the viewpoint of the *Tao*, things, though different, yet are united and become one.

The *Ch'i Wu Lun* says again: "To make a distinction is to make some construction. But construction is the same as destruction. For things as a whole there is neither construction nor destruction, but they turn to unity and become one." For example, when a table is made out of wood, from the viewpoint of that table, this is an act of construction. But from the viewpoint of the wood or the tree, it is one of destruction. Such construction or destruction is so, however, only from a finite point of view. From the viewpoint of the *Tao*, there is neither construction nor destruction. These distinctions are all relative.

The distinction between the "me" and the "non-me" is also relative. From the viewpoint of the *Tao*, the "me" and the "non-me" are also united and become one. The *Ch'i Wu Lun* says: "There is nothing larger in the world than the point of a hair, yet Mount T'ai is small. There is nothing older than a dead child, yet Peng Tsu [a legendary Chinese Methuselah] had an untimely death. Heaven and Earth and I came into existence together, and all things with me are one." Here we again have Hui Shih's dictum: "Love all things equally, Heaven and Earth are one body."

Knowledge of the Higher Level

This passage in the *Ch'i Wu Lun*, however, is immediately followed by another statement: "Since all things are one, what room is there for speech? But since I have already spoken of the one, is this not already speech? One plus speech make two. Two plus one make three. Going on from this, even the most skillful reckoner will not be able to reach the end, and how much less able to do so are ordinary people! If proceeding from nothing to something we can reach three, how much further shall we reach, if we proceed from something to something! Let us not proceed.

Let us stop here." It is in this statement that the *Ch'i Wu Lun* goes a step further than Hui Shih, and begins to discuss a higher kind of knowledge. This higher knowledge is "knowledge which is not knowledge."

What is really "one" can neither be discussed nor even conceived. For as soon as it is thought of and discussed, it becomes something that exists externally to the person who is doing the thinking and speaking. So since its all-embracing unity is thus lost, it is actually not the real "one" at all. Hui Shih said: "The greatest has nothing beyond itself and is called the Great One." By these words he described the Great One very well indeed, yet he remained unaware of the fact that since the Great One has nothing beyond itself, it is impossible either to think or speak of it. For anything that can be thought or spoken of has something beyond itself, namely, the thought and the speaking. The Taoists, on the contrary, realized that the "one" is unthinkable and inexpressible. Thereby, they had a true understanding of the "one" and advanced a step further than did the School of Names.

In the *Ch'i Wu Lun* it is also said: "Referring to the right and the wrong, the 'being so' and 'not being so': if the right is really right, we need not dispute about how it is different from the wrong; if the 'being so' is really being so, we need not dispute about how it is different from 'not being so.' . . . Let us forget life. Let us forget the distinction between right and wrong. Let us take our joy in the realm of the infinite and remain there." The realm of the infinite is the realm wherein lives the man who has attained to the *Tao*. Such a man not only has knowledge of the "one," but also has actually experienced it. This experience is the experience of living in the realm of the infinite. He has forgotten all the distinctions of things, even those involved in his own life. In his experience there remains only the undifferentiable one, in the midst of which he lives.

Described in poetical language, such a man is he "who chariots on the normality of the universe, rides on the transformations of the six elements, and thus makes excursion into the infinite." He is really the independent man, so his happiness is absolute.

Here we see how Chuang Tzu reached a final resolution of

the original problem of the early Taoists. That problem is how to preserve life and avoid harm and danger. But, to the real sage, it ceases to be a problem. As is said in the *Chuang-tzu:* "The universe is the unity of all things. If we attain this unity and identify ourselves with it, then the members of our body are but so much dust and dirt, while life and death, end and beginning, are but as the succession of day and night, which cannot disturb our inner peace. How much less shall we be troubled by worldly gain and loss, good-luck and bad-luck!" (Ch. 20.) Thus Chuang Tzu solved the original problem of the early Taoists simply by abolishing it. This is really the philosophical way of solving problems. Philosophy gives no information about matters of fact, and so cannot solve any problem in a concrete and physical way. It cannot, for example, help man either to gain longevity or defy death, nor can it help him to gain riches and avoid poverty. What it can do, however, is to give man a point of view, from which he can see that life is no more than death and loss is equal to gain. From the "practical" point of view, philosophy is useless, yet it can give us a point of view which is very useful. To use an expression of the *Chuang-tzu,* this is the "usefulness of the useless." (Ch. 4.)

Spinoza has said that in a certain sense, the wise man "never ceases to be." This is also what Chuang Tzu means. The sage or perfect man is one with the Great One, that is, the universe. Since the universe never ceases to be, therefore the sage also never ceases to be. In the sixth chapter of the *Chuang-tzu,* we read: "A boat may be stored in a creek; a net may be stored in a lake; these may be said to be safe enough. But at midnight a strong man may come and carry them away on his back. The ignorant do not see that no matter how well you store things, smaller ones in larger ones, there will always be a chance for them to be lost. But if you store the universe in the universe, there will be no room left for it to be lost. This is the great truth of things. Therefore the sage makes excursions into that which cannot be lost, and together with it he remains." It is in this sense that the sage never ceases to be.

Methodology of Mysticism

In order to be one with the Great One, the sage has to transcend and forget the distinctions between things. The way to do this is to discard knowledge, and is the method used by the Taoists for achieving "sageliness within." The task of knowledge in the ordinary sense is to make distinctions; to know a thing is to know the difference between it and other things. Therefore to discard knowledge means to forget these distinctions. Once all distinctions are forgotten, there remains only the undifferentiable one, which is the great whole. By achieving this condition, the sage may be said to have knowledge of another and higher level, which is called by the Taoists "knowledge which is not knowledge."

In the *Chuang-tzu* there are many passages about the method of forgetting distinctions. In the sixth chapter, for example, a report is given of an imaginary conversation between Confucius and his favorite disciple, Yen Hui. The story reads: "Yen Hui said: 'I have made some progress.' 'What do you mean?' asked Confucius. 'I have forgotten human-heartedness and righteousness,' replied Yen Hui. 'Very well, but that is not enough,' said Confucius. Another day Yen Hui again saw Confucius and said: 'I have made some progress.' 'What do you mean?' asked Confucius. 'I have forgotten rituals and music,' replied Yen Hui. 'Very well, but that is not enough,' said Confucius. Another day Yen Hui again saw Confucius and said: 'I have made some progress.' 'What do you mean?' asked Confucius. 'I sit in forgetfulness,' replied Yen Hui.

"At this Confucius changed countenance and asked: 'What do you mean by sitting in forgetfulness?' To which Yen Hui replied: 'My limbs are nerveless and my intelligence is dimmed. I have abandoned my body and discarded my knowledge. Thus I become one with the Infinite. This is what I mean by sitting in forgetfulness.' Then Confucius said: 'If you have become one with the Infinite, you have no personal likes and dislikes. If you have become one with the Great Evolution [of the universe], you are one who merely follows its changes. If you really have achieved this, I should like to follow your steps.' "

Thus Yen Hui achieved "sageliness within" by discarding knowledge. The result of discarding knowledge is to have no knowledge. But there is a difference between "*having-no* knowledge" and "having *no-knowledge*." The state of "*having-no* knowledge" is one of original ignorance, whereas that of "having *no-knowledge*" comes only after one has passed through a prior stage of having knowledge. The former is a gift of nature, while the latter is an achievement of the spirit.

Some of the Taoists saw this distinction very clearly. It is significant that they used the word "forget" to express the essential idea of their method. Sages are not persons who remain in a state of original ignorance. They at one time possessed ordinary knowledge and made the usual distinctions, but they since forgot them. The difference between them and the man of original ignorance is as great as that between the courageous man and the man who does not fear simply because he is insensible to fear.

But there were also Taoists, such as the authors of some chapters of the *Chuang-tzu,* who failed to see this difference. They admired the primitive state of society and mind, and compared sages with children and the ignorant. Children and the ignorant have no knowledge and do not make distinctions, so that they both seem to belong to the undifferentiable one. Their belonging to it, however, is entirely unconsciousness. They remain in the undifferentiable one, but they are not conscious of the fact. They are ones who *have-no* knowledge, but not who have *no-knowledge*. It is the latter acquired state of *no-knowledge* that the Taoists call that of the "knowledge which is not knowledge."

Selections
from the *Chuang Tzu*

Translated by James Legge

ON DEATH

(Book XVIII)

4. When *K*wang-ʒze went to *Kh*û, he saw an empty skull, bleached indeed, but still retaining its shape. Tapping it with his horse-switch, he asked it, saying, 'Did you, Sir, in your greed of life, fail in the lessons of reason, and come to this? Or did you do so, in the service of a perishing state, by the punishment of the axe? Or was it through your evil conduct, reflecting disgrace on your parents and on your wife and children? Or was it through your hard endurances of cold and hunger? Or was it that you had completed your term of life?'

Having given expression to these questions, he took up the skull, and made a pillow of it when he went to sleep. At midnight the skull appeared to him in a dream, and said, 'What you said to me was after the fashion of an orator. All your words were about the entanglements of men in their lifetime. There are none of those things after death. Would you like to hear me, Sir, tell you about death?' 'I should,' said *K*wang-ʒze, and the skull resumed: 'In death there are not the distinctions of ruler above and minister below. There are none of the phenomena of the four seasons. Tranquil and at ease, our years are those of heaven and earth. No king in his court has greater enjoyment than we have.' *K*wang-ʒze did not believe it, and said, 'If I could get the Ruler of our Destiny to restore your body to life with its

Reprinted from James Legge, tr., *The Sacred Books of China*, Part II: The Writings of Chuang Tzu, in *The Sacred Books of the East*, edited by F. Max Müller, Vol. XL (1891).

bones and flesh and skin, and to give you back your father and mother, your wife and children, and all your village acquaintances, would you wish me to do so?' The skull stared fixedly at him, knitted its brows, and said, 'How should I cast away the enjoyment of my royal court, and undertake again the toils of life among mankind?'

THE FULL UNDERSTANDING OF LIFE

(Book XIX)

1. He who understands the conditions of Life does not strive after what is of no use to life; and he who understands the conditions of Destiny does not strive after what is beyond the reach of knowledge. In nourishing the body it is necessary to have beforehand the things appropriate to its support; but there are cases where there is a superabundance of such things, and yet the body is not nourished. In order to have life it is necessary that it shall not have left the body; but there are cases when the body has not been left by it, and yet the life has perished.

When life comes, it cannot be declined; when it goes, it cannot be detained. Alas! the men of the world think that to nourish the body is sufficient to preserve life; and when such nourishment is not sufficient to preserve the life, what can be done in the world that will be sufficient? Though all that men can do will be insufficient, yet there are things which they feel they ought to do, and they do not try to avoid doing them. For those who wish to avoid caring for the body, their best plan is to abandon the world. Abandoning the world, they are free from its entanglements. Free from its entanglements, their minds are correct and their temperament is equable. Thus correct and equable, they succeed in securing a renewal of life, as some have done. In securing a renewal of life, they are not far from the True Secret of their being. But how is it sufficient to abandon worldly affairs? and how is it sufficient to forget the business of life? Through the renouncing of worldly affairs, the body has no more toil; through

forgetting the business of life, the vital power suffers no diminution. When the body is completed and the vital power is
restored to its original vigour, the man is one with Heaven.
Heaven and Earth are the father and mother of all things. It is
by their union that the body is formed; it is by their separation
that a new beginning is brought about. When the body and
vital power suffer no diminution, we have what may be called
the transference of power. From the vital force there comes
another more vital, and man returns to be the assistant of Heaven.

On Identifying the Tâo

(Book XXII)

6. Tung-kwo ʒze asked Kwang-ʒze, saying, 'Where is what
you call the Tâo to be found?' Kwang-ʒze replied, 'Everywhere.'
The other said, 'Specify an instance of it. That will be more
satisfactory.' 'It is here in this ant.' 'Give a lower instance.' 'It is
in this panic grass.' 'Give me a still lower instance.' 'It is in this
earthenware tile.' 'Surely that is the lowest instance?' 'It is in
that excrement.' To this Tung-kwo ʒze gave no reply.

Kwang-ʒze said, 'Your questions, my master do not touch the
fundamental point of the Tâo. They remind me of the questions addressed by the superintendents of the market to the
inspector about examining the value of a pig by treading on it,
and testing its weight as the foot descends lower and lower on
the body. You should not specify any particular thing. There is
not a single thing without the Tâo. So it is with the Perfect Tâo.
And if we call it the Great Tâo, it is just the same. There are the
three terms,—"Complete," "All-embracing," "the Whole." These
names are different, but the reality sought in them is the same;
referring to the One thing.

'Suppose we were to try to roam about in the palace of Nowhere;—when met there, we might discuss about the subject
without ever coming to an end. Or suppose we were to be together in the region of Non-action;—should we say that the Tâo

was Simplicity and Stillness? or Indifference and Purity? or
Harmony and Ease? My will would be aimless. If it went
nowhere, I should not know where it had got to; if it went and
came again, I should not know where it had stopped; if it went
on going and coming, I should not know when the process would
end. In vague uncertainty should I be in the vastest waste. Though
I entered it with the greatest knowledge, I should not know how
inexhaustible it was. That which makes things what they are has
not the limit which belongs to things, and when we speak of
things being limited, we mean that they are so in themselves.
The Tâo is the limit of the unlimited, and the boundlessness of
the unbounded.

'We speak of fulness and emptiness; of withering and decay.
It produces fulness and emptiness, but is neither fulness nor
emptiness; it produces withering and decay, but is neither withering nor decay. It produces the root and branches, but is neither
root nor branch; it produces accumulation and dispersion, but is
itself neither accumulated nor dispersed.'

SUPERIOR MAN AND THE TÂO

(Book XII)

2. The Master said, 'It is the Tâo that overspreads and sustains
all things. How great It is in Its overflowing influence! The
Superior man ought by all means to remove from his mind all
that is contrary to It. Acting without action is what is called
Heaven-like. Speech coming forth of itself is what is called a
mark of the true Virtue. Loving men and benefiting things is
what is called Benevolence. Seeing wherein things that are different yet agree is what is called being Great. Conduct free from
the ambition of being distinguished above others is what is called
being Generous. The possession in himself of a myriad points of
difference is what is called being Rich. Therefore to hold fast
the natural attributes is what is called the Guiding Line of government; the perfecting of those attributes is what is called its

Establishment; accordance with the Tâo is what is called being Complete; and not allowing anything external to affect the will is what is called being Perfect. When the Superior man understands these ten things, he keeps all matters as it were sheathed in himself, showing the greatness of his mind; and through the outflow of his doings, all things move and come to him. Being such, he lets the gold lie hid in the hill, and the pearls in the deep; he considers not property or money to be any gain; he keeps aloof from riches and honours; he rejoices not in long life, and grieves not for early death; he does not account prosperity a glory, nor is ashamed of indigence; he would not grasp at the gain of the whole world to be held as his own private portion; he would not desire to rule over the whole world as his own private distinction. His distinction is in understanding that all things belong to the one treasury, and that death and life should be viewed in the same way.'

3. The Master said, 'How still and deep is the place where the Tâo resides! How limpid is its purity! Metal and stone without It would give forth no sound. They have indeed the power of sound in them, but if they be not struck, they do not emit it. Who can determine the qualities that are in all things?

'The man of kingly qualities holds on his way unoccupied, and is ashamed to busy himself with the conduct of affairs. He establishes himself in what is the root and source of his capacity, and his wisdom grows to be spirit-like. In this way his attributes become more and more great, and when his mind goes forth, whatever things come in his way, it lays hold of them and deals with them. Thus, if there were not the Tâo, the bodily form would not have life, and its life, without the attributes of the Tâo, would not be manifested. Is not he who preserves the body and gives the fullest development to the life, who establishes the attributes of the Tâo and clearly displays It, possessed of kingly qualities? How majestic is he in his sudden issuings forth, and in his unexpected movements, when all things follow him!—This we call the man whose qualities fit him to rule.

'He sees where there is the deepest obscurity; he hears where there is no sound. In the midst of the deepest obscurity, he alone sees and can distinguish various objects; in the midst of a soundless abyss, he alone can hear a harmony of notes. Therefore where one deep is succeeded by a greater, he can people all with things; where one mysterious range is followed by another that is more so, he can lay hold of the subtlest character of each. In this way in his intercourse with all things, while he is farthest from having anything, he can yet give to them what they seek; while he is always hurrying forth, he yet returns to his resting-place; now large, now small; now long, now short; now distant, now near.'

On Non-Action

(Book VII)

6. Non-action makes its exemplifier the lord of all fame; non-action serves him as the treasury of all plans; non-action fits him for the burden of all offices; non-action makes him the lord of all wisdom. The range of his action is inexhaustible, but there is nowhere any trace of his presence. He fulfils all that he has received from Heaven, but he does not see that he was the recipient of anything. A pure vacancy of all purpose is what characterises him. When the perfect man employs his mind, it is a mirror. It conducts nothing and anticipates nothing; it responds to what is before it, but does not retain it. Thus he is able to deal successfully with all things, and injures none.

The Seal of Virtue Complete

(Book V)

1. In Lû there was a Wang Thâi who had lost both his feet; while his disciples who followed and went about with him were as numerous as those of Kung-nî. Khang Kî asked Kung-nî about him, saying, 'Though Wang Thâi is a cripple, the disciples who follow him about divide Lû equally with you, Master. When

he stands, he does not teach them; when he sits, he does not discourse to them. But they go to him empty, and come back full. Is there indeed such a thing as instruction without words? and while the body is imperfect, may the mind be complete? What sort of man is he?'

Kung-nî replied, 'This master is a sage. I have only been too late in going to him. I will make him my teacher; and how much more should those do so who are not equal to me! Why should only the state of Lû follow him? I will lead on all under heaven with me to do so.' Khang Kî rejoined, 'He is a man who has lost his feet, and yet he is known as the venerable Wang;—he must be very different from ordinary men. What is the peculiar way in which he employs his mind?' The reply was, 'Death and life are great considerations, but they could work no change in him. Though heaven and earth were to be overturned and fall, they would occasion him no loss. His judgment is fixed regarding that in which there is no element of falsehood; and, while other things change, he changes not. The transformations of things are to him the developments prescribed for them, and he keeps fast hold of the author of them.'

Khang Kî said, 'What do you mean?' 'When we look at things,' said Kung-nî, 'as they differ, we see them to be different, as for instance the liver and the gall, or Khû and Yüeh; when we look at them, as they agree, we see them all to be a unity. So it is with this Wang Thâi. He takes no knowledge of the things for which his ears and eyes are the appropriate organs, but his mind delights itself in the harmony of all excellent qualities. He looks at the unity which belongs to things, and does not perceive where they have suffered loss. He looks on the loss of his feet as only the loss of so much earth.'

Khang Kî said, 'He is entirely occupied with his proper self. By his knowledge he has discovered the nature of his mind, and to that he holds as what is unchangeable; but how is it that men make so much of him?' The reply was, 'Men do not look into running water as a mirror, but into still water;—it is only the still water that can arrest them all, and keep them in the contemplation of their real selves. Of things which are what they are by the influence of the earth, it is only the pine and cypress which are the best instances;—in winter as in summer brightly green. Of those which were what they were by the influence of Heaven, the most correct examples were Yâo and Shun; fortunate in thus maintaining their own life correct, and so as to correct the lives of others.

'As a verification of the power of the original endowment, when it has been preserved, take the result of fearlessness,—how the heroic spirit of a single brave soldier has been thrown into an army of nine hosts. If a man only seeking for fame, and able in this way to secure it, can produce such an effect, how much more may we look for a greater result from one whose rule is over heaven and earth, and holds all things in his treasury, who simply has his lodging in the six members of his body, whom his ears and eyes serve but as conveying emblematic images of things, who comprehends all his knowledge in a unity, and whose mind never dies! If such a man were to choose a day on which he would ascend far on high, men would seek to follow him there. But how should he be willing to occupy himself with other men?'

THE GREAT MAN

(Book VI)

1. He who knows the part which the Heavenly in him plays, and knows also that which the Human in him ought to play, has reached the perfection of knowledge. He who knows the part which the Heavenly plays knows that it is naturally born with him; he who knows the part which the Human ought to play proceeds with the knowledge which he possesses to nourish it in the direction of what he does not yet know:—to complete one's natural term of years and not come to an untimely end in the middle of his course is the fulness of knowledge. Although it be so, there is an evil attending this condition. Such knowledge still awaits the confirmation of it as correct; it does so because it

is not yet determined. How do we know that what we call the Heavenly in us is not the Human? and that what we call the Human is not the Heavenly? There must be the True man, and then there is the True knowledge.

2. What is meant by 'the True Man'? The True men of old did not reject the views of the few; they did not seek to accomplish their ends like heroes before others; they did not lay plans to attain those ends. Being such, though they might make mistakes, they had no occasion for repentance; though they might succeed, they had no self-complacency. Being such, they could ascend the loftiest heights without fear; they could pass through water without being made wet by it; they could go into fire without being burnt; so it was that by their knowledge they ascended to and reached the Tâo.

The True men of old did not dream when they slept, had no anxiety when they awoke, and did not care that their food should be pleasant. Their breathing came deep and silently. The breathing of the true man comes even from his heels, while men generally breathe only from their throats. When men are defeated in argument, their words come from their gullets as if they were vomiting. Where lusts and desires are deep, the springs of the Heavenly are shallow.

The True men of old knew nothing of the love of life or of the hatred of death. Entrance into life occasioned them no joy; the exit from it awakened no resistance. Composedly they went and came. They did not forget what their beginning had been, and they did not inquire into what their end would be. They accepted their life and rejoiced in it; they forgot all fear of death, and returned to their state before life. Thus there was in them what is called the want of any mind to resist the Tâo, and of all attempts by means of the Human to assist the Heavenly. Such were they who are called the True men.

3. Being such, their minds were free from all thought; their demeanour was still and unmoved; their foreheads beamed simplicity. Whatever coldness came from them was like that of autumn; whatever warmth came from them was like that of

spring. Their joy and anger assimilated to what we see in the four seasons. They did in regard to all things what was suitable, and no one could know how far their action would go. Therefore the sagely man might, in his conduct of war, destroy a state without losing the hearts of the people; his benefits and favours might extend to a myriad generations without his being a lover of men. Hence he who tries to share his joys with others is not a sagely man; he who manifests affection is not benevolent; he who observes times and seasons to regulate his conduct is not a man of wisdom; he to whom profit and injury are not the same is not a superior man; he who acts for the sake of the name of doing so, and loses his proper self is not the right scholar; and he who throws away his person in a way which is not the true way cannot command the service of others.

4. The True men of old presented the aspect of judging others aright, but without being partisans; of feeling their own insufficiency, but being without flattery or cringing. Their peculiarities were natural to them, but they were not obstinately attached to them; their humility was evident, but there was nothing of unreality or display about it. Their placidity and satisfaction had the appearance of joy; their every movement seemed to be a necessity to them. Their accumulated attractiveness drew men's looks to them; their blandness fixed men's attachment to their virtue. They seemed to accommodate themselves to the manners of their age, but with a certain severity; their haughty indifference was beyond its control. Unceasing seemed their endeavours to keep their mouths shut; when they looked down, they had forgotten what they wished to say.

They considered punishments to be the substance of government, and they never incurred it; ceremonies to be its supporting wings and they always observed them; wisdom to indicate the time for action, and they always selected it, and virtue to be accordance with others, and they were all-accordant. Considering punishments to be the substance of government, yet their generosity appeared in the manner of their infliction of death. Considering ceremonies to be its supporting wings, they pursued by means of them their course in the world. Considering wisdom to indicate the crime for action, they felt it necessary to employ it in the direction of affairs. Considering virtue to be accordance with others, they sought to ascend its height along with all who had feet to climb it. Such were they, and yet men really thought that they did what they did by earnest effort.

5. In this way they were one and the same in all their likings and dislikings. Where they liked, they were the same; where they did not like, they were the same. In the former case where they liked, they were fellow-workers with the Heavenly in them; in the latter where they disliked, they were co-workers with the Human in them. The one of these elements in their nature did not overcome the other. Such were those who are called the True men.

Death and life are ordained, just as we have the constant succession of night and day;—in both cases from Heaven. Men have no power to do anything in reference to them;—such is the constitution of things. There are those who specially regard Heaven as their father, and they still love It (distant as It is);—how much more should they love That which stands out Superior and Alone! Some specially regard their ruler as superior to themselves, and will give their bodies to die for him;—how much more should they do so for That which is their true Ruler! When the springs are dried up, the fishes collect together on the land. Than that they should moisten one another there by the damp about them, and keep one another wet by their slime, it would be better for them to forget one another in the rivers and lakes. And when men praise Yâo and condemn Kieh, it would be better to forget them both, and seek the renovation of the Tâo.

6. There is the great Mass of nature;—I find the support of my body on it; my life is spent in toil on it; my old age seeks ease on it; at death I find rest in it;—what makes my life a good makes my death also a good. If you hide away a boat in the ravine of a hill, and hide away the hill in a lake, you will say that the boat is secure; but at midnight there shall come a strong man and carry it off on his back, while you in the dark know nothing

about it. You may hide away anything, whether small or great, in the most suitable place, and yet it shall disappear from it. But if you could hide the world in the world, so that there was nowhere to which it could be removed, this would be the grand reality of the ever-during Thing. When the body of man comes from its special mould, there is even then occasion for joy; but this body undergoes a myriad transformations, and does not immediately reach its perfection;—does it not thus afford occasion for joys incalculable? Therefore the sagely man enjoys himself in that from which there is no possibility of separation, and by which all things are preserved. He considers early death or old age, his beginning and his ending, all to be good, and in this other men imitate him;—how much more will they do so in regard to That Itself on which all things depend, and from which every transformation arises!

7. This is the Tâo;—there is in It emotion and sincerity, but It does nothing and has no bodily form. It may be handed down by the teacher, but may not be received by his scholars. It may be apprehended by the mind, but It cannot be seen. It has Its root and ground of existence in Itself. Before there were heaven and earth, from of old, there It was, securely existing. From It came the mysterious existences of spirits, from It the mysterious existence of God. It produced heaven; It produced earth. It was before the Thâi-kî, and yet could not be considered high; It was below all space, and yet could not be considered deep. It was produced before heaven and earth, and yet could not be considered to have existed long; It was older than the highest antiquity, and yet could not be considered old.

WEBBED TOES

(Book VIII)

1. A ligament uniting the big toe with the other toes and an extra finger may be natural growths, but they are more than is good for use. Excrescences on the person and hanging tumours

are growths from the body, but they are unnatural additions to it. There are many arts of benevolence and righteousness, and the exercise of them is distributed among the five viscera; but this is not the correct method according to the characteristics of the Tâo. Thus it is that the addition to the foot is but the attachment to it of so much useless flesh, and the addition to the hand is but the planting on it of a useless finger. . . .

3. The presumption is that benevolence and righteousness are not constituents of humanity; for to how much anxiety does the exercise of them give rise! Moreover when another toe is united to the great toe, to divide the membrane makes you weep; and when there is an extra finger, to gnaw it off makes you cry out. In the one case there is a member too many, and in the other a member too few; but the anxiety and pain which they cause is the same. The benevolent men of the present age look at the evils of the world, as with eyes full of dust, and are filled with sorrow by them, while those who are not benevolent, having violently altered the character of their proper nature, greedily pursue after riches and honours. The presumption therefore is that benevolence and righteousness are contrary to the nature of man:—how full of trouble and contention has the world been ever since the three dynasties began!

And moreover, in employing the hook and line, the compass and square, to give things their correct form you must cut away portions of what naturally belongs to them; in employing strings and fastenings, glue and varnish to make things firm, you must violently interfere with their qualities. The bendings and stoppings in ceremonies and music, and the factitious expression in the countenance of benevolence and righteousness, in order to comfort the minds of men:—these all show a failure in observing the regular principles of the human constitution. All men are furnished with such regular principles; and according to them what is bent is not made so by the hook, nor what is straight by the line, nor what is round by the compass, nor what is square by the carpenter's square. Nor is adhesion effected by the use of glue and varnish, nor are things bound together by means of strings and bands. Thus it is that all in the world are produced what they are by a certain guidance, while they do not know how they are produced so; and they equally attain their several ends while they do not know how it is that they do so. Anciently it was so, and it is so now; and this constitution of things should not be made of none effect. Why then should benevolence and righteousness be employed as connecting links, or as glue and varnish, strings and bands, and the enjoyment arising from the Tâo and its characteristics be attributed to them?—it is a deception practised upon the world. Where the deception is small, there will be a change in the direction of the objects pursued; where it is great, there will be a change of the nature itself. How do I know that it is so? Since he of the line of Yü called in his benevolence and righteousness to distort and vex the world, the world has not ceased to hurry about to execute their commands; —has not this been by means of benevolence and righteousness to change men's views of their nature? . . .

5. When I pronounce men to be good, I am not speaking of their benevolence and righteousness;—the goodness is simply their possession of the qualities of the Tâo. When I pronounce them to be good, I am not speaking of what are called benevolence and righteousness; but simply of their allowing the nature with which they are endowed to have its free course. When I pronounce men to be quick of hearing, I do not mean that they hearken to anything else, but that they hearken to themselves; when I pronounce them to be clear of vision, I do not mean that they look to anything else, but that they look to themselves. Now those who do not see themselves but see other things, who do not get possession of themselves but get possession of other things, get possession of what belongs to others, and not of what is their own; and they reach forth to what attracts others, and not to that in themselves which should attract them. But thus reaching forth to what attracts others and not to what should attract them in themselves, be they like the robber Kih or like Po-î, they equally err in the way of excess or of perversity. What I am ashamed of is erring in the characteristics of the Tâo, and

therefore, in the higher sphere, I do not dare to insist on the practice of benevolence and righteousness, and, in the lower, I do not dare to allow myself either in the exercise of excess or perversity.

MISCELLANEOUS APHORISMS

The Great Tâo does not admit of being praised. The Great Argument does not require words. Great Benevolence is not officiously benevolent. Great Disinterestedness does not vaunt its humility. Great Courage is not seen in stubborn bravery.

The Tâo that is displayed is not the Tâo. Words that are argumentative do not teach the point. Benevolence that is constantly exercised does not accomplish its object. Disinterestedness that vaunts its purity is not genuine. Courage that is most stubborn is ineffectual. These five seem to be round and complete, but they tend to become square and immovable. Therefore the knowledge that stops at what it does not know is the greatest. Who knows the argument that needs no words and the Way that is not to be trodden? (Book II)

13. To be unthought of by the foot that wears it is the fitness of a shoe; to be unthought of by the waist is the fitness of a girdle. When one's wisdom does not think of the right or the wrong of a question under discussion, that shows the suitability of the mind for the question; when one is conscious of no inward change, or outward attraction, that shows the mastery of affairs. He who perceives at once the fitness, and never loses the sense of it, has the fitness that forgets all about what is fitting. (Book XIX)

9. Yang-ʒze, having gone to Sung, passed the night in a lodging-house, the master of which had two concubines;—one beautiful, the other ugly. The ugly one was honoured, however, and the beautiful one contemned. Yang-ʒze asked the reason, and a little boy of the house replied, 'The beauty knows her beauty, and we do not recognise it. The ugly one knows her ugliness, and we do not recognise it.' Yang-ʒze said, 'Remember it, my disciples. Act virtuously, and put away the practice of priding

yourselves on your virtue. If you do this, where can you go to that you will not be loved?' (Book XX)

8. Kwang-ʒze said, 'If a man have the power to enjoy himself in any pursuit, can he be kept from doing so? If he have not the power, can he so enjoy himself? There are those whose aim is bent on concealing themselves, and those who are determined that their doings shall leave no trace. Alas! they both shirk the obligations of perfect knowledge and great virtue. The latter fall, and cannot recover themselves; the former rush on like fire, and do not consider what they are doing. Though men may stand to each other in the relation of ruler and minister, that is but for a time. In a changed age, the one of them would not be able to look down on the other. Hence it is said, "The perfect man leaves no traces of his conduct."

'To honour antiquity and despise the present time is the characteristic of learners; but even the disciples of Khih-wei have to look at the present age; and who can avoid being carried along by its course? It is only the Perfect man who is able to enjoy himself in the world, and not be deflected from the right.' (Book XXVI)

5. The penumbrae once asked the shadow, saying, 'Formerly you were looking down, and now you are looking up; formerly you had your hair tied up, and now it is dishevelled; formerly you were sitting, and now you have risen up; formerly you were walking, and now you have stopped:—how is all this?' The shadow said, 'Venerable Sirs, how do you ask me about such small matters? These things all belong to me, but I do not know how they do so. I am like the shell of a cicada or the cast-off skin of a snake;—like them, and yet not like them. With light and the sun I make my appearance; with darkness and the night I fade away. Am not I dependent on the substance from which I am thrown? And that substance is itself dependent on something else! When it comes, I come with it; when it goes, I go with it. When it comes under the influence of the strong Yang, I come under the same. Since we are both produced by that strong Yang, what occasion is there for you to question me?' (Book XXVII)

6. The sage looks on what is deemed necessary as unnecessary, and therefore is not at war in himself. The mass of men deem what is unnecessary to be necessary, and therefore they are often at war in themselves. Therefore those who pursue this method of internal war, resort to it in whatever they seek for. But reliance on such war leads to ruin. (Book XXXII)

1. There is a limit to our life, but to knowledge there is no limit. With what is limited to pursue after what is unlimited is a perilous thing; and when, knowing this, we still seek the increase of our knowledge, the peril cannot be averted. There should not be the practice of what is good with any thought of the fame which it will bring, nor of what is evil with any approximation to the punishment which it will incur:—an accordance with the Central Element of our nature is the regular way to preserve the body, to maintain the life, to nourish our parents, and to complete our term of years. (Book III)

'Do you not know the fate of the praying mantis? It angrily stretches out its arms, to arrest the progress of the carriage, unconscious of its inability for such a task, but showing how much it thinks of its own powers. Be on your guard; be careful. If you cherish a boastful confidence in your own excellence, and place yourself in collision with him, you are likely to incur the fate of the mantis.' (Book IV)

CHAPTER V

Eastern Ethical
and Social Practice

D. T. SUZUKI

I

To understand what lies underneath Eastern* culture and moral practice it is necessary to know the three principal forms of thought prevailing in the East: Confucianism, Taoism, and Buddhism. The first two are native to China, whereas the last is an importation from the neighboring country, India, in the first century of the Christian era.

Confucianism is concerned chiefly with moral life and politics, that is, with worldly affairs so called. While Taoism is also politically minded, there is much of religion in it, for instance, when it refers to the "Mysterious Mother." Buddhism, when it was first transplanted to China, encountered some resistance from the native scholars, chiefly the Confucians, but proved itself strong enough to be gradually recognized not only by the people but also by the intellectuals. The reason is that Buddhism has what the Chinese mind lacks—metaphysics and spiritual feelings. This fact first repelled the Chinese but later attracted them.

Besides, in the Taoist way of thinking and feeling there is something closely related to the Buddhist trends of thought: love of Nature, poetic imagination, transcendentalism, a mystic ap-

Reprinted from D. T. Suzuki, "Basic Thoughts Underlying Eastern Ethical and Social Practice," in *Philosophy and Culture: East and West,* edited by Charles A. Moore (Honolulu: University of Hawaii Press, 1962), pages 428–444. Used by permission of the publisher.
* This term will be used here in a very narrow sense, for I wish to limit the applicability of my thought to the Far Eastern area, that is, China and Japan.

preciation of reality. Buddhism also has much thought affiliating itself with Confucianism, for instance, when it is not so amoralistic as Taoism. But it was the Taoists who first approached Buddhism and adopted a great deal of its way of life and finally developed a religious system akin to it. Not only that, but, when the Chinese began in the seventh century to establish their own forms of Buddhism, they exhibited a great deal of originality. The Ching-t'u (Jōdo), Hua-yen (Kegon), Ch'an (Zen), and T'ien-t'ai (Tendai) are such forms. In them we can detect the imaginative depths of the Chinese mind as well as its speculative penetration. The Chinese perhaps did not realize that all these qualities lay dormant in them until the qualities were finally brought brilliantly to the surface of their consciousness.

As I consider the Zen form of Buddhism more important in many ways than the other forms, such as the Jōdo, I wish to regard Zen as representing Buddhism generally when I talk about the Buddhist influence over Eastern, and especially Japanese, moral life.

Zen flourished in China from the seventh century throughout the T'ang (610–905) and the Sung (960–1278), and even down to the Ming (1369–1628). In Zen we find the best that Chinese culture can offer to the world harmoniously blended with the best of the Indian speculative mind.

In the following, let me take up the Buddhist philosophy of Emptiness and contrast it with the Western way of thinking, for Zen also bases its *Welt-* and *Lebens-Anschauung* on it.

II

One, at least, of the most fundamental differences between East and West as far as their way of thinking is concerned is that the Western mind emphasizes the dualistic aspect of reality while the Eastern mind basically tends to be advaitist. Advaitism is not the same as monism; it simply asserts that reality is non-dualistic. Monism limits, whereas advaitism leaves the question open, and refuses to make any definite statement about reality. It is not-two, which is not the same as one. It is both yes and no, yet it is neither the one nor the other.

The West lives in a world separated into two terms: subject and object, self and not-self, yes and no, good and evil, right and wrong, true and false. It is therefore more logical or scientific, where yes cannot be no and no cannot be yes, where a square is not a triangle, where one is not two, where "I" and "thou" are eternally separated and can never be merged, where God creates and the creature forever remains created, where "our Father . . . art in heaven" and we mortals are groveling on earth. The Western mind abhors paradoxes, contradictions, absurdities, obscurantism, emptiness, in short, anything that is not clear, well-defined, and capable of determination.

Advaitism is not a very clear concept, however, and I should like to have another term to make my position better defined. When I say that reality is not dualistic, that a world of subject and object is not final, and that there is a something which is neither subjective nor objective, and further that this something is not to be subsumed under any category born of the dualistic concept of subject and object, I may be stamped as a mystic with all his scientifically unacceptable qualifications. Whatever this may mean, the mystic has a very concrete and therefore a very positive experience of ultimate reality which according to him cannot be conceptualized after the ordinary rules of logical thinking. Logic, as we understand it, has its limitation and cannot expect to catch every fish in its net.

All our sense-experiences are limited and definite, and the intellect based on them is also limited and definable. They all belong in the world of subject and object, seeing and seen, thinking and thought, that is, in the world of dualities. Here reality is always subjected to a separation; it is never grasped in its suchness or isness, or in its totality. Logicians and scientists deal with reality in its inevitably separated and therefore limited aspect. Therefore, there is always a something left over after their studies and measurements. They are not conscious of this something; in fact, they insist that there is nothing left behind, that they have everything they want to study. They go even so far as to declare that if there is anything left they have nothing to do with it, for it can never be scooped up with their logical shovel.

In fact, there are some minds that can never be satisfied with so-called logical accuracies and mathematical measurements, for they have the feeling or sense of a something which persistently claims their attention and which can never be "accurately" determined. This something is described by Baudelaire as "the steely barb of the infinite." They cannot rest until this disquieting something is actually held in their hands in the same way as we pick up a piece of stone or listen to a singing bird. Whatever name we may give to this mysterious something—God, or Ultimate Reality, or the Absolute, or the *Ātman,* or the Self, or Brahman, or Tao, or Heaven, or Reason, or the Infinite, or Emptiness, or Nothing—it is always bafflingly before us or behind the duality of "I and thou," or of the self and not-self, or subject and object, or God and the creation.

I may provisionally call this mysterious something the First Person, "I." It cannot be logically determined, temporally chronicled, spatially located. You might say, "That is too vague, too obscure, and we cannot deal with such an unknowable." Naturally, it cannot be clear and definable as far as our intellection is concerned. It is "O taste and see." The tasting-and-seeing is not intellectual; it is perceptual and personal and cannot be brought out to the open market of conceptualization. But its presence in our mind is undeniable and its persistent call for our conscious attention is authentically attested in the history of thought. For this no specifications are needed.

Let me repeat: the First Person, "I," is not the subject standing in contrast to the object; it is not the self opposing the not-self; nor is it the creator looking at his creation. It can never be caught up in any form of intellectual duality, because it is that which produces all dualities and which hides itself somewhere as soon as dualities are taken notice of. It is, therefore, outside the pale of our logical comprehension. The only way to catch it is by means of a paradox or contrary diction—"the clear light of the

void," or "rays of darkness," or "eternal present," or "pure darkness is pure light," or *"todo y nada"* (all and nothing), or $O = \infty$,
and so on.

Zen is rich in this kind of vocabulary, as is explained in my
works on Zen.

There is no doubt that this mysterious First Person is not an
object of knowledge. But, if it is not, how can one take hold of
it so that one can say, "I have it now!"? An "intuition" does not
seem to be an adequate term for this kind of experience. "Feeling" is liable to be misunderstood, unless a specifically defined
sense is given to it. I like to take it in the most primary sense,
somewhat in the way the eye sees and the ear hears.

The difference between sense-perception and "primary" feeling-
experience is: in the former there is a sense-subject and its object,
but, in the latter, subject and object are not differentiated—subject is object, and object is subject, and yet there is no particu-
larizable substance to be known as such, as a something. What
I can state, though only tentatively, in this "primary" experience
is that, when I hear or see, it is my whole being wherein hearing
is seeing and seeing is hearing, because in the totality of my being
there are no such sense-differentiations as one observes in one's
sense-perception.

That is to say, one's whole being is there where the hearing or
the seeing takes place and there is no sense-particularization.
One's whole being is the ear or the eye, and with it the totality
of being hears or sees itself in the hearing or seeing. There is
nothing in it that is vague or obscure or chaotic. In truth, the ear
then hears and the eye sees in the real sense of the term.

Daitō Kokushi, one of the greatest Zen masters of Japan, composed a poem on the subject:

> *When the ear sees,*
> *And the eye hears,*
> *One cherishes no doubts:*
> *How naturally the rain drips*
> *From the eaves!*

This is a typically Zen poem, one might say. How could the rain-drops from the eaves be heard as natural when the sense functions in such a crazily confused manner as stated above? But we must remember that our ordinary hearing or seeing is a specialized sense-function taking place at a specified area where a specified set of nerves converge for the performance of a particular limited form of activity. A totalistic hearing or seeing, on the other hand, eventuates at the deepest level of one's being, where hearing is seeing and seeing hearing. If this functional interfusion should come to pass at the localized terminal, there would be an utter confusion of the senses. What might be called the totalization of particular senses, including intellection, transforms all the brutal mechanistic laws of "necessity" into something full of meaning. Life then ceases to be a mere repetition of biological events governed by the so-called laws of Nature.

This may be called Eastern subjectivism, though the term frequently lends itself to gross misinterpretation. What I mean by subjectivism is not opposed to objectivism, which generally characterizes Western thought. Eastern subjectivity is an absolute one. It is a position transcending all forms of opposition and separation. Buddhist philosophy designates it as "Emptiness" (*śūnyatā* in Sanskrit, *k'ung* in Chinese, and *kū* in Japanese). I understand there was a Western philosopher who called it "subjectum," which corresponds to the "First Person" or Lin-chi's *jen* ("person" or "I").

III

The philosophy of Emptiness is full of meaning. As I state repeatedly, it is not the philosophy of sheer nothingness; it is the philosophy of infinite possibilities, of a nothing filled with fullness of things, in which "nothing is lost and nothing is added." And there is no contradiction whatever when I say that "Emptiness" is the First Person, "I," and that the First Person, "I," is Emptiness. . . .

I have no time here to explore all the implications that can be discovered in the philosophy of Emptiness. Suffice it to give two of the most significant: (1) Being and becoming are one. (2) Necessity and freedom are one. As long as we hold to the dualistic way of thinking, statements like these are highly contradictory or utterly impossible, and, psychologically as well as morally, we shall find ourselves constantly in one form or another of nervous tension and asked to come to a decision. Fortunately, Buddhism is not a system of philosophy; it simply makes use of philosophy in order to satisfy our intellectual requirements. It tells us that there is a higher field of discipline where we can find our original home. I may call it an ethico-aesthetic experience of reality. Judaeo-Christian mythology will supply us with an illuminating parallel to illustrate what I mean by the "ethico-aesthetic."

When God as creator came out of the Godhead (as Emptiness), he did not ask the question "Why?," nor did he complain about the task of looking after his work. He saw light separating itself from darkness, and said, "Good!" It is not our business as human beings to fathom the meaning of this utterance on the part of the creator, for it is the most mystically pregnant exclamation anyone endowed with the power of expressing himself can make while viewing any work, human or divine.

The eye confronts a mass of spring foliage and declares it green. Insofar as we cannot go any further than that, we are still on the logically mechanistic level of necessity. We may be human but are far from being divine. It is only when we can pronounce "Good!" that we can approach the "psychology" of the creator, which is what I term "ethico-aesthetic." The "good" here has no moral implication pure and simple. It corresponds to what we call in the East *myō* in Japanese (*miao* in Chinese). When we understand it, the whole universe, including everything in it, good and evil, right and wrong, subject and object, you and me, goes through a transformation, which is marvelously phenomenal.

Advaitism, or the philosophy of Emptiness, is still an intellectual and therefore a conceptual term and does not mean much to the Oriental mind, which is ever yearning for the deepest and most fundamental in the world we live in. The logically true or the morally good is never satisfactory, never fully thirst-quenching. We must come to the realization of the *myō*, the ultimately good, while surveying the creation in its infinite wholeness. Let us study the *myō* for a while.

To understand what the *myō* means is to understand the working of Japanese psychology, or that which lies behind Japanese culture and Japanese behavior. The term appears in Lao Tzu's *Tao-te ching* and also in Chuang Tzu's work. Perhaps it is originally Taoist. Buddhism adopted it, and *saddharma* (true law) was translated as *miao-fa* (*myōhō*) in A.D. 407 by Kumāra-jīva. The best English equivalent one can find for this term "*myō*" is "mystery" or "mysterious." But "mystery" or "mysterious" has certain intellectual overtones, which is inevitable, seeing that the Western mind is not so well acquainted with the realm of discipline where the idea of the *myō* plays a predominant role.

The *myō* being a Taoist term, it is best for us to know something more about Lao Tzu. It is possible that the *myō* was used before his time, but it was he who made the most of it. In the first chapter of the *Tao-te ching* the author refers to the *myō* as something characteristic of Tao. Tao is beyond any form of designation or definition. As soon as one begins to define it, Tao ceases to be Tao. But, as we cannot leave it without designating it somehow, we call it Tao and make it manifest as "being" and "non-being," as something contradicting itself. This is Tao determining itself.

By means of "non-being" we have a glimpse of the *myō*, and by means of "being" we have an objective world of multiplicities and limitations (*chiao, kyō*). The world of being is subject to quantitative measurements, whereas the world of non-being is unlimited. Unlimited and therefore infinite is this world of absolute non-being. We human beings live in two worlds, limited and yet unlimited, finite and yet infinite. This living in two worlds is called *gen* (*hsüan* in Chinese). And for this reason Lao Tzu's philosophy is known as the teaching of the *hsüan* (*gen*), and we have compounds like these: *hsüan-hsüeh* (doctrine of the *hsüan*), *hsüan-lan* (survey of the *hsüan*), *hsüan-t'an* (discussion on the *hsüan*), *hsüan-chih* (principle of the *hsüan*), *hsüan-men* (doorway to the *hsüan*), etc. When Taoism was made a pseudo State-religion early in the T'ang, Lao Tzu was canonized in A.D. 666 as Hsüan-yüan huang-ti (the emperor of the most abstruse philosophy).

Gen (*hsüan*) literally means "dark," "reddish black," "the color of the sky," which derivatively came to signify "impenetrable," "unfathomable," "inexpressible," "mysterious," etc. When this *gen* is personified, it is called the "Mother." All things come from the Mother and return to her. The Mother is "the creator of the ten thousand things." In the West, the creator is the Father, the Heavenly Father, the Almighty God of wrath and jealousy, but in the East the creator is the Mother, the Mother Earth, the Great Earth, or, as Lao Tzu has it, the "Valley Spirit," or the "Mysterious Female." (This difference between East and West provides us with a number of interesting topics for discussion.)

Gen (*hsüan*) and *myō* (*miao*) are largely synonymous, with perhaps this distinction: *gen* has a more objective sense, while *myō* is more subjective; *myō* is more psychological and *gen* more ontological; *myō* is the way human minds react to the presence of *gen*. When we see a wonderfully executed, most inspiring work of art, we describe it as *myō* and not *gen*. The impenetrable depths of the sky are *gen* but not *myō*. All things designable can be designated as *myō* but issue from what is *gen*. Sometimes the two characters form a compound. In this case, *genmyō* may be tentatively translated as "deeply (or unfathomably) mysterious."

The character *myō* (*miao*) was originally written as a composite of *gen* (*hsüan*) and *shō* (*shao*), which latter means "young," "small," "weak," "wanting," etc. But later the *gen* was replaced by the character *jo* (*nü*), meaning "a woman," and then *myō* came to be associated with a young maiden. But the original meaning was never lost, that is, an aesthetic appreciation of something immeasurably deep and defying description of any kind. The *myō* is thus not to be caught up by the analytical meshes, however fine, of scientific study, for there is something warm and living and full of creativity, which can only be experienced individually, personally, and is not to be conceptualized.

The *myō* is, then, definable as the feeling reflecting the mystic experience of Identity (*gendō, hsüan-tung*), in which nothingness (*jōmu, chang-wu*) and somethingness (*jōu, chang-yu*) are indistinguishably merged as one, though differentiated in name. The *gen* is its ontological name, and the *myō* is its psychological, or, rather, aesthetic reaction. When the mystic experience of Identity is actually attained in its pure totalistic aspect, each particular experience one may have in the realm of finites will participate in the general *myō* feeling for "the mystery of being" (*hsüan chih yu hsüan*). Hence "the doorway of all *myō* (*shūmyō no mon, chung-miao chih men*)."

In ordinary language, the *myō* experience is essentially the outcome of understanding the obscurest depths of eternal Tao (*jōdō, chang-tao*) or eternal *Logos* (*jōmei, chang-ming*), which expresses itself in the finite world of particulars (*yūmei, yu-ming*). The finite, namable world of particulars ultimately returns to the infinite Nameless (*mumei, wu-ming*), which is called by Lao Tzu "the Mother of all things." By "returning," however, is not meant "to stay returned"; it means that there is a close interrelationship between the Infinite and the finites, the Mother and the child (*eiji, ying-erh* or *eigai, ying-hai*). So, says Lao Tzu, the Mother and the child are not to be separated. The understanding of this Identity constitutes the feeling of *myō*. It goes without saying that the Identity is not to be numerically conceived, but is on the transcendental level of the Nameless. We may call it the mystical experience of the Darkness. It would be a great mistake to try to treat it along the line of intellectual analysis.

The serious oversight which is likely to be committed by scientists or logicians is to reduce everything to mathematical measurements and give the result in numbers or in signs. They forget altogether that the essential nature of the feeling is subjective and that when it is objectified it ceases to be itself and turns into a concept which has no life whatever. The feeling that is not alive is no feeling. Especially is this the case with the feeling that arises in connection with the totality of things, which cannot be finitely comprehended. A circle with an infinitely extending circumference is one of such cases; an infinite series of finite numbers is another. A serial infinity may be mathematically symbolized and treated accordingly. An infinity as a concrete totality is not only beyond the pale of intellection but incapable of becoming an object of feeling in the ordinary sense. An infinite totality may be symbolized to a certain degree or may have its analogical representation. As long as our intellect and senses are limited to finite experiences, an infinity must be said to be altogether outside their comprehension. Yet, we have a feeling for the Infinite, and this feeling is at the basis of all finite and particular feelings. We only "vaguely" feel its presence, though we ordinarily fail to bring it to the surface of our consciousness.

When I say a feeling of the Infinite, I use the term "feeling" in its deepest and most fundamental sense. I often used "intuition" in such cases, but I now find it somewhat inaccurate because intuition has still an epistemological taint, as I stated before, while an experience of the Infinite is not to be subsumed under the same category. It is *sui generis*. It is no wonder that so-called religious-minded people ascribe this experience to a power higher than themselves.

Western people try to approach Tao objectively, as I said before, and therefore inevitably epistemologically. On the other hand, the Eastern approach is from the inside; that is, it is subjective, and by "subjective" I mean from the point of view of the thing-in-itself-ness of a thing, or simply its isness. To see a thing subjectively, therefore, means to see it as it is, in its suchness, in its just-so-ness. What we ordinarily call "subjective" is, strictly speaking, not subjective, for it is still objective inasmuch as it is conceived in opposition to an object. No subject is possible without its object, and to this extent there is in the subject something of objectivity. I like to point out that there is a something, though not definitely designable as this or that, even before the differentiation of subject and object. This is one of the first questions the Zen master would require us to answer: "What does your face which you had even before you were born look like?" This "face" which every one of us has, or this something which transcends all forms of dualistic opposition, is that which creates "the ten thousand things." It may be called the Absolute or Ultimate Reality, or Emptiness (as Buddhists have it). Those who hold this view cannot be called subjectivists as the term is commonly understood.

I may add one more word and say that the identification of subject and object where self-knowledge or self-realization takes place is in actuality the self-determining of Emptiness, or the Godhead's turning into God as the creator. By this turning, the Godhead becomes self-conscious in the way Emptiness comes to self-realization.

When I make this kind of statement, I am said to be vague, approaching nonsense. But, when you actually have it, you know what it is and will realize that there is nothing clearer, simpler, and, at the same time, deeper.

When one asserts that the seer is the seen and the seen is the seer, we may declare him nonsensical, because logically A is A and is never not-A. Moreover, practically speaking, the eye cannot see itself—it requires a mirror to see itself. But, in actuality this kind of seeing is not at all seeing itself, but seeing its reflection, which is by no means its self, as it is in its isness, or in its nakedness.

The West excels in describing an object in its relatedness to others, in analyzing it epistemologically, following logical steps one after another, and in coming to a certain form of conclusion, which, however, is not a conclusion, because it is never conclusive or final. One "conclusion" reached by one philosopher is sure to be contested by another, indefinitely.

The East excels in seeing reality or Tao from the inside, from within, in its just-so-ness, without doing any violence to it. Easterners have been so trained since the first awakening of consciousness.

This awakening has taken two separate courses in its development: the one is the Western way and the other the Eastern. We can say that the West is extrovert, while the East is introvert or introspective or self-analyzing or not at all analyzing. The West is not unconscious of this self-analyzing process, the discipline prevailing in the East. But the West has been doing this cursorily, sporadically, or spasmodically. We see in the West some splendid specimens of it, such as Plato, Plotinus, Eckhart, St. John of the Cross, and so on. But they have been looked upon as abnormal, eccentric, and unacceptable.

A system of discipline more or less methodical has been going on since of old in China as well as in India. To give an example from the *Chuang Tzu:*

Yen-ch'eng Tzu-yu said to Tung-kuo Tzu-chi: Since I received your instruction, in one year I gained simplicity; in the second year I knew how to adjust myself as demanded; in the third I felt no impediments; in the fourth I objectified myself; in the fifth I had an attainment; in the sixth the spirit came to me; in the seventh I was in conformity with Heaven; in the eighth I had no thought of life and death; finally, in the ninth year, I attained to Great *Miao.*

As long as we are in a dualistic world of birth and death, right and wrong, good and evil, subject and object, we cannot realize what the *myō* is; we feel it only when we come in contact with the Infinite, where we are free from all forms of restriction and inhibition. To accomplish this, it may take nine years or more, but one will attain it if one does not relax his efforts.

Instantaneity and eternity, *saṁsāra* and Nirvāṇa, this world of transiency and the Pure Land of permanent peace, are great contrasts. We live in the former and desire the latter. The desire is strong, but its object is at a great distance. It is impossible to cross the distance. Some say that this distance is the soul of the beautiful and to contemplate the beautiful is bliss. This view, however, is not the one held by Eastern thinkers. Chuang Tzu would advise us to attain what is known as *tso-wang,* "sitting-forgetting," or *sang-wou,* "losing the self." Chuang Tzu is not a Buddhist; therefore, he does not go any further than to state that the self is to be lost or forgotten. Buddhists declare that there is no self from the beginning, that the mirror has never been soiled with dust, and that therefore there is no need of trying to clean it. When we get rid of the delusions arising from finite existences, the "self" is purified, and the "Original Person" reveals himself. It is he who enjoys the ethico-aesthetic feeling of the *myō.*

Tso-wang is defined by Chuang Tzu: "It is freeing oneself from the body, getting rid of the intelligence, and, further, thus, by separating oneself from form and removing the intellect, identifying with the Great Thoroughfare (*ta-t'ung*)." *Sang-wou* is given the following description: It is "as if absent-mindedly going beyond the opposition of subject and object, as if the body were like a dead tree and the mind like cold ashes, and no longer looking like one's former self." According to Chuang Tzu, when this state of mind is attained, one is in communion with *t'ien-chün* (heavenly equity), or *t'ien-i* (heavenly unity), which means that one goes beyond the humanly finite discrimination of good and bad, right and wrong, and lives in the field of infinity, where things move in their just-so-ness. Everything has its place, its destiny, its function, and, so long as it does its work in the way its nature requires though it may not be conscious of it, there is nothing that will interfere with its movements.

In regard to the experience of Identity of Heavenly Unity, Chuang Tzu has the following to say about the wise man who achieves such transcendence of dualistic difficulties:

It is only the wise man who knows how to make use of the principle of Identity through the maze of contrary ideas. He does not uphold his own views as absolutely correct; he surrenders himself to that which transcends all individual differences. By so doing he objectifies himself. By objectifying himself he passes over obstacles. By passing over obstacles he attains Identity and with this he is contented. He has no cravings for anything else. He rests with himself now, and he does not know why it is so. This is Tao.

This is one of the difficult and obscure passages in the *Chuang Tzu*, and I have added a few words to make it more intelligible to modern readers. The translation is inevitably an interpretation and open to discussion.

The principle of Identity to which Chuang Tzu resorts in order to unify or merge the controversies that have been going on around him has its concrete symbolization in the person of Nan-kuo Tzu-chi. This person is introduced at the beginning of Chuang Tzu's discourse on the subject, that is, in Book II of his work. Nan-kuo Tzu-chi is probably Chuang Tzu's imaginary

creation. He is found to be leaning against the table as if lost to
the whole world. He looks so absent-minded that he is no longer
like his former self, which was involved in the whirlpools of
subject and object, right and wrong, good and bad.

To such a one, metaphysically speaking, the whole universe is
no bigger than the tip of a hair; P'eng Tsu, historically renowned
for his long life of 800 years, is not any older than the baby who
dies even before weaning; "heaven-and-earth and I are of the
same age; the ten thousand things and I are all one." From the
moral point of view, he is a wise man or a perfect man. He is
not concerned with worldly affairs of gain and loss; he lives outside the dust and filth of a finite life; he is the living example
of *miao-tao*.

IV

Living is the art of creativity demonstrating itself. Creativity
is objectively seen as necessity, but from the inner point of view
of Emptiness it is "just-so-ness" (*jinen* or *shizen* in Japanese and
tzu-jan in Chinese). *Jinen* is literally "by-itself-so" and may be
regarded as equivalent to spontaneity or naturalness, but in *jinen*
we see the innerliness of things more emphatically brought out.
When the human mind is perfectly attuned to this innerliness,
the feeling of the *myō* is awakened in a manner somewhat as
when the tongue touching sugar tastes it sweet.

Objectively speaking, the *myō* may be represented as the
straight line of time drawn tangent to a circumferenceless circle
of Emptiness. The point at which the time-line touches the curve
is the absolute present, or eternal now, or here-now. All the past
converges here and all the future issues from here, but the "here,"
which is really "here-now," is Emptiness itself—Emptiness infinitely rich in content and inexhaustibly creative. Chuang Tzu
calls it the "heavenly storehouse." The *myō* is the human way of
expressing this experience.

Emptiness, like the Godhead, being the source of inexhaustible
creativity, is not to be conceived as empty nothingness, inert,
inane, and eternally quiescent, and absorbed in aesthetic contemplation. The *myō* is not such a state of contemplation. It is in

every form of motion, in every phase of action, not only individually but totalistically in it. When this is experienced, necessity is freedom, and freedom is necessity. When hungry I eat, when thirsty I drink. "Tao is no more than our everyday-mindedness." "What does Heaven say?" asks Confucius, "yet the four seasons go on, and the ten thousand things grow up. What does Heaven say?" Thus everything goes on along the line of "just-so-ness."

The *myō* is also applied to works of art. However technically perfect, they do not awaken in us the sense of the *myō;* there must be something that goes beyond the technique, that is to say, something that enlivens every display of skill. When this enlivening agency of creativity is present, we have the *myō.*

Life, as long as it is confined to the animal and to the vegetative, is necessity; but man is free and creative and proceeds to make the universe look beautiful and lovable. To man, the universe is not something rigidly, mercilessly, and altogether impersonally controlled by so-called laws of Nature.

Beauty is not primarily objective. Nature, symbolic of necessity, becomes beautiful and the source of joy when man's mind rises above things finite, and, soaring up to the Infinite, surveys the world therefrom. It is a mistake to think that what is beautiful is limited to a human work of imagination. The universe is also a work of art, though not human; it is beautiful when it is seen from the point of view where the iron chain of necessity and obedience, of law and irresistibility, is shattered, that is to say, when one enters into the spirit of creativity, as "God makes himself necessity," to use the terminology of Simone Weil.

When this takes place, we have the *myō,* the feeling of beauty, not objectively perceived but innerly growing out of one's being. The *myō,* therefore, is a subjective and psychological term. It is the sense of harmony, which is not necessarily objectively demonstrable, but which is felt innerly when all the finites are seen in something infinitely transcending them while not losing their particularization. When this *myō* is felt in the way one lives we have a life of no-striving, which Buddhists consider as superseding all the moral values we finite beings esteem.

It is not quite true that the East looks upon ethical values as insignificant because the absolute reality is above all forms of relativity. The East, no doubt, pays the highest regard to the Ultimate, but that does not mean that ethics is neglected. In this respect, Chinese Buddhism is eloquent in disproving the charge, in that Chinese mentality is firmly rooted in the Great Mother Earth. The Chinese look up to Heaven as much as the people in the West, but they never forget the Earth. Confucius as well as Lao Tzu and Chuang Tzu and other Taoists make frequent references to Heaven and Heavenly Reason, but for that reason they never neglect relating to our earthly affairs and human relations. Their Heaven always remains in intimate communion with things going on on earth. Indeed, it is Heaven that looks down upon us below instead of our looking up to it.

Buddhism made its start in India and was known for being ethically minded. But, as it developed into the Mahāyāna system of thought, it became more speculative and transcendental and showed a decided tendency to flee from the world. But, when it struck root deeply in China, we find it intimately affiliated with Confucianism as well as with Taoism, supplying them with what they needed, that is, a philosophical background. In Chinese Buddhism, we thus discover the best in Indian Buddhism organically functioning in the Chinese practical mind. For instance, Zen Buddhism, which swayed China from the early T'ang (618–907) to the late Ming (1368–1644), for about nine hundred years, is the embodiment of Chinese and Indian thought happily amalgamated.

Buddhism does not try to find meaning outside of life, for living itself is meaning. Meaning is not added to life from the outside. When one knows what life is, one knows that there is nothing of value beyond the living of it. How to live, however, is an art. In this respect every one of us is an artist, a creative artist. The painter may need brushes, canvas, paints, and other materials to produce fine specimens of art. So with sculptors and others known as artists. But we, most ordinary and probably prosaic people, deeply concerned with worldly affairs and far from being artists of any denomination whatever, are also artists in the genuine sense of the term. Besides, we have no need for such external materials as are required by professional artists. Everything we wish to have is already in us, with us, and waiting to be utilized. We are each and all born artists. We are creators of the *myō*.

Inasmuch as life, or how to live it, is an art and every one of us is meant to be an artist of high grade—and who knows we are not already such!—we must try our best to attain the *myō* in our daily living. When a Zen master was asked what Tao is, the answer was "Everyday-mindedness." When another master was further asked, "What is the meaning of it?" he said, "When you wish to sleep you sleep, when you wish to sit up you sit up." Is this not leading a life of "just-so-ness," following the natural order of things in our daily life? Where is the *myō*? Where is the art? This is the very point, however, where the *myō* is beyond our intellection.

Some may ask, "There are many people who cannot eat even when hungry, cannot sleep even when tired. What about them?" Such questions are asked because the questioner is still groveling in the mud of finitudes and dualities. The *myō* is appreciated only when one can stand at the highest peak of the Himalayas and at the same time walk along the very bottom of the Pacific Ocean. The idea, in modern expression, is that a world of finites is to be understood as the Infinite limiting itself, or, in Buddhist terminology, as the self-determination of Emptiness. The following incident extracted from the history of Zen, I hope, will, to a certain extent, illustrate the point.

Yakusan (Yüeh-shan Wei-yen) once gave the sermon: "Where the intellect fails to reach, do not try to make any statement [on the matter]. If you do, the horns will grow on your head."

Dōgo (Tao-wu Yüan-chih) [or brother Chih] then left the room.

Ungan (Yün-yen T'an-ch'eng) later asked the master, "Why did not Brother Chih react to your remark, O Master?"

Said the master, "It is Chih the monk who knows all about it. Go and ask him."

Ungan, following the master's advice, came to Brother Chih and said, "How is it that you did not react at all to our master's remark the other day?"

Dōgo responded, "I have a headache today. You had better ask the master himself."

When Ungan passed, Dōgo remarked, "Ungan did not know what's what, after all. I regret that I did not tell him all about it then. In spite of all this, he deserves to be called a disciple of our master, Yakusan."

Daigu Shūshi (Ta-yü Shou-chih) of Kinshū later gave this comment: "Ungan did not know what's what. As for Dōgo's knowing it, he regrets that he did not at the time tell Ungan all about it. Tell me now whether or not Dōgo really had it?"

This Zen story may not seem to be very intelligible. The only reference to anything abstract, and perhaps intelligible, is Yakusan's statement about the intellect. Though he does not expressly mention the subject about which he is talking, we know that it is about the final reality or the ultimate truth, and he goes on to say that it is beyond one's intellectual grasp and that if one attempts to give it anything approaching a conceptual definition one will surely miss it. The rest of the story makes no reference whatever to the main subject except one's having a headache and the other's regretting and the third's evading. As for the commentator, he is anxious to know whether or not Dōgo understood the whole affair. All that we can get out of the whole transaction is what seems to be a trivial episode in the life of a monastery. But is this really so? What is there in it that makes Zen people so concerned with it?

I will give another example to elucidate what makes Zen masters so concerned with details of our daily life, which passes on without attracting much attention on our part. It may be necessary for the philosopher to maneuver an imposing army of abstract ideas and erudite references when he wants to demonstrate the truth of a proposition, to establish the significance of human values, to confirm the objectivity of knowledge, etc. But, to the Zen master, such a parade of concepts does not mean very much. He is content with offering tea to a visitor, with bidding a fare-thee-well to a departing friend. When a philosopher comes to the master ready to discuss with him something weighty, the master has no hesitation in telling the intruder that he has a headache. The headache is really the answer to whatever question may be coming. If the philosopher understands it, it is all right with him and he may be grateful for the master's kindness. If not, woe unto him!—he has "another thirty years" to ponder the matter.

When Ryūtan Sōshin first came to Dōgo to study Zen, Dōgo gave him no special teaching about it. Some time passed, and Sōshin grew impatient and approached the master and asked him about Zen. Dōgo said, "Ever since you came to me, I have been teaching you in Zen every day." Sōshin was puzzled and wished to be enlightened on the matter. Dōgo said, "When you bring me a cup of tea in the morning, do I not take it gratefully? When you give me something to eat when mealtime comes, do I not accept it? When you greet me, do I not return it? When have I not instructed you in the essentials of Zen?" Sōshin dropped his head and began to reflect. The master lost no time in saying, "When you want to see, see at once—no deliberation whatever!" This instantly helped Sōshin open his mind. Sōshin then asked how to nourish it further. Dōgo's answer was: "Saunter along self-sufficiently in accordance with your nature; be free and uninhibited in response to the situation in which you find yourself. Only do away with thoughts arising from your limited knowledge, and there is no realization specifically to be termed supreme."

"To do away with one's limited thoughts" means to recognize rightly the relativity of all knowledge and, further, to see deeply into the source of being or to survey the open field of Emptiness. There is no other revelation to be known as supreme or divine. As Buddhists say, the moon of Suchness shines by itself when the clouds of ignorance (i.e., *wu-ming,* or *avidyā,* that is relative knowledge) are dispersed. A life cleansed of all accretions is one of *anābhogacaryā,* a life of no-striving.

Baso's saying, "Everyday-mindedness," is explained by himself in the following way:

Tao does not need any form of discipline, only have it not defiled. What are the defilements? Have no thought of birth and death. Have no contrivances. Have no purposiveness. These are the defilements.

If one wishes to understand instantly what Tao is, everyday-mindedness is Tao. What is "everyday-mindedness"? It is not to strive after anything. It is neither right nor wrong. It is neither to take up nor to let go. It is to be neither nihilistic nor positivistic. It is not to make any distinction between the commoner and the wise man.

In the *sūtra* we read: "It is not the life of the ordinary man, it is not the life of the saint—that is the life of the *bodhisattva*." As we at present walk, rest, sit, lie down, respond to various situations, or meet people of all classes—Tao is in all this.

To recapitulate: *Anābhogacaryā* is, as one Chinese translator has it, a life of no strivings, of no usefulness, of no effectiveness. This corresponds to: Lao Tzu's *wu-wei* or *wu-wei erh wu-pu-wei* ("By doing nothing, all things are done," or "Everything is done by non-doing"); Chuang Tzu's *wu-yung chih yung* (usefulness of non-usefulness); Chao-chou Ts'ung-shen's "Stone-bridge which carries horses as well as donkeys"; Lin-chi's *wu-shih chih jên* (a man of no-work); Hakuin's "Hiring an idiotic wise man who tries to fill the well with snow"; Bankei's *pu-sheng jen* ("Man of the Unborn") and the *chieh-k'ung jen* ("Man of Emptiness"), to the exposition of which the whole Prajñā-pāramitā literature is devoted.

A man of *anābhogacaryā*, then, is one who lives the *myō* in its ethico-aesthetic sense, as well as in its ontological sense. All the moral values and social practice, Buddhists claim, come out of this life of no-strivings, of just-so-ness, of Suchness, which is Emptiness. When all the defilements and accretions are wiped away, purged, purified, the original light of creativity will illumine one's whole being, and whatever one does will be "good."

The Dhammapada reads:

> *Not to do any evil,*
> *To promote the good,*
> *To purify one's own mind,—*
> *This is the Buddha's teaching.*

CHAPTER VI

The Religions of Japan

In quite different ways, three religions have contributed to the formation of the basic patterns of Japanese culture. Shintoism is the native religion of the Japanese and expresses their traditions, temperament, and national style of life. Confucianism entered Japan from China but never functioned forcefully as a separate religious movement. The principal impact of Confucianism upon Japanese culture and history has been in the areas of law and education, not in the spheres of religious ideas, sentiments, or ceremonies. Confucian ideals appealed mainly to the aristocratic class, and, hence, never gained widespread popular support in Japan; however, they played a major role in shaping social institutions and political life. Buddhism, another foreign import, has been a prominent religious and civilizing force in the history of Japan. For almost a thousand years Buddhism was the national religion of the Japanese. During that period it transformed the appreciation of the Japanese for their national traditions as these were expressed in Shintoism and revitalized the spiritual life of Japan.

SHINTOISM

It is difficult to ascertain whether the term "Shintoism" refers more accurately to a cultural or to a religious phenomenon. "Shinto" is a Sino-Japanese term meaning "the way of the spirits," a term first used during the period when Buddhism was establishing itself in Japan. It was probably used originally to distinguish the old native traditions from the new, more sophisticated import. In a larger sense, Shinto refers to the traditional manner in which the Japanese have ordered their personal and communal lives for over twenty-five hundred years. Of course, in twenty-five hundred years, Japan has changed drastically in many ways, but there can be no doubt that a continuing thread of tradition binds the modern Japanese to his primitive ancestor.

The claim frequently advanced by scholars that Shintoism grew out of a primitive ancestor worship is probably wrong. Although, generally speaking, ancestor worship was part of the practices of the primitive cult, the primitive religion of Japan was a rather disorganized polytheism in which ancestral spirits, heroes, nature spirits, and other vaguely defined occult forces were venerated and worshiped.

Shintoism is essentially a religion of joy and celebration. The superior beings that are worshiped range from ancestors to legendary heroes, from the sun-goddess to the god of food. All the revered subjects of the Shinto faith are approached as ancestoral or parental figures by the Japanese; that is, with reverence, awe, and respect.

Shinto worship organizes itself around the "kami": Shinto actually means the "kami way," and the Japanese have worshiped kami for over two millennia. "Kami" is one of those loaded terms which carry a diversity of meaning. The great Japanese scholar Motoori says, regarding the definition of "kami":

Speaking in general, *kami* signifies in the first place the deities of heaven and earth that appear in the ancient records and also the spirits worshipped at the shrines.

It seems hardly necessary to add that it also includes human beings. It also includes such objects as birds, beasts, trees, plants, seas, mountains, and so forth. In ancient usage, anything whatsoever which was outside the ordinary, which possessed superior power or which was awe-inspiring was called *kami*. Eminence here does not refer to the superiority of nobility, goodness or meritorious deeds. Evil and mysterious things, if they are extraordinary and dreadful, are called *kami*.

It is also evident that among human beings who are called *kami* the successive generations of sacred emperors are all included. The fact that emperors are called "distant *kami*" is because from the point of view of common people they are far-separated, majestic and worthy of reverence. In a lesser degree we also find, in the present as well as in ancient times, human beings who are *kami*. . . .

Furthermore, among things which are not human, the thunder is always called "sounding-*kami*." Such things as dragons, the echo, and foxes, inasmuch as they attract attention, are wonderful and awe-inspiring, are also *kami*. In popular belief the echo is called a mountain goblin. . . .

In the *Nihongi* and the *Manyoshu* the tiger and the wolf are also spoken of as *kami*. Again, there are cases in which peaches were given the name, August-Thing-Great-*Kami*-Fruit, and a necklace was called August-Storehouse-Shelf-*Kami*. There are further instances in which rocks, stumps of trees and leaves of plants spoke audibly. These were all *kami*. There are again numerous places in which seas and mountains are called *kami*. This does not have reference to the spirit of the mountain or the sea, but *kami* is here used directly of the particular mountain or sea. This is because they were exceedingly awe-inspiring.[1]

If "kami" describes such a wide diversity of objects, then the term does not basically refer to a particular set of objects, but rather to the qualitative aspects of experience. Kami as much characterizes the experiences of awe, fascination, mystery, horror, dread, and so on, as it does specific things which literally evoke these experiential qualities.

The Shinto faith seems to be an established vehicle in which the Japanese, over the centuries, have attempted to preserve and cultivate their experience of the "holy," or that which strikes awe, terror, mystery, and respect into the hearts of men. Viewed thusly, the worship of kami celebrates the mystery of things, and is an occasion for the recognition and evocation of the experience of the holy. Thus, the term "kami" denotes the world of the sacred, the world of holy powers, special personages, and occult

---

[1] Toyokai Motoori (ed.), *Motoori Norinaga Zenshu* ("Complete Works of Motoori Norinaga") (Tokyo, 1901), Vol. 1, pp. 150–152.

events, all of which stand in direct contrast to the mundane, secular world of everyday life. When viewed in this manner, Shintoism can be seen as that system of right belief, ritual, and human comportment expressing the kami-experience of the Japanese people throughout their history.

The history and development of the Shinto faith in Japan cannot be disassociated from Buddhism's taking root and its subsequent growth in Japanese soil. Pre-Buddhistic Shinto had been a loose, disorganized system of nature and ancestor worship supported by a fantastic mythology concerning the genesis of the spirits and strange legends about the origin of the world. Its prayers and sacrifices had been aimed at obtaining temporal prosperity for the living. However, with the introduction of Buddhism into Japan in the sixth century A.D., the old, indigenous faith was challenged by a sophisticated rival that brought with it a complex, speculative scheme, an intense moral devotion, and a proven capacity to accommodate itself to new cultures and new spiritual needs. The presence of a vigorous new religion made the Japanese more self-conscious and even defensive about their indigenous religious customs. During the seventh and eighth centuries, Buddhism made rapid inroads into the popular support of Shintoism despite periods of suppression and harassment. By the ninth century A.D., Buddhism was recognized as the national religion of Japan, and Shintoism went into a period of semi-obscurity due to its inability to expand and enrich itself through a healthy confrontation with this new religious force.

Movements began, however, in the ninth century A.D., that had as their goal the unification of Buddhism with Shinto tradition. One of these, called Ryobu-Shinto ("Two Aspect Shinto") literally fused the two religions. Shinto gods (kami) were viewed by this compromise faith as incarnations of Buddhas and Bodhisattvas. Of great interest is the fact that both Buddhist leaders *and* Shinto priests supported this amalgamation of the two faiths. Shinto gods and legends were so ill-defined and amorphous that they were readily assimilated into the Buddhist pantheon. The sun-goddess, worshiped in Shinto as the ancestress of the imperial family, was identified with Vairocana, the Great-Sun, the ultimate Buddha-reality. Buddhism took possession of all Shinto shrines and temples (except the sacred shrine at Ise) during this period, and for a millennium was the spiritual mentor of Japan. Two Buddhist sects, the Tendai and Shingon, demonstrated the ability of the Mahayana form of Buddhism to assimilate native faiths. They also showed how Buddhism always shaped itself according to its relations with the culture of the land in which it thrived. We shall defer our more detailed attention to the Tendai and Shingon sects until we consider the growth of Japanese Buddhism as a whole.

Japan witnessed a resurgence of Shintoism beginning in the latter part of the eighteenth century, culminating in 1868 with the declaration of Shinto as the state religion. Buddhism was thus deposed as custodian of all Shinto shrines and temples, which once again reverted back to the control of the Shinto priests under the protection and supervision of the government. With the revival of Shintoism in the nineteenth century, the theocratic base of Japanese political life, latent in the Shinto worship of the emperor as incarnate deity, emerged as an overt principle of national solidarity. Shintoism replaced Buddhism as the religious foundation of the Japanese state, reconfirming a continuity between the ancient traditions and the modern Japanese people and their aspirations.

The Shintoism that had been preserved by the tolerance of the Buddhists during their thousand-year reign in Japanese history now associated itself more directly with the central government and its vision of the destiny of the Japanese people. Ancient myths and cosmogonies became the religious apologies for political aspirations, e.g., the territorial expansion of the Japanese state. The nationalistic and chauvinistic aspects of Shinto have received special attention as a consequence of World War II. The Japanese government found Shintoism to be a reliable instrument for uniting the Japanese people and inflaming their patriotic spirit. Following the disestablishment of national Shinto in 1945, all Shinto shrines reverted back to a private status, no longer enjoying governmental support and no longer under the direct supervision of a government agency. The propagation of Shinto in educational institutions was prohibited and the government's requirement of attendance at Shinto festivals and ceremonies as proof of patriotism was rescinded. Nevertheless, most Shinto shrines continued to be centers of religious worship and ceremony, and the domestic shrines of the Shinto faith were completely untouched by the directives of the Allies at the conclusion of World War II. In one census taken in 1963, over sixty-six million Japanese professed faith in the Shinto religion. Shintoism may have been destroyed as a state religion, but it obviously was not obliterated as the expression of the communal and national life of faith of the Japanese.

It is interesting to note that in that same census, taken in 1963, in which sixty-six million Japanese professed Shintoism as their religious preference, fifty-four million Japanese preferred Buddhism. Since these figures exceed the population of the Japanese nation by twenty-four million people (Japan's population in 1963 was ninety-six million), one is able to see in a concrete way that, for the Japanese, the practice of Shintoism does not disqualify one from practicing and believing in Buddhism and vice versa. Westerners are prone to think of religious affiliation as a matter of exclusive membership, whereas in the East, particularly in China and Japan, affiliations by individuals in religious sects are typically plural. Most divisions in Western religions are strongly doctrinal or creedal, whereas most divisions in popular religions of the East are matters of different styles of worship or different ways of approaching divinity.

JAPANESE BUDDHISM

Buddhism was introduced to Japan in A.D. 552 by an emissary sent to the mikado of Japan by the king of Korea. This ambassador brought with him a graven image of the Buddha and several volumes of Mahayanist scripture. Setting aside a special place for the study of this new faith, the Japanese emperor initiated the

Buddhist movement in Japan. Although the early efforts to establish Buddhism in Japan met with stiff resistance from the Shintoists, by the seventh century the Buddhist movement had grown to the point where it had forty-six temples and monasteries in Japan and a monastic order of approximately fourteen hundred monks. As previously indicated, during the eighth century, Buddhism became the state religion of Japan and continued as such until the revival of Shintoism in 1869.

A number of factors contributed to the success that Buddhism enjoyed in its competition with Shintoism to win the allegiance of the Japanese. Buddhism presented a set of lofty, spiritual ideals, such things as charity, humanity, sympathy, self-control, and moderation, which were far superior to any ideals to be found in Shintoism. To the heart burdened by the misery of life and grown weary of the world, Buddhism offered hope for complete liberation, or at least a respite in a Buddhist paradise. In its sculpture, art, architecture, ritual, and monastic organization, it appealed to other dimensions of the human personality which were relatively ignored by Shintoism. In general, Buddhism deepened the spiritual life of the Japanese, stimulated their speculative interest in religious concerns, and refined their religious sentiments.

Most of the major sects of Japanese Buddhism were modeled after schools of Chinese Buddhism. The Japanese Buddhists placed themselves under the tutelage of Chinese Buddhism during the early stages of the development of the religion in Japan. While we cannot trace the immense complexities of Buddhist history in Japan, we can examine the major sects both in terms of their origin and principal doctrines.

1. *The Tendai School.* This school, founded in the early part of the ninth century A.D. by Saicho, derives from the Chinese school known as T'ien-t'ai. Saicho was a Japanese Buddhist who established a monastery on Mount Hiei which became the most powerful center for the dissemination of Buddhist culture and learning in Japanese history. In 804, he was sent to China by the emperor to seek out an authoritative truth in Buddhism and

returned bearing scriptures and tracts of the T'ien-t'ai (in Japanese, "Tendai") School of Chinese Buddhism. The authoritative Buddhist scripture for the Tendai School is the Lotus Sutra. This sutra's teachings point to the fact that the Buddha and the eternal truths of Buddhism are continually being manifested in concrete realities—in the historical Gautama, in every human being and blade of grass, and even in the kami of the Shinto faith. The whole purpose of life is to realize the Buddha-nature within oneself so that everyone can participate in the Buddha's saving love and work. The realization of the Buddha-nature within requires intensive moral discipline, in fact, necessitates the imitation of the Buddha's life. The historical Buddha is a "Condescension-body," a concrete, conditioned manifestation of eternal reality and truth which has "condescended" to appear in human form so that we can have faith. While these are the general features of Tendai doctrine, it is quite difficult to be more specific, since Tendai was quite eclectic and even disposed to adopt opposing views as partial revelations of Buddhist truth rather than enter into conflict with them. The Tendai School is the breeding ground for many of the minor sects of Japanese Buddhism, for example the Eisai, Dogen, Honen, Shinran, and Nichiren.

2. *The Shingon School.* The Shingon and Tendai schools were very closely associated in Japan. There was much interchange of doctrine and practice between the two, perhaps because they flourished in Japan at the same time and both enjoyed the favor of the imperial court. Kukai is credited with founding Shingon in Japan following his visit to China in 804–806. The Buddhism that he encountered in China was that of the Chen-yen School, a Tantric sect emphasizing sacred spells, magic, a sophisticated pantheism, and the worship of Vairocana. Legend informs us that when Kukai died in 835, he was actually in a state of samadhi (intense trance) and had himself buried alive. Even in the modern age, Kukai receives the adoration and faith of many people who believe that he had extraordinary powers and that he emerges periodically from his state of contemplation to work miracles.

Shingon builds upon the idea that Buddha, called Maha-Vairocana, is the essence of all things; indeed, he comprises the whole cosmos. Ordinary bodies, words, and thoughts are manifestations of the body, word, and thought of Vairocana. These are called the "three mysteries" (body, word, and thought), and the purpose of Shingon ritual is to permeate us with these "mysteries," to vitalize in us the Supreme Illuminator, Vairocana. Every single event in nature, from the slightest sound to the largest star, is a manifestation of Buddha Vairocana, and the task of the devoted Buddhist is to learn to decipher the language of cosmic action. Shingon ritual is extraordinarily symbolic in almost every aspect of its action, language, and even in the dress of the worshiper and the priest. Shingon in its worship attempts to present a mystical, but concrete, representation of Buddhist truth, rather than teaching extensive reliance upon meditation as do many other schools of Buddhism. It does this by its two basic mandalas, one representing Vairocana in ideal form surrounded by all of his emanations, including various saints, Buddhas, and still further manifestations in the forms of mythological figures and symbols; another representing the dynamic and creative powers of Vairocana represented as groups of deities, goblins, demons, heroic humans, and beasts, in the center of which lies a red lotus symbolizing the Buddha-heart of the universe. Taken together, these mandalas represent the life and being of Vairocana, the creative and sustaining source of all the world and of every divine being manifested in the world.

Shingon appealed to the Japanese because it was a marvelous unity of rich art, mystical speculation, profound spirituality, elaborate ritual, and the promise of magical powers. Its founder, Kukai (called posthumously Kobo Daishi), is the most popular and well-known figure in the history of Japanese Buddhism.

3. *Amidism.* The Japanese school associated with the worship of Amida (Amitabha in India and China) derives from the Chinese Buddhist sect known as Ch'ing-t'u (in Japanese, Jodo). Worship of Amida is prevalent in almost every form of Chinese and Japanese Buddhism but only in Japan did it develop into an

organized, popular sect. Although faith in Amida, the Savior of the Western Paradise, was part of the early sects in Japanese Buddhism, the true founder of the religion of the Pure Land in Japan was Honen (1133–1212). The sect propagating this religion usually is called Jodo.

Jodo is a religion of simple piety and faith. Its cardinal tenet is that salvation may be achieved by faith in or meditation upon Amida, whose compassionate nature and overabundance of merit guarantees to all who approach him salvation in his Pure Land of bliss. The religious life, as taught by the Jodo sect, was to be lived in absolute devotion to Amida and in confidence that Amida's accumulated merit could be turned over to the faithful to work for their salvation. According to Honen's teaching, all that was required to obtain admission to purgatory (the region bordering on the Pure Land) was to repeat the formula "namu Amida Butsu," or "reverence to Amida Buddha." This sacred formula, called the Nembutsu, was presumed to be a manifestation of that piety and faith which lay at the heart of Jodo. If a faithful worshiper repeated the formula eighteen times, he was assured of entrance into paradise and eventually the realization of Nirvana or Buddhahood.

The sects organized primarily around the worship of Amida, the religion of the Pure Land, are often referred to as the Buddhist "shortcut" schools. They did provide an easy, intelligible faith for the masses, uncomplicated by ritual, excessive moral demands, and difficult philosophy. Honen's formulation of the Jodo faith was simple and undogmatic, and as a result, he managed to avoid conflicts with other major Buddhist sects. Following his death, however, his disciples began to define the doctrines more precisely with the result that many subsects developed within Jodo. Some of these subsects emphasized "salvation by the grace of Amida alone" to the neglect of morality, while others concentrated upon formal rules for pietistic worship.

4. *Zen.* Zen Buddhism in Japan is a derivative of the Chinese school of Ch'an. Zen was introduced into Japan in the twelfth century by Eisai (1141–1215). Equally important in introducing

Zen methods and doctrines was Dogen (1200–1253). Zen, in conformity with Ch'an, denied that scriptures could communicate the truth of Buddhism and affirmed that the deepest truth of Buddhism occurs by a special transmission from Buddha to his disciples and then from disciple to disciple. Zen places great emphasis upon the primacy of the religious experience of satori, which is an instantaneous realization of truth, a blinding illumination. All activities in Zen are subordinate to the purpose of realizing enlightenment. Once attained, the truth of enlightenment cannot be communicated or taught.

Of all the sects of Buddhism in Japan, Zen probably expresses the Japanese character more than any other. It has exerted a powerful influence in the arts and thus has played a fundamental role in shaping the aesthetic elements of Japanese culture.

CHAPTER VII

Shintoism

On Shinto

Masaharu Anesaki

GENERAL FEATURES OF SHINTO

"In that Land there were numerous deities (or spirits) which
shone with a lustre like that of fireflies, and evil deities which
buzzed like flies. There were also trees and herbs which could
speak." This is said of the Japanese archipelago when the founder
of the nation meditated descending from heaven to the country.
And it is said in another connection: "The God who originally
founded this country is the God who descended from Heaven
and established this State in the period when Heaven and Earth
became separated, and when the trees and herbs had speech."
Imagine a religion amounting to the worship of these deities or
spirits and lacking almost any system of moral teachings or metaphysical doctrines. It cannot but be called "primitive," if not in a
strictly anthropological sense. Certain systems have, from time to
time, been established on the basis of those primitive ideas, and
indeed attempts, more or less successful, have been made to lay
the foundation of a national life on the worship of the "Deity

Reprinted from Masaharu Anesaki, *History of Japanese Religion* (Kegan Paul,
Trench, Trubner & Co., 1930), pages 19–47. Copyright 1930 by Kegan Paul,
Trench, Trubner & Co. Used by permission of the publisher.

who originally established this State." The beliefs and practices pertaining to those deities and spirits remain even in these days of the twentieth century a living force among the people, and represent the basic elements of their religious and social life, out of which new offshoots of religion or quasi-religion may and do arise. The whole complex of beliefs and worship is known by the name of *Shinto,* which means the "Way of the Gods (or Spirits)," and it may be called the national or popular religion of the Japanese, as it was their ancient and indigenous religion.

The designation was, however, made in the sixth century in order to distinguish the native religion from Buddhism, and its being called a "Way" may be due to the influence of Taoism, the Chinese religion of the "Way." Now the latter is a religion which regards supernormal attainments in corporeal life as the ideal aim or ultimate potentiality of human beings, in contrast to the social and moral teachings of Confucianism. A combination of naturalism and supernaturalism, it exercised a great influence upon popular beliefs in China and Korea, and it is no wonder that the Shinto theorists found in it congenial features and adopted some Taoist ideas and practices. However this may be, Shinto is fundamentally not so much a religious system as a complex of ancient beliefs and observances which have remained comparatively unchanged through the vicissitudes of history, despite the impacts of foreign systems like Buddhism and Confucianism. Thus it is not quite unnatural that the advocates of Shinto even nowadays call their religion "The Way after the manner of the Gods," or "as it was practised by the Gods" (*Kami nagara no Michi*). But on the other hand we must not forget that attempts have repeatedly been made to organize these primitive beliefs into a national or State religion centred round the adoration of the sovereign as the descendant of the "Deity who established the State," particularly the Sun-goddess, the supreme deity of the Shinto religion. Though a clear line of demarcation can never be drawn between these two aspects of Shinto, the primitive and popular on the one side, and the national and official on the other, the distinction and connection between them can be compared to those between the mystery gods and the Olympian gods of the Greeks, as shown by Miss Harrison in her *Themis*. The history of Shinto is a series of reactions between these two factors, to speak in a broad way, as influenced by the development of the national life in its social and political organization, and also in reaction to the overwhelming influence of Buddhism and Confucianism.

Now, the deity or spirit is called *Kami* which, though of disputed etymology, means "superior" or "sacred" or "miraculous." Any object or being which evoked a thrill of emotion, whether affectionate or awe-inspiring, appealing to the sense of mystery, might be regarded as a Kami and accorded due respect. Some of the Kami were thought to reside in the heavens, others to sojourn in the air or in the forests, to abide in the rocks, in the fountains, or to manifest themselves in animals or human beings. Princes and heroes were Kami manifest in human form, or any person might become a Kami by exhibiting supernormal powers. These gods were, as a later Shinto theorist said, men in the age of the gods, while human beings are gods in the age of men. As a matter of fact, only an artificial line can be drawn between the Age of the Gods and that of Men; and gods, spirits, men, and any natural objects or phenomena pass easily, even in the later age of men, from one realm to the other. "In the beginning" men and animals were gods, and plants and rocks had speech; but even now, according to the Shinto conception, it is not entirely otherwise. Thus it is no wonder that out of this stuff any sort of gods can be enthroned, and that crude mysteries, often vigorous in their nascent state, come to command a certain amount of influence.

These deities or spirits were more or less personified and called such-and-such *Mikoto* (August One), or *Nushi* (Master), *Hiko* (Lord) or *Hime* (Lady), but their individuality was not always distinct. In some cases a person or an object was regarded as a Kami in itself, but in many other cases men or objects were respected as Kami on account of their having been possessed by a certain divinity or spirit. Here again no clear distinction can be drawn between these two categories of sacred beings, nor was personification necessary in worshipping a divinity. It is also to be noted that sex distinction never played a very important part either in worship or in mythology, and that the attributes and functions of the deities were easily variable and interchangeable.

In short, Shinto as a religion was an unorganized worship of spirits. It was rooted in the instinctive being of human nature feeling itself in communion with the living forces of the world and showed its vitality in the communal cult. For the worship was often connected with local legends and communal customs, and the deities thus worshipped were mostly considered to be the ancestral or tutelary spirits of the communes. Thus the communal cult was the pivot upon which the traditions and life of the people moved, wherein gods or spirits, animals and trees, even rocks and streams, were believed to be in living communion with men. In some cases, however, stories of the Kami were told as mere stories or poetic fancies about the occurrences of nature related in the fashion of human events. There were awesome mysteries in the worship side by side with playful elements in the myths; traditions and conventions played as great a part as the basic manifestations of passions and instincts, and all these factors were often so mixed that Shinto comprises religion and customs, poetry and folklore, politics and magic, among other things.

But one point to be specified in conclusion is that it was pre-eminently the religion of an agricultural people. The frequent manifestation of spirits of plants and corn, the intimate relationship existing between the people and the communal deities, the close ties binding the divinities with things of nature, all this indicates the life of an agricultural people settled down in close communities. And when it had been more or less organized in the course of several centuries up to the eighth, emphasis was laid on the supremacy of the Sun-goddess, who was naturally adored as the protectress of agriculture and as the ancestress of the ruling family. Thus the Shinto religion is not a primitive one in the strict sense, but has the traits of national religion glorifying the unity of the nation under the rulership of the emperor identified with the guardianship of the great goddess.

SHINTO MYTHOLOGY

The Primordial Chaos and the Growth of Life

There was no definite theogony in Shinto, yet a certain cycle of cosmological myths may be discerned. Three deities are said to have sprung out of the primeval chaos which was like an ocean of mud veiled in darkness. The head of the triad was the Heavenly-Central-Lord (*Ame-no-minaka-nushi*), or the Eternal-Land-Ruler (*Kuni-toko-tachi*), while the two subordinates were the High-Producing (*Taka-mi-musubi*), and the Divine or Mysterious-Producing (*Kami-mi-musubi*). This latter couple seem to have symbolized the male and female principles of generation and are sometimes identified with the Divine-Male (*Kami-rogi*) and the Divine-Female (*Kami-romi*), *i.e.*, the Divine-Father and the Divine-Mother who are constantly invoked in the rituals. This first triad, however, vanished without leaving posterity, and was followed by a series of similar ones, who were generated spontaneously independently from one another. All of them came out of the primeval chaos and vanished without trace. However, their titles indicate that they were intended to personify powers of spontaneous generation, such as mud, vapour, germs, were thought to be.

These deities are called the celestial deities in seven generations, in distinction from those who are said to have worked on earth, the earthly deities. It is an interesting question whether the former belonged to the category of those deities no more worshipped, forgotten deities, or were mere abstractions borrowed from outside. Though a conclusive solution of the problem can perhaps never be expected, the present writer inclines to the former alternative, from some analogies in other religions.

The last couple of the series were the Male-who-Invites (*Izanagi*) and the Female-who-Invites (*Izana-mi*). They are said to have descended to earth by order of the celestial deities, in order to produce the terrestrial world. Most probably they were conceived to be the earthly manifestations of the male and female principles in the primeval triad. They united and gave birth to many things, to the Japanese archipelago, first of all, and to things or spirits, such as waters, winds, mountains, fields, mists, foods, fire, and so on. This was evidently conceived as sexual generation, while on the other hand a belief in spontaneous generation and metamorphosis is betrayed even in the stories of the birth of their children; these two modes of generation were believed to exist side by side. All things produced were called Kami, deities or spirits, though only a few of them were actually worshipped. Sex distinction is made among them, but it plays no important part in the mythology and cult, probably because the Japanese mind had not yet attained a state of definite personification.

Finally, the divine couple begat the rulers of the world, the Heaven-Illumining Goddess (*Ama-terasu Ohmi-kami*), the Moon-Ruler (*Tsuki-yomi*) and the Valiant-Swift-Impetuous Hero (*Takéhaya Susanowo*). The realm of light, including heaven and earth, was assigned to the Sun-goddess, the reign of night to the Moon-god, while the ocean, together with the domain of hidden things, was entrusted to the rule of the Swift-Impetuous. The Moon-god never played a prominent part; the rule of the universe was divided between the two others, a division which was to have very great importance in mythical narratives where it is possible to discern a reflection of some political and social events, as we shall see further.

Thus the divine couple were the originators of life on earth, but life was associated with its necessary counterpart, death. The mythology tells us how the Female deity came later to be the genius of evil and death, having died on giving birth to fire and gone to a subterranean abode where death and darkness prevailed. Death in this case was apparently conceived as through fever, and considered to be the first instance of mortality. The Male deity, like Orpheus, pursued his lamented consort to her dark abode, tried to look at her by lighting a torch, to the dismay of the Female, because decomposition was taking place in her body. This act of impudence enraged the Female, and she caused the hosts of evil spirits and furies to pursue the Male in order to confine him in the realm of death and darkness. Having repulsed the pursuers, the Male reached the boundary between the dark world and the realm of light, where he blocked up the passage with a huge rock, and the two deities exchanged words across the barrier. The Female threatened to kill a thousand people in his domain, while the Male retorted by saying that he would give birth to five hundred more than that every day. This story was evidently intended for an explanation of the proportion of births and deaths in the human world. Thus, after all, death was unable to supersede life, yet the fear of death is expressed in the story, and ills and dangers are therein identified with pollution, to be expiated by purification. The act of purification is said to have been inaugurated then by the Male deity who, having escaped the snare of death, washed himself in the sea. Various kinds of evil spirits came out of the dirt and stain which he had brought from the dark region. These evil spirits are believed to be still lingering among men and to cause all kinds of evil and trouble.

The Two Rulers of the World

We hear nothing definite about the end of the Male progenitor, except that he finally hid himself, or is abiding in the Solar Palace of Youth (*Hi-no-waka-miya*). After the disappearance of the primeval couple the world was transferred to the dual rule of the Sun-goddess and the Swift-Impetuous, the latter of whom showed many traits of a storm-god. The Sun-goddess, or the Heaven-illumining Lady, was bright and beautiful in features, unrivalled in dignity, benign, honest, and meek in temper. She ruled wisely and brilliantly the realm assigned to her, giving light and life to all, and she also protected the rice-fields by constructing irrigation canals. Besides, she is represented as the organizer of religious rites, especially those in observance of the rules of purity. In short, she was the presiding deity of peace and order, of agriculture and the food supply. Herein we can detect a representation of the rôle womanhood played in the early rise of peaceful social order and agricultural pursuits. On the other hand, her brother, the Swift-Impetuous, was wild, arrogant, and disobedient. He cried in wild fury, disregarded all his duties, and raged in the air between heaven and earth. The

details of his atrocities against his sister in heaven remind us
strongly of storm-gods in other mythologies. His cry and fury are
said to have been instigated by his longing for the abode of
his mother, who had become the genius of death and darkness.
In this respect the Storm-god is often identified with the mighty
evil spirit ruling the invisible world—a feature which, as we shall
presently see, is inherited by his posterity.

The contest of the two deities is depicted in two scenes, one
on the Heavenly River-basin of Peace (*Ama-no-Yasugawara*)
and the other in the arbour where the Sun-goddess was preparing for the great feast of harvest, the foremost of Shinto festivals.
The former can be taken as symbolic of the contest between sun
and storm, and yet each of the deities is said to have given birth
to children by the "inspiration" of the other, or by exchanging
respiration and jewels. The latter story of sacrilege represents
evidently a conflict in social order, but the story culminates in a
scene reminding us of a solar eclipse. It runs as follows:

The Swift-Impetuous ravaged the domain of his sister by
destroying the rice-fields cultivated by her, and finally by an act
of sacrilege, polluting the sacred observance instituted by her.
The Sun-goddess, greatly distressed by the wanton acts of her
brother, but not combating him, hid herself in a cave, whereby
the entire world was deprived of light, and disorder ran riot.
Eight million deities assembled in front of the cave and at last
succeeded in inducing her to come out, by performing charms
and a ceremonial dance. When light and order had been restored
by the reappearance of the goddess, all the assembly burst into a
cry of joy, at the resonance of which heaven and earth trembled.
This is the climax of the mythical narrative, and therein we see
the triumph of light over darkness, of peace and order over
savagery and destruction. This triumph of the Sun-goddess over
the Storm-god secured her the rule of the world, and the belief
in her as the supreme deity was associated with the tradition that
the ruling family descended from the Sun-goddess.

The triumph of light over darkness was accomplished by hosts
of the Kami, who stood loyally on the side of the Sun-goddess in
her resistance against the opposing power. This narrative has

two aspects in its bearings upon the belief and life of the people. As a myth of solar phenomena, it represents the beliefs of an agricultural people and their reverence for the sun as the source of life, as well as their practice of exorcism in case of a solar eclipse. Politically, the same beliefs resulted in the predominance of a certain family or tribe, who worshipped the goddess as their progenitrix, and in the allegiance of other tribes to that family. Thus, the Sun-goddess embodied life-giving power and wise rulership at the same time. In the former aspect she is associated with a male counterpart, the High-Producing Deity, who accompanies her as her hidden or higher entity. There is, however, also a female partner, the Abundance-Bounty Goddess (*Toyo-uke no Kami*), who is even to-day worshipped beside her at Isé, the most holy of the Shinto sanctuaries. The political rôle attributed to the Sun-goddess is no less important, the belief in the divine origin of the ruling family being symbolized by the insignia of the imperial throne, a mirror, a sword, and a bead, all believed to have been handed by her to her posterity. We shall see later how these three treasures led Shinto theologians to ethical and cosmological speculations. The Sun-goddess may be called the supreme deity of the Shinto religion, and her worship occasionally gave rise to a kind of monotheism in the course of Shinto history.

On the other hand the outrageous Storm-god was banished to a remote region by the hosts assembled before the "heavenly cave." The place of exile is located in the province of Izumo on the northern coast of Japan, facing the eastern side of the Korean peninsula; it was there, in fact, that a tribe claiming their descent from the Storm-god established themselves and resisted for a while the rule of the Solar Race. As the ancestor of the Izumo tribe, the Swift-Impetuous played the rôle of pioneer and colonizer, and a story says that he planted, from his hair and beard, the mountains in the province of Kii on the southern side of Japan.

The Storm-god and his sons are regarded as rulers of Izumo and at the same time as agents of mysterious things, including even evil-doings. This is a natural consequence of the conception that the Storm-god was an associate or chief of the spirits inhabiting the subterranean world; quite naturally the primitive mind invoked the genius of evil for the purpose of averting ills and calamities. One of the sons of the Storm-god was the Great Evildoer (*Oh-Magatsumi*), the source of all evils, while another son, the Great Land-master (*Oh-Kuninushi*), worked for the welfare of the people in association with his partner, the Small Prince of Renown (*Sukuna-biko*), who is regarded as the chief of medicine-men. On this account the deities belonging to the Izumo group were worshipped when a pestilence raged or any disaster took place.

The opposition between the contending powers did not, as we might have expected, develop into a dualism like that of the ancient Persian religion, to which Shinto has some similarities. On the contrary, a compromise in the way of a division of spheres was arranged between the two deities and their descendants. The rule of the actual world in a theocratic government was entrusted to the descendants of the Sun-goddess, while the mysterious side of the religion, including magic, divination, exorcism, was left to the care of the Storm-god and his children. This pact of division is said to have been made between the children of the Storm-god and the generals sent to them by the Sun-goddess, that the "realm of the visible" should belong to the latter and the "domain of the invisible" to the Storm-god. Thus, a division between the Olympian gods and the mystery gods, to borrow an analogy from Greek religion, was decided once for all—a division which was destined to determine the nature and function of the official Shinto religion as the worship of the Sun-goddess and other deities believed to care for the welfare of the people in worldly matters. This function of the official cult, national and communal, was a strength in the sense that Shinto worship was ever closely related with the political and social life of the nation, but it was a weakness at the same time, as the official Shinto alienated itself more and more from the mysteries of religious life. The consequence was that Shinto in general has always had a tendency to formalism and officialism, and that, whenever a reaction against this formalism took place, resort was had to the occult side of the religion, and appeal made to the superstitious ideas and practices of the people.

RELIGION AND SOCIAL LIFE

National Cult and Communal Life

The general tendency of the Shinto religion at the dawn of the historical period was towards the domination of the Sun-goddess over the numerous local deities and miscellaneous spirits. This was made possible by the growing power of the ruling family (the descendants of the Sun-goddess), the several sub-jugated clans bringing their respective clan cults under the hegemony of the Sun-goddess. Thus the growth of national unity was a political and religious issue, and was symbolized in a central seat of worship dedicated to the Great Deity (*Oh-mi-kami*), which was established at Isé on the sea-coast facing the east. Even to-day Isé remains the holy of holies of the Shinto cult. Moreover, the worship and predominance of the Sun-goddess were accelerated by the progress of agriculture, because she was regarded as the greatest protectress of agriculture, and because the Japanese people seem to have made a rapid transition from a life of hunting and fishing to one of agriculture, especially of rice culture. Herein religious beliefs worked together with political and economic conditions. This connection is best shown in the ritual of the Harvest-prayer Festival (*Toshigoi no Matsuri*). After the invocation of various deities, it says:

More especially do I humbly declare in the mighty presence of the Great Heaven-shining Deity who dwells in Isé. Because the Great Deity has bestowed on him (the sovereign) the lands of the four quarters over which her glance extends as far as where the walls of Heaven rise, as far as where the bounds of Earth stand up, as far as the blue sky extends, as far as where the white clouds settle down; by the blue sea-plain, as far as the prows of ships can reach without letting dry their poles and oars; by land, as far as the hoofs of horses can go, with tightened baggage-cords, treading their way among rock-beds and tree-roots where the long roads extend, continuously widening the narrow regions and making the steep regions level, in drawing together, as it were, the distant regions by throwing over them (a net of) many ropes—therefore let the first-fruits for the Sovran Deity be piled up in her mighty presence like a range of hills, leaving the remainder for him (the sovereign) tranquilly to partake of.

Moreover, whereas you bless the Sovran Grandchild's reign as a long reign, firm and enduring, and render it a happy and prosperous reign, I plunge down my neck cormorant-wise in reverence to you as our Sovran's dear, divine ancestress, and fulfil your praise by making these plenteous offerings on his behalf.

Here we see pictured all the clansmen coming together to pray for harvest and welfare, joining in the worship of the genius of life and growth, the progenitrix of the ruling family. Similarly instituted was the thanksgiving for harvest, the Festival of First Fruits (*Nii-name*), celebrated at midnight in the late autumn, observed annually even to-day. It is the most solemn and mysterious of all the Shinto ceremonies, the deity worshipped being unknown or unmentioned and all the performance being carried on in darkness, except for a few torches in the holy precinct. The Sun-goddess herself is believed to have served in this ceremony as the chief priestess, and hence the Emperor alone always serves as the chief priest. His person is in direct communion with the unnamed Deity, or he is identified with the Deity, and what he performs in the worship remains a sealed mystery to all but himself. Yet all those who participate in the ceremony outside the inner sanctuary are supposed to share the mysterious union, in darkness and to ancient music.

The supremacy of the Sun-goddess had thus been established, but it never suppressed the tribal cults and the communal life of the clans. The whole history of Japan, in its social and political aspects, exhibits a series of compromises as well as conflicts of the two forces, union and division, the national principle and the clan interest. Similarly there were changes of religious ideas tending alternately to unity and plurality, or monotheistic and polytheistic tendencies; these two phases are indicated by the tenacious persistence of the tribal and local cults beside the national cult of the Sun-goddess, while the simple pure faith of the people often led them to a monotheistic worship of the supreme deity.

The people settled in agricultural pursuits along valleys or on lake-sides were separated from one another by hills and inlets, and the groups made up compact communities bound by clan kinship and communal traditions. The clan was called *uji,* which meant birth or blood relationship, and each of the clans kept to its native soil and communal cult. The clan deity (*uji-gami*) was conceived as the progenitor of the *uji,* or as the tutelary spirit of the locality; in many cases the local chthonian deity was identified with the ancestral. Many clans derived their descent from a certain nature-god, such as the spirit of water or of wind, as there was no sharp distinction between a deity of nature and a spirit of the dead. The clan cult was the centre of the communal life, resting on the communion of the deity and the people, as well as on the common beliefs, observances, and traditions, all closely knit into the daily life of the people and their attachment to the soil they inherited.

The clan deity was usually represented by a symbol and enshrined in a simple sanctuary erected at a spot commanding the best view of the locality, and in many cases occupying a strategic point. The sanctified spot was carefully guarded and kept scrupulously clean. The simple, sober-looking shrine standing in the dim light of the woods inspired the people with the presence of a divine spirit. The sacred grove furnished a prominent landmark in every locality and was associated with the legendary lore of the community, its ancestors and heroes, or genii and fairies. The communal sanctuary was also the place where periodical celebrations and social gatherings were held, all connected with various phases of social life as well as with the change of the seasons and the associated festivities. Thus the Shinto religion was deeply rooted in the soil of the national spirit, patriotism in the narrower but original sense. Just as men lived in communion with the gods and they together made up the communal life, so nature and the physical surroundings played a no less important part in moulding religious sentiment. These remarks hold true to a great extent concerning village life in modern Japan. This aspect of Shinto may be called the Hellenic feature in Japanese life, because the religious and social life of the people is manifested in festivities and in connection with the poetry of nature.

Shinto, in this way, derived its continuity largely from its function as a communal cult, in which the observance of rites and customs was supported by the sanction and tradition of the community. The reason for the sanctity of traditional rules was that they were believed to have originated in divine or ancestral ordinances. The most important of the observances was that of purity and ablution in ceremonies as well as in daily life. The worst offence was violation of the rules of purity. Impurities were of various kinds, such as birth, blood, disease, corpses; contact with any of these required ablution, usually by bathing in a stream, often accompanied by fasting. Unconscious or involuntary offences were washed away, while conscious offences were expiated by penance or fines paid to the community in the presence of the divine spirit. Cases of civil and penal offences were decided by ordeal, "divine punishment," generally banishment. Thus, morality, religious observances, laws and customs were interwoven, and their inculcation rested upon the shoulders of the community, represented by an assembly of priests and elders. Grave offences on the part of any member of the community were believed to draw divine wrath upon the whole community, and therefore propitiation was required from the community as well as from the individual. However, these ordinances were rarely formulated but were mostly handed down in traditional customs. This is one of the reasons why the priesthood has played little part outside merely ceremonial observances.

Tribal Ethics, Authority of the Community

Scrupulous fidelity to tradition is everywhere a characteristic of tribal religion. Its morality is based upon the sanctity of the communal life amounting to the adoration of blood kinship and the observance of social rules. The individual is almost nothing in the face of the community, and unreasoning submission to social sanction is the essential condition of individual life. Authority and tradition, not the person and conscience, are the ultimate foundation of morality which, though remaining still in force, are being modified by the influence of modern civilization on village life. This has been the strength and at the same time the weakness of Japanese morality. It was the force that solidified the feudal régime and still sustains the solidarity of the people as a body. On the other hand, the lack of individual initiative and the tyranny of the community over the individual have often produced evils, and the history of the nation has exhibited in many phases the conflict between group control and individual freedom.

There was in the primitive society of the Japanese no systematic teaching of morality nor any definite codification of social and political institutions. This was yet to be achieved, awaiting the help of Chinese civilization. Philosophical elaboration of ideas and beliefs was far beyond the ken of the primitive faith, and it was Buddhism that supplemented this defect.

Shinto morality emphasized the virtue of submission, while its aggressive aspect was exhibited in valour and militancy. Clan division was necessarily associated with strife, even among the clans adhering to the central authority of the ruling family. Combat was regarded as the affair of the whole clan, and therefore of the clan deity. Thus people fought with religious zeal, and it was everyone's duty to do his best according to the ordinance of tradition, and to die for the clan or its chief. Submission was not mere renunciation but demanded action and valour. The old saying, "Face the flying arrows, never turn thy back towards them," represented this temperament. A warrior poet of the eighth century sang:—

> Serve our Sovran at sea,
> Our sodden corpses leaving to the salt sea,
> Serve our Sovran by land,
> Our corpses leaving amid the wild-waste bushes;
> Rejoice to die in our dread Sovran's cause,
> Never looking back from the border of the battles.

This he sang, to be sure, as an old tradition among his clansmen, and the wording is not his own. Though loyalty towards the sole sovereign was a product of gradual growth, service done for the clan and valour in its cause were coeval with the communal cult of the Shinto religion. We shall see later how these militant qualities manifested themselves in the twelfth century, in connection with the rise of the military men in the provinces and the consequent foundation of a feudal régime.

The military aspect of Shinto morality is shown in the instances of swords, spears, bows and arrows being worshipped as deities or as their symbols. Naturally, Susanowo, the raging spirit of Storm, represented this militant aspect, and it is said that he presented to his sister, the Sun-goddess, a sword which he had discovered in the body of the dragon slain by him. This sword is believed to have later been used by Prince Yamato-takeru, or Japan-valiant, in his military expeditions, and it is now enshrined in a sanctuary.[1] More mythical personifications of the warlike spirit are the Sharp-Cutting-Lord (*Futsu-nushi*), and the Valiant-August-Thunder (*Take-mika-zuchi*), who are said to have subjugated the unruly gods of Izumo at the behest of the Sun-goddess. These deities are worshipped at Kashima and Katori in eastern Japan, as the tutelary spirits of outposts against the Ainus in the northeast, and it is possible that they commemorate certain fighters. A rock is shown in Kashima which is said to have been thrust by the August-Thunder deep into earth as the sign of his firm grasp of the country. It is interesting to see that further development of the warlike spirit was always associated with the worship of the patrons of military families, while the Sun-goddess played the rôle of peace-maker, as the progenitrix of the ruling family and the presiding deity of agriculture. Thus, the militant aspect of Japanese morality was a manifestation of

---

[1] This sword is one of the three Insignia of the Throne. The two others are a mirror and a crooked ornamental bead, believed to symbolize the soul of the Sun-goddess, its sagacity and clemency respectively. The mirror is deposited in the sanctuary of Isé and the bead or jewel is in the personal possession of the Emperor. Further on we shall see the symbolic doctrines concerning these three as propounded by the later Shinto theorists.

the Shinto religion as a tribal cult, whereas national unity as embodied in the worship of the Sun-goddess represented the peace-loving disposition of the people and their submission to the sovereign.

Idea of the Soul

Belief in spirits was the basis of the ancient Shinto religion; but in spite of this, the conception of the human soul and its future conditions was very vague. Yet undoubtedly there existed an idea of the soul and belief in its future life. The Land of Gloom (*Yomotsu-kuni*) or the Bottom-Land (*Sokotsu-kuni*), where the Female-who-Invites reigned as the genius of ills and death, was a kind of Hades. Apparently it was conceived to be somewhere in the subterranean world. In the heavenly world, the Plain of High Heaven (*Takama-no-hara*), celestial beings reside, presided over by the Sun-goddess. Probably the human soul was thought to go after death to one of these regions, but the legends speak of future life only in connection with deities or great men. Possibly the souls of common mortals were believed to vanish sooner or later. Objects excavated from ancient tombs show that various utensils and even human beings were buried beside the remains of a dead lord or lady, undoubtedly with the intention that he or she might enjoy comfort and service in the future life. Only a faint idea of an eternal life is indicated by the name *Toko-yo,* or "Perpetual Country," which is sometimes identified with the heavenly plains, but oftener believed to mean a country beyond the sea where oranges grow. At any rate, the soul, if it continued to exist at all, was believed to sojourn among its former fellow-beings for an indefinite period, and both the Heavenly Plain and the Bottom-Land were considered to be not very far away from this world.

Perhaps more important than the question of the future life was the activity of the soul apart from its bodily confinement. The soul was believed to be composed of two parts, one mild, refined, and happy, the other rough, brutal, and raging (the mild, *nigi-mitama,* and the rough, *ara-mitama*). The former cares for its possessor's health and prosperity, while the latter performs adventurous tasks or even malicious deeds. Either of them can leave the body and appear to the astonishment of its possessor himself. The *nigi-mitama* is also designated as, or subdivided into, *saki-mitama* (happy, prosperous) and *kushi-mitama* (wondrous, mysterious). This is the ordinary interpretation, but the author is inclined to identify this dual division with the one stated above. It is not clear whether every deity or human being was believed to possess double souls, or powerful persons only. Certain, however, it is that the idea of the soul was associated with breathing, and it is called *tama,* which means a precious or mysterious thing (globular in form as a rule). Another name for the soul, *tama-shii,* seems to mean "mysterious breathing," and probably the word *shinu,* to die, the departure of breath. According to the popular belief, which prevails even nowadays, the soul quits the body at the moment of death; it may often be seen lingering as a pale fire-ball flying in darkness.

Cult and Priesthood

The Shinto sanctuary was very simple, as was quite natural in a rather primitive religion, yet remarkably simpler than in many other religions. Its simplicity is due not merely to the preservation of its primitive character, but in many cases to deliberate purity and intentional austerity. The deity was worshipped, in the remote ages of prehistoric antiquity, at a hallowed ground enclosed by trees or fences planted around a square and marked off by a sanctified rope of straw. The enclosure was either temporary or permanent and called *himorogi,* which is explained in various ways, often in mystic interpretations by later Shintoists, but it seems to have meant an abode of the deity. There were also sacred grounds surrounded by stones, like Stonehenge of the Druids (they were called *iwa-ki,* stone enclosure, or *kōgo,* divine abode), the remains of which are found mostly in western Japan. These primitive sanctuaries were gradually replaced by the shrines which mark the Shinto sanctuaries of to-day. But these shrines are mostly built in wooded places and preserve the atmosphere of primitive nature-worship.

The construction of the shrine is extremely simple—straight

pillars thrust into the earth, covered by a thatched roof. There is no decorative effect, except the conventionalized ends of the beams projecting in an oblique cross over the angle of the roof. A shrine of this kind is called *yashiro, i.e.,* miniature of a dwelling-house, and its model is evidently taken from a human abode. The architecture can hardly be called artistic, yet the unvarnished pillars exhibit a singularly attractive simplicity and the whole structure an archaic sobriety. The situation of the sombre-looking shrine among old trees in the dim light of wooded places contributes very much to the austerity of the sanctuary. This sequestered solemnity is characterized by words such as *kōgōshi,* "godlike, very godlike," or *kami-sabi,* "divinely serene." The Shinto Japanese have never built a stone cathedral; their holy places were temples of nature wherein a group of huge trees rivalled a Gothic tower.

Every hallowed spot of ground or sanctified object is marked off by a straw rope, as referred to above, from which pieces of paper hang. It is called *shime-nawa,* or demarcation rope, and its purpose is to keep off evil influences. Another symbol of sanctity is a small pole of wood or bamboo, in which is inserted a piece of paper or cloth, so cut that the two parts hang down on the two sides of the pole and each part looks plaited. This is called *nusa* (or *gohei*) and was originally an offering of cloth, which was converted to a symbol of sanctity or divinity. Another sign of a Shinto sanctuary is the *tori-i* which stands at the entrance to every sanctuary. It is a simple structure, either in wood or stone, made up of two quadrangular beams laid horizontally above the head and supported by two round columns. This is the portal, and it stands at the entrance to a long avenue of trees, and at intervals as well as in front of the shrine. A temporary entrance is occasionally constructed by making a large ring by binding sheaves of a kind of reed. Thus, the portals, the avenue, and the woods, together with the shrine and various sacred symbols, make up a Shinto sanctuary. A well or rock is sanctified within the precinct for the use of the deity; and similarly a fountain is provided for the purification of the worshippers.

Equally simple, austere, and quiet are Shinto ceremonials. In the shrine there is no image but only a symbolic representation of the deity called "spirit-substitute" (*mitama-shiro*), usually a mirror or a *nusa*. The offerings consist of food stuffs, such as fish, fowl, cereals, vegetables, always uncooked—arrayed together with *saké* drink and some other objects. No flower is offered but green leaves of the tree *sakaki*—probably in contradistinction to the abundant flowers of Buddhist rites. There are traces of human sacrifice both in the ceremonies and in the legends, but it ceased to be practised long before the historical period, and any bloody sacrifice is carefully avoided, because it means pollution.

The ceremony proper consists of bringing offerings one after another, reciting a ritual, and then taking away the offerings. Private prayers may be offered, but the regular ritual is always public. The priests serving in these ceremonies glide in and out of the sanctuary with quiet footsteps, silence being strictly observed. Besides these austere services, however, dances are performed with songs and musical accompaniment in a separate building, in the presence of the worshippers. The dance is either a simple movement or it portrays scenes from myths. The motion of the dancer is usually horizontal and a jump or other abrupt movement is scarcely ever seen—although it is a feature of most of the secular dances. The representation of the stories gave rise, as in other countries, to dramatic performances, while the primitive dances are carefully preserved. Torches are used in festivals, but exclusively for light, no kind of explosive fireworks being used. In this way Shinto ceremonial is peculiarly pure and solemnly quiet. These features give to it an archaic sobriety, and the Shintoists are proud of this as an evidence of its direct derivation from the celestial world. But as a matter of fact there are some boisterous services in local performances, and the quiet feature of the official rites was chiefly derived from the solemnity of court ceremonies.

There were periodical festivities as well as occasional ceremonies performed in front of a shrine or in the family. The greatest of the public festivals are those of the Harvest and the Purification. At the Feast of Harvest, offerings from the new crops are made every autumn to the Sun-goddess and once after the coronation ceremony of each reign. The Harvest is the most solemn ceremony, being celebrated at midnight at a fixed date in late autumn, now the 23rd of November. The rice to be offered on this occasion is taken from a special rice-field, sanctified by ritual, and cultivated by hallowed virgins. The Purification is performed twice a year, for the purpose of washing away the pollution, physical and moral, incurred during the preceding half-year. This was, in the ancient days, performed at the court by the priestly family Nakatomi, and the ritual is known by that name—the Nakatomi Ritual. But the ceremony may be performed in any other place, within a sacred precinct or on the river-bank, and the members of the community are expected to attend it. The performance consists in sprinkling water, reciting the ritual, and swinging the symbolic *nusa,* while human figures made of rice-straw are thrown into the stream, the effigies representing the stained substance of the attendants. The *nusa* was, as we have said, originally an offering, but it was adapted to symbolize the deity and to represent the divine potency, therefore evil influences were averted by swinging it.

The Nakatomi Ritual recited on the occasion of the periodical ablution is a good example of the religious and moral sentiments of Shinto. We cite some passages:

Give ear, all ye Imperial Princes, Princesses, Ministers of State, and functionaries who are here assembled, and hearken every one to the Great Purification by which at this year's interlune of the sixth (or twelfth) month he deigns to purge and absolve all manner of faults and transgressions which may have been committed by those who serve in the Imperial Court . . . all those who do duty in the various offices of State.

                    .   .   .   .   .

Now of the various faults and transgressions to be committed by the celestial race destined more and more to people this land of his peaceful rule, some are of Heaven, to wit, the breaking down of divisions between rice-fields, filling up of irrigation channels, removing water-pipes, sowing seed over again, planting skewers, flaying alive, flaying backwards. These are distinguished as Heavenly offences.

Earthly offences which will be committed are the cutting of living bodies, the cutting of dead bodies, leprosy, *kokumi,* incest of a man with his mother or daughter, with his mother-in-law or step-daughter, bestiality, calamities from creeping things, from the high gods and from high birds, killing animals, bewitchments.

Whensoever they may be committed, let the Great Nakatomi, in accordance with the customs of the Heavenly Palace, cut Heavenly saplings at the top and cut them at the bottom, and make thereof a complete array of one thousand stands for offerings. Then let him recite the mighty ritual words of the celestial ritual.

When he does so, the Gods of Heaven, thrusting open the adamantine door of Heaven and cleaving the many-piled clouds of Heaven with an awful way-cleaving will lend ear. The Gods of Earth, climbing to the tops of the high mountains and to the tops of the low mountains, sweeping apart the mists of the high mountains and the mists of the low mountains, will lend ear.

When they have thus lent ear, all offences whatsoever will be annulled, from the Court of the Sovran Grandchild to the provinces of the four quarters of the Under-Heaven.

As the many-piled clouds of Heaven are scattered by the breath of the Wind-Gods; as the morning breezes and the evening breezes dissipate the dense morning vapours and the dense evening vapours; . . . as yonder thick brushwood is smitten and cleared away by the sharp sickle forged in the fire, so shall all offences be utterly annulled.

Therefore he (the Mikado) is graciously pleased to purify and cleanse them away. The Goddess called *Se-oritsu-hime* (The-Lady-who-descends-the-Rapids), who dwells in the rapids of the swift streams whose cataracts tumble headlong from the tops of the high mountains and from the tops of the low mountains will bear them out into the great sea-plain. Thereupon the Goddess called *Haya-aki-tsu-hime* (Rapid-Open-Channel-Lady), who dwells in the myriad meetings of the tides of the myriad brine-paths of the myriad ways of the currents of the boisterous sea will swallow them up. And the God *Ibukido-nushi* (Breath-Blowing-Lord), who dwells in the Breath-blowing-place, will puff them away to the Root-country, the Bottom-country. Then the Goddess *Haya-sasura-hime* (Swift-Banishment-Lady), who dwells in the Root-country, the Bottom-country, will banish and abolish them. When they have been so destroyed, every one, from the servants of the Imperial Court to the four quarters of the Under-Heaven, will remain void of all offences whatsoever.

Here we see the offences "of Heaven," that is, pertaining to agriculture, and those "of Earth," mostly physical pollutions, enumerated side by side with offences connected with sexual relations. This list of offences clearly shows the rather primitive stage of social and ethical ideas; the method of casting out those pollutions is correspondingly naïve, consisting simply in performing a ceremony believed to have magical efficacy.

Besides the public ceremonies and the private prayers, spells and charms were much in vogue, and divination and augury were practised. The divine and magical efficacy of objects connected with the ceremonies was believed in and made use of, mostly against evil spirits. Swinging the *nusa,* making fire of wood used in the ceremonies, partaking of food or drink offered to the gods—these were believed to confer miraculous powers. Certain austerities were practised with the intention of expelling evils and purifying oneself, such as bathing in cold streams, hard mountain climbing, or abstaining from sexual intercourse. Magic, exorcism, and other occult practices were performed by persons who had passed certain stages of ascetic training. These practices were later combined with and elaborated by Buddhist occultism and gave impetus to many superstitious beliefs and customs. We shall see (in the third period) the rise of the mountaineer priests, who still later became promulgators of the various forms of popular Shinto in which reverence towards invisible spirits and devils played a large part.

Priestly families have existed from an unknown antiquity, the Nakatomi and the Imbé being the foremost. Whatever these names may have meant, most probably the former performed public services in the court and represented the bright side, so to speak, of the Shinto religion, while the latter attended the propitiatory services and practised occultism. The chief priest at a service was, and is, called *kan-nushi,* the "god-man" or the chief of the priests, and he presided over the ceremonies; under him there were *negi,* reciters, *hafuri,* service-men, and *kan-nagi,* dancers. Women also served as priestesses and they were expected to be virgins, though not necessarily for life. The most important of the priestesses was a royal princess who served the Sun-goddess at Isé. There were similar priestesses in other sanctuaries recruited from noble families, while the dancers were women of no rank.

The Shinto priest is to-day clad in a broad mantle-like costume, with large sleeves, usually white, and the dancing virgins are clad in white robes with long red skirts. These are of later origin, being the court dresses dating from the tenth century; the ancient priestly robes are entirely lost.

In spite of the existence of the priestly families and professional priests, sacerdotal services were not limited to them, but every ruler or patriarch played a priestly rôle. Another point to be noticed here is that the Shinto priests seldom played such a prominent part in politics as the Buddhist. The descendants of the Nakatomi became, after the seventh century, ministers of State and majordomos of the ruling family; this was not because of their priesthood, for in fact they had abandoned their priestly function when they began to control politics. To-day the Shinto priest is often chauvinist and his ambition is rising under the protection of the reactionary government.

Selections from Shinto Literature

"Human Immortality"

"The Yemishi rebelled. Tamichi was sent to attack them. He was worsted by the Yemishi, and slain at the harbour of Ishimi. Now one of his followers obtained Tamichi's armlet and gave it to his wife, who embraced the armlet and strangled herself. When the men of that time heard of this they shed tears. After this the Yemishi again made an incursion and dug up Tamichi's

Reprinted from W. G. Aston, *Shinto: The Way of the Gods* (London: Longmans, Green, and Co., 1905).

tomb, upon which a great serpent started up with glaring eyes
and came out of the tomb. It bit the Yemishi, who were every
one affected by the serpent's poison, so that many of them died,
and only one or two escaped. Therefore the men of that time
said: 'Although dead, Tamichi at last had his revenge. How can
it be said that the dead have no knowledge?' "

Nihongi, A.D. 367

"CREATION MYTH"

"Izanagi and Izanami stood on the floating bridge of Heaven,
and held counsel together, saying 'Is there not a country beneath?'
Thereupon they thrust down the 'Jewel-Spear of Heaven' (Ame
no tama-boko) and groping about with it, found the ocean. The
brine which dripped from the point of the spear coagulated and
formed an island which received the name of Onogoro-jima or
the 'Self-Coagulating Island.' The two deities thereupon descended and dwelt there. Accordingly they wished to be united
as husband and wife, and to produce countries. So they made
Onogoro-jima the pillar of the centre of the land."

Nihongi

"MONOTHEISTIC TENDENCIES"

"A man of the neighbourhood of the River Fuji, in the East
Country, named Ohofube no Ohoshi, urged his fellow villagers
to worship an insect, saying: 'This is the God of the Everlasting
World. Those who worship this God will have long life and
riches.' At length the wizards (kannagi) and witches (miko)
pretending an inspiration of the Gods, said: 'Those who worship
the God of the Everlasting World will, if poor, become rich, and,
if old, will become young again.' So they more and more per-
suaded the people to cast out the valuables of their houses, and
to set out by the roadside sake, vegetables, and the six domestic
animals. They also made them cry out: 'The new riches have
come!' Both in the country and in the metropolis people took the

insect of the Everlasting World and, placing it in a pure place, with song and dance invoked happiness. They threw away their treasures, but to no purpose whatever. The loss and waste was extreme. Hereupon Kahakatsu, Kadono no Hada no Miyakko, was wroth that the people should be so much deluded, and slew Ohofube no Ohoshi. The wizards and witches were intimidated, and ceased to persuade people to this worship. The men of that time made a song, saying:

> Udzumasa
> Has executed
> The God of the Everlasting World
> Who we were told
> Was the very God of Gods.

"This insect is usually bred on orange trees, and sometimes on the hosoki. It is over four inches in length, and about as thick as a thumb. It is of a grass-green colour with black spots, and in appearance very much resembles the silkworm."

Nihongi, A.D. 644

"Creation Myth"

"The two deities having descended on Onogoro-jima erected there an eight fathom house with an august central pillar. Then Izanagi addressed Izanami, saying: 'How is thy body formed?' Izanami replied, 'My body is completely formed except one part which is incomplete.' Then Izanagi said, 'My body is completely formed and there is one part which is superfluous. Suppose that we supplement that which is incomplete in thee with that which is superfluous in me, and thereby procreate lands.' Izanami replied, 'It is well.' Then Izanagi said, 'Let me and thee go round the heavenly august pillar, and having met at the other side, let us become united in wedlock.' This being agreed to, he said, 'Do thou go round from the left, and I will go round from the right.' When they had gone round, Izanami spoke first and exclaimed, 'How delightful! I have met a lovely youth.' Izanagi then said,

'How delightful! I have met a lovely maiden.' Afterwards he said, 'It was unlucky for the woman to speak first.' The child which was the first offspring of their union was the Hiruko (leech-child) which at the age of three was still unable to stand upright, and was therefore placed in a reed-boat and sent adrift."

"FOOD GODDESS"

"She was rejoiced, and said, 'These are the things which the race of visible men will eat and live.' So she made the millet, the panic, the wheat, and the beans the seed for the dry fields, and the rice she made the seed for the water-fields. Therefore she appointed a Mura-gimi (village-lord) or Heaven, and forthwith sowed for the first time the rice-seed in the narrow fields and in the long fields of Heaven."

"PRAYER TO SUN-GODDESS"

"By order of the Mikado we declare with deepest reverence in the spacious presence of (with awe be her name pronounced) the Sovran Great Heaven-shining Deity, whose praises are fulfilled in the Great Shrine, whose pillars are broad-based on the nethermost rocks, and whose cross beams rise aloft to the Plain of High Heaven on the bank of the River Isuzu in Uji, of Watarahi in Ise, as follows:—

"Since the past sixth month reports have been received from the Dazaifu that two pirate-ships of Shiraki appeared at Aratsu, in the district of Naka, in the province of Chikuzen, and carried off as plunder the silk of a tribute-ship of the province of Buzen. Moreover, that there having been an omen of a crane which alighted on the arsenal of the Government House, the diviners declared that it presaged war with a neighbouring country. Also that there had been earthquakes with storms and floods in the province of Hizen by which all the houses had been overturned and many of the inhabitants swept away. Even the old men affirmed that no such great calamity had ever been heard of before.

"Meanwhile news was received from the province of Michinoku of an unusually disastrous earthquake, and from other provinces grave calamities were reported.

"The mutual enmity between those men of Shiraki and our Land of Yamato has existed for long ages. Their present invasion of our territory, however, and their plunder of tribute, show that they have no fear of us. When we reflect on this, it seems possible that a germ of war may spring from it. Our government has for a long time had no warlike expeditions, the provision for defence has been wholly forgotten, and we cannot but look forward to war with dread and caution. But our Japan is known as the country of the Gods. If the Gods deign to help and protect it, what foe will dare to approach it? Much more so, seeing that the Great Deity in her capacity (with awe be it spoken) as ancestress of the Mikado bestows light and protection on the Under-Heaven which he governs. How, therefore, shall she not deign to restrain and ward off outrages by strangers from foreign lands as soon as she becomes aware of them?

"Under these circumstances, we (the names of the envoys follow) present these great offerings by the hands of Komaye, Imbe no Sukune, Vice-Minister of the Bureau of Imbe, who, hanging stout straps on weak shoulders, has purely prepared and brought them hither. Be pleased graciously to hearken to this memorial. But if unfortunately such hostile acts as we have spoken of should be committed let the (with awe be it spoken) Great Deity, placing herself at the head of all the deities of the land, stay and ward off, sweep away and expel the enemy before his first arrow is shot. Should his designs ripen so far that his ships must come hither, let them not enter within our borders, but send them back to drift and founder. Suffer not the solid reasons for our country being feared as the Divine Country to be sodden and destroyed. If, apart from these, there should be danger of rebellion or riot by savages, or of disturbance by brigands at home, or again of drought, flood or storm, of pestilence or famine such as would cause great disaster to the State or deep sorrow to the people, deign to sweep away and destroy it utterly before it takes form. Be pleased to let the Under-Heaven

be free from alarms and all the country enjoy peace by thy help
and protection. Grant thy gracious favour to the Sovran Grandchild, guarding his august person by day and by night, firm and
enduring as Heaven and Earth, as the Sun and the Moon.

"Declared with deep reverence"

Prayer addressed to Sun-Goddess in 870 by envoys despatched
to Ise

"SACRIFICE TO RIVER-GODS"

"A.D. 379. This year, at a fork of the River Kahashima, in the
central division of the Province of Kibi, there was a great water-
dragon which harassed the people. Now when travellers were
passing that place on their journey, they were sure to be affected
by its poison, so that many died. Hereupon Agatamori, the
ancestor of the Omi of Kasa, a man of fierce temper and of great
bodily strength, stood over the pool of the river-fork and flung
into the water three whole calabashes, saying: "Thou art continually belching up poison and therewithal plaguing travellers.
I will kill thee, thou water-dragon. If thou canst sink these
calabashes, then will I take myself away, but if thou canst not
sink them, then will I cut thy body to pieces.' Now the water-
dragon changed itself into a deer and tried to draw down the
calabashes, but the calabashes would not sink. So with upraised
sword, he entered the water and slew the water-dragon. He
further sought out the water-dragon's fellows. Now the tribe of
all the water-dragons filled a cave in the bottom of the pool.
He slew them every one, and the water of the river became
changed to blood. Therefore that water was called the pool of
Agatamori."

"A.D. 323. In order to prevent the overflowing of the Northern
river the Namuta embankment was constructed. At this time
there were two parts of the construction which gave way and
could not be stopped up. Then the Emperor had a dream, in
which he was admonished by a God, saying: 'There are a man
of Musashi named Koha-kubi and a man of Kahachi named

Koromo no ko, the Muraji of Mamuta. Let these two men be sacrificed to the River-God, and thou wilt surely be enabled to close the gaps.' So he sought for these two men, and having found them, offered them to the River-God. Hereupon Koha-kubi wept and lamented and plunging into the water, died. So that embankment was completed. Koromo no ko, however, took two whole calabashes, and standing over the water which could not be dammed, plunged the two calabashes into the mid-stream and prayed, saying: 'O thou River-God who hast sent the curse (to remove which) I have now come hither as a sacrifice! If thou dost persist in thy desire to have me, sink these calabashes and let them not rise to the surface. Then shall I know that thou art a true God, and will enter the water of my own accord. But if thou canst not sink the calabashes, I shall, of course, know that thou art a false God, for whom why should I spend my life in vain?' Hereupon a whirlwind arose suddenly which drew with it the calabashes and tried to submerge them in the water. But the calabashes, dancing on the waves, would not sink, and floated far away over the wide waters. In this way that embankment was completed, although Koromo no ko did not die. Accordingly Koromo no ko's cleverness saved his life. Therefore the men of that time gave a name to these two places, calling them 'Koha-kubi's Gap' and 'Koromo no ko's Gap.' "

Nihongi

CHAPTER VIII

New Religions
of Japan

HARRY THOMSEN

The New Religions

One of the most significant religious developments in postwar Japan is undoubtedly the emergence of the so-called "new religions," the *shinko shukyo*. Mushrooming into prominence at the end of the Second World War, the new religions at present claim to have about eighteen million believers, or one out of every five Japanese. Although this figure may be subject to doubt, no serious observer can afford to ignore the present influence and future potential power of the new religions. It is even possible that the emergence of these religions is the third major milestone in the history of Japanese religion—the first milestone being the introduction of Buddhism in the sixth century, and the second, the appearance of the popular branches of Buddhism in the 13th century.

NEITHER NEW NOR RELIGION

The term "new religions" has been subject to much discussion, and there is no denying the fact that it is a misleading and inaccurate name. Consequently new names have been suggested—for

Reprinted from Harry Thomsen, *The New Religions of Japan* (Rutland, Vermont: Charles E. Tuttle Company, Inc., 1963), pages 15–31, 79–80, 82–83, 87–94, 101–103, 156–172. Used by permission of the publisher.

example, "modern religions," "modern religious movements," etc.—however, the current term continues to be "new religions."

As for age, the new religions are *not* startlingly new. Some of them, like Tenrikyo, Omotokyo, and Konkokyo started in the 19th century, and even those that came into existence after the Second World War more often than not have a long history behind them within the framework of Shinto or Buddhism. Still, compared to the age of the so-called established religions (Buddhism, Shinto, and Christianity), the "new religions" may be considered rather new.

As for the content of the new religions, it follows that in the strict sense of the word they also cannot be called new. Mainly their doctrines and teachings are simply popularized versions of Shinto and Buddhism. However, there is one important new element in the new religions, namely Christianity, or rather Christian doctrines and teachings taken out of their original context and more or less skilfully mixed with thoughts from Buddhism and Shinto.

In form the new religions *are* most certainly new. One of the main characteristics of the new religions is that they endeavor to present their teaching in a new and striking way with new rites, new buildings, new methods of evangelism, and new interpretations of anything old.

As for calling them religions, it must be pointed out that a large number of the new religions do not meet any definition of the word that includes a regular doctrinal system, an established liturgy, and a certain measure of stability in organization. However, Shinto, which is generally handled as a religion, does not measure up to many definitions of religion either. Further these groups are recent developments, and those that are not already strictly speaking religions are, mainly, moving toward the status of religion. In any case, Tenrikyo and a few others are established to the point where there can be little objection to applying the term religion now. Due to their extraordinary variety there may be no term completely satisfactory, but since the term "new religions" is already in current use, it will be used in this book.

Where there may be some doubt as to its correctness, justification will be offered in the appropriate place.

NUMERICAL STRENGTH

It is difficult to give the exact number of the new religions, not to mention giving the number of their believers. Practically all figures available are those supplied by the religions themselves, and although some of these figures are accurate, most of them cannot be relied upon. The numbers given in the *Year Book of Religions* (Shukyo Nenkan), published by the Ministry of Education, cannot be trusted either since they are only reproductions from reports submitted to the ministry by the religious groups concerned.

The number of new religions registered with the Ministry of Education at present is 171. A little more than one-third of them are registered under Shinto, about one-third under Buddhism, two or three under Christianity, and the rest (thirty) are simply listed as "miscellaneous." Besides the 171 new religions, which are found in most prefectures of the country, there are many smaller religious groups found in only one prefecture and accordingly are registered only on the prefectural level. The exact number within the latter category is not known.

The believers of the thirty new religions listed as "miscellaneous religions" by the Ministry of Education totaled 3,597,599 as of January 1, 1958. The followers of the remaining 141 new religions listed under Shinto, Buddhism, and Christianity run to a little less than 15,000,000, making a total of 18,000,000. However, as mentioned above, the figures have been reported by the new religions themselves and cannot be heavily relied upon. The only thing that can be said with certainty is that the actual number of believers is not above the figures quoted.

Approximately eight percent of the believers belong to the bottom of the social pyramid—farmers and workers. However, the percentages were much higher in this field some years ago since several new religions have made serious attempts to attract the middle class and the intelligentsia. Prime example of this is Tenrikyo, which partly due to its enormous library and its educational program, has succeeded in attracting a fair number of people from the top of the pyramid. On the whole the vast majority of new religions seem to concentrate on the farmers and workers in the first stage of their development and then gradually shift some of the emphasis to the middle and upper classes as the religions in question get older and more firmly established.

The main strength of the new religions is concentrated in the cities of Tokyo, Kyoto, Osaka, and the rural areas of Kyushu, Hokkaido, Okayama Prefecture, Hiroshima Prefecture, and Yamaguchi Prefecture.

The financial strength of the new religions is considerable. The budget of Tenrikyo for 1958 was 880,000,000 yen; that of Rissho Kosei Kai, 600,000,000 yen; PL Kyodan, 380,000,000 yen; Konkokyo, 300,000,000 yen. The rate of increase for the budgets of the various new religions is considerably faster than for the established religions, and the contributions of each member are generally much higher. Tenrikyo, Sekai Kyusei Kyo, and some others are extremely wealthy. The total financial strength of the new religions makes them a factor to reckon with in the future life of the nation.

REASONS BEHIND DEVELOPMENT

The majority of the new religions have their roots in prewar Shinto and Buddhism: the fifty-five old Buddhist denominations and the thirteen old Shinto sects. But while the new religions have such a historical background, their postwar acceleration, their fantastic mushrooming in the space of a few years must be accounted for. The defeat in the war is the key. This can be divided into three facets: a reaction against estranged religion; an answer to a crisis; and a new freedom made possible by the removal of religious restrictions.

The times of crisis during and after World War II led, on a

world-wide scale, to the emergence of all kinds of religions and sects which might minister to the needs of man. The defeat of Japan, the first in its long history, left the nation in a state of moral and economic chaos. War's destruction and defeat's blow to national self-confidence combined to create for many a need for religion. Some turned to Shinto, Buddhism, and Christianity to satisfy these needs. But many more found their answer in the new religions.

On the whole there was a religious vacuum at the end of the war. Shinto, with its connection to the head of state, the Emperor, suffered a great loss of face on defeat. Buddhism was not a vital religion—a situation that had been true for many years before the war. Christianity stood ready to enter the spiritual vacuum, but only a small number of people thought they could find their answer in it, probably partly because Christianity was yet felt to be a foreign religion. In the midst of this situation of disillusionment and turmoil what seems to have happened is that events have shaped up to put Japan on the threshold of a period of religious development that bears a striking resemblance to that of 13th-century Japan.

This seeming historical parallel may become clearer with a brief review of the events of the second great milestone in the history of Japanese religion—the birth of the popular Buddhist sects in the 13th century.

By 1200, the seven schools of Nara Buddhism, as well as the later sects of Shingon and Tendai Buddhism, were waning. They had never reached the level of the common people and, in the hands of the privileged courtiers and clergy, had become increasingly corrupt and lacking in vitality by the end of the Heian period. Political foment and a rising national feeling only widened the already large gap between the involved, ceremonious, and esoteric doctrines and practices of Buddhism and the unlearned and uninitiated masses. The farmer and the worker needed bread instead of stones, however beautiful the stones might be. Against this background and within the space of sixty years, arose the popular sects of Jodo, Shin, and Nichiren Buddhism, which taught about salvation in terms that anyone could understand and showed a way towards this salvation that even the most sinful could follow. Within a few decades they had become the religions of the farmer and the worker. And Zen, with its practical approach to Buddhism, became a sect of high appeal to the rising warrior class.

The parallels are not hard to see. The established religions at war's end were generally in a state of impotency as far as the masses were concerned, or outside forces had combined to destroy their confidence in the old way. Buddhism was out of the race. Shinto had been part and parcel of the ultra-nationalism of the war and fell into disrepute at surrender, its tremendous influence on education and social behavior being withdrawn soon after. Christianity suffered from its connection with the West and had been hampered by the wartime government. Whatever efforts at retrenching they could muster could not immediately fill the vacuum. The removal of religious restrictions that occurred under the Occupation in 1945 was the final event that allowed the budding new religions to grow and multiply. The 1939 Religious Bodies Law had held all such development in check.

Once the way was clear the new religions, with their easy-to-understand doctrines of popular appeal, began to spread among the people—mainly among farmers and workers, but also getting a foothold in the upper levels of Japanese society. This emergence may be more momentous than most religious observers seem to think, so that today we may stand at the third great milestone in the history of Japanese religion.

CHARACTERISTICS

No foolproof classification of the new religions is possible due to their extraordinary variety. The following eight characteristics will vary in degree of strength and importance in the different religions, and in the case of a few religions some of the points may be misleading. However, to some extent they constitute the major characteristics of the 171 new religions.

1. They Center Around a Religious Mecca

In the case of most of the larger new religions an imposing headquarters has been constructed, a central point where all the believers go on special occasions. There is the huge Tenrikyo headquarters near Nara, which in its architecture points back to the past of Japan. There is the impressive center of Soka Gakkai near Mt. Fuji, which reflects the modern day in its large ferro-concrete building. There is the colossal headquarters of Rissho Kosei Kai, scheduled for completion in 1964, which combines the past and the present in its architecture with a modernistic ferro-concrete building that is topped by ancient Indian-style temple domes. The Rissho Kosei Kai headquarters will house more than 50,000 people and will probably be the largest building for religious use in the Far East.

The importance of the impressive headquarters is manifold. The centers, with the various ceremonies taking place there, lend to the religion a special atmosphere; they are a bulwark against frequent secessions—a weakness of several new religions; they give the believers a center towards which to proceed on pilgrimages and festive occasions; and they give to the faithful a sense of pride, dignity, and a feeling of being part of something big.

2. They Are Easy to Enter, Understand, and Follow

With a few notable exceptions, these organizations are exceedingly easy to enter—there are no entrance examinations, no special requirements, no baptisms, and no promises. It is true that in a few religions there is an entrance fee, and in the case of a few others of these that the prospective member needs recommendation by a present member. Once entered, the main requirement is to pay the monthly fee, which might be five or ten yen, and to buy various religious articles—such as, the sutras or holy scriptures of the particular religion, a shoulderband, a rosary, or some other object.

One of their most important characteristics is the simple and uncomplicated doctrinal structure, which makes it possible for even the most unlearned farmer or worker to understand. Nothing is regarded as useful unless it can be understood by everybody belonging to the religion. We are reminded of Nelson's words: "The speed of a fleet is that of its slowest ship," although the new religions turn the words around to have a more positive ring: "the slower the doctrinal speed, the more efficient the religion."

In so far as the dogmas of Buddhism have been taken over by these groups they have been simplified and are expressed in a terminology that can be grasped by anybody—for example: "God's world and that of maggots [non-believers] are as different as two trains passing each other going in opposite directions. The celestial ship is about to depart for Heaven from a maggot harbor while the maggot ship of mud is floundering. If you realize that you are on board the ship of mud, the only thing for you to do is to transfer to the ship of God."

Often the doctrine is coupled with a kind of visual demonstration, and in this way difficult Buddhist doctrines which were formerly understood by only a small minority have become popularized. Thus the *muga* (non-self) doctrine of Buddhism is demonstrated, or given expression, by the *muga no odori* (non-self dance) in the group known as the Dancing Religion (Odoru Shukyo). And in Tenrikyo the removal of the dust (sin or evils) from the heart is illustrated by sweeping hand movements, and this forms part of the daily worship.

The service in the new religions usually consists of the following elements: some ceremonies, often colorful and interesting, and wherever possible typical of the religion in question; a speech or sermon; and the *zadankai* (a get-together). The speech, which could be called a popular sermon (formerly regarded as the monopoly of Christianity), is simple and easy to understand. It is applied to everyday problems and often is mixed with humorous anecdotes. The zadankai is probably the most important part of the service. Over a cup of tea the believers experience a sense of fellowship and belonging, they exchange testimonies, and discuss common problems, such as, how to educate their children, how to become happy, how to win new followers.

3. They Are Based on Optimism

In contrast to Buddhism (or at least to original Buddhism) the new religions are basically optimistic. There is no room for life-pessimism and negativism. Life is beautiful, and there is always a sun above the clouds.

Man is regarded as "a being of happiness," and several of the new religions call themselves "religions of happiness." "How to Live a Happy Life" or "Towards Happiness" are titles used for many books and pamphlets. The happiness is emphasized by numerous festivals, often on a stupendous scale. Thus PL Kyodan has the greatest display of fireworks seen anywhere in the nation on the occasion of their annual summer festival, and the annual celebrations of such groups as Tenrikyo, Rissho Kosei Kai, and Kurozumikyo have become nationally known.

The aura of *festivitas,* the stupendous festivals, and the various colorful dances and ceremonies undoubtedly account for much of the popular appeal of the new religions to the Japanese, with whom the pessimism of Buddhism has never harmonized.

4. They Want to Establish the Kingdom of God on Earth, Here and Now

Practically all the new religions claim to be working for, or to be able to attain, the establishment of the Kingdom of God on earth—not in the distant uncertain future, but right here and now. They promise freedom from various evils: "Sickness, poverty, and unhappiness will become things of the past, and a happy life with the fulfillment of every human need lies ahead." Kitamura Sayo, the foundress of the Dancing Religion, expresses this in the following way: "If you come to God's world, you will find all the necessary supplies you need piled up in quantities ready to be allocated. Greedy self-deluded fools are groping around in the dark and are failing to take in these rich heavenly supplies. Come and see the Kingdom of God! There is no worry, agony, sickness, or suffering in God's land. There you can enjoy a heavenly life with the body you now possess. God's Kingdom is nowhere remote. It sprouts in your heart and grows within yourselves."

Innumerable quotations could be added. The following is the seventh article in the creed of Seicho no Ie: "We wish to overcome diseases and all other miseries of mankind by a true conception of man's life, by a true way of living, and by a true method of education; and we want to devote ourselves to propagating the idea that all men are children of God, in order to establish on earth the Heaven of Mutual Love and Assistance." It should also be noted that Tenrikyo at an early stage of its development owed part of its growth to the promise of painless childbirth, and the Soka Gakkai has spread among the rank and file coal miners in Hokkaido and elsewhere by promising freedom from disease, safety from mine accidents, and automatic wage raises without resorting to strikes.

Healing by faith and prevention of sickness by faith are main characteristics of the new religions. In connection with this various forms of magic have been practiced in some groups, often resulting in much-publicized sudden deaths. Although numerous accounts of miraculous healings are published in the respective religious news organs every day—quite a few cases—especially those due to nervous diseases, probably authentic—there is no doubt that a large number of the believers go to an untimely grave because they refrain from consulting a doctor. Still, faith-healing remains one of the main attractions, a fact that may be partly explained by the ancient connection between religion, the healing of diseases, and the reversal of disasters.

As the various organizations gradually develop and change their emphasis from farmers and workers to the middle and upper classes, a change takes place in the doctrine of faith-healing. Thus Soka Gakkai at first discouraged its followers from consulting doctors. "Don't waste your money on the doctors," they said, "go to Soka Gakkai." But now the motto seems to be "first go to the doctor, and if he cannot cure it, then come to Soka Gakkai." Tenrikyo too has changed its emphasis on faith-healing, which has now come from being one of the main doctrines to its present more peripheral status. Tenrikyo and a few others have even built hospitals, whose doctors more often than not are non-believers.

The promise of a heaven on earth has been particularly emphasized by Sekai Kyusei Kyo (formerly Meshiyakyo), which has built two miniature prototypes of an earthly paradise, one in Atami and one in Hakone, both well-known Japanese resort areas. The one in Atami is situated on a hill commanding a beautiful view of Atami bay and is combined with an art museum designed to convey to the believers the feeling of happiness through beauty. The other in Hakone also has an impressive museum of art objects as well as one of the most beautiful gardens in Japan.

In the "Kingdom of God," world peace is a necessity, and accordingly this is emphasized in the official writings of practically every new religion. In some cases the emphasis on world peace seems genuine, but in other cases it seems to be more an appeal to popular sentiment than a central dogma. Near Hiroshima it is prerequisite for any religion that wants popular support to emphasize world peace and recommend itself as a means towards this goal.

5. They Emphasize that Religion and Life Are One

In most of the new religions the believers are taught that religion in itself has no value if it is not intimately connected with daily life to the point where they merge into one. Thus Ittoen, a new religious movement, refuses to be called a religion but uses the term *seikatsu* (life, living).

The connection of life and religion works both ways: religion being thought of in terms of daily life, and daily life being filled with religious contents. Kitamura Sayo of the Dancing Religion expresses it in this way: "Religion is not merely to worship and believe in God, but also to advance along the Road to God by practicing God's teaching. Human life is holy, and therefore one's home and community are the places where the soul must be polished. No religion can exist which is not intimately related to one's daily life." Miki Tokuchika, leader of PL Kyodan, expresses the same idea in the terminology characteristic of his religion: "Life is art, and every occupation and every action must be carried out artistically. Man is an artist, and God is the artist of artists." Taniguchi Masaharu, founder and leader of Seicho no Ie, maintains that many religions are only book-and-church religions and cannot be applied to practical life.

An interesting attempt to express the union of life and teaching in religious terminology, while at the same time intimating that Christianity does not practice this union, is found in the Dancing Religion. The title used for one of their most important books, the biography of the founder, has the same pronunciation as the word used by the Christians for the Bible, namely *seisho*. But whereas the Chinese characters used by the Christians mean holy writing, the characters used by the Dancing Religion convey the meaning of living book. Similarly the words used for "faith" have the same pronunciation in the two religions, but whereas the *shinko* of Christianity has the meaning of to believe, or to worship, the characters used by Kitamura Sayo convey the meaning of holy action.

This characteristic has been treated in length because of its importance when the success and popular appeal of the new religions are estimated. It must also be pointed out in this connection that most of these religions are lay movements.

Many new religions are well known for their emphasis on social services of various kinds. Best known in this respect are Ittoen, Tenrikyo, and Rissho Kosei Kai. Ittoen members, living in the village of Kosenrin near Kyoto, go out one day a week to clean toilets in the neighboring towns and villages in what they call "prayer in action" or "prayer for world peace." Rissho Kosei Kai sends its members out every week to clean various public places in Tokyo, and Tenrikyo believers twice a year clean the huge park in Nara, close to their headquarters. It should also be mentioned that Reiyukai recently constructed a large hall at the cost of 200,000,000 yen and presented it to the city of Tokyo for social welfare work.

6. *They Rely Upon a Strong Leader*

Most of the new religions are centered around a leader who is so closely identified with his religion that his death usually causes drastic changes and in several cases has led to the dissolution of the religion.

Whereas the relationship between the believers is thought of in horizontal terms, the relationship between the leader and the believers is vertical and is based on the *oyako* principle, the absolute authority of father over son. This authority cannot be questioned, and to some extent it may be said that whereas democracy is evident in the relationship between the believers, the old feudalism lingers on in the relationship between leader and believer. Some observers point out that the reverence paid to the emperor to the end of World War II has been transferred to these leaders.

In about sixty of the new religions the authority of the leader is based on a revelation in which the divinity of the religion appeared and asked the leader to initiate the movement. The authority of the leader based upon such a close connection with the divinity leads the believers to regard the founder as divine. Thus Kitamura Sayo of the Dancing Religion is called Goddess (*Ogami-sama*), and her son is known as the young god.

These *ikigami* (living gods), found in the streets or fields of today's Japan, have their roots in the history of Japanese religion, where the distinction between God and man never has been very clear. To the Japanese there never was a Jahveh of Sinai, there never was the gulf between man and God which is found in the West. In Japanese religion man and God have always been regarded as a whole. In Buddhism, man is conceived of as having inside of him the Buddha-seed or as being Buddha himself. And in Shinto the term *kami* (god) is given to men as well. Consequently in Japanese religion the man-God conception has more or less leveled out the difference between man and God—man being the image of God, and God being the image of man. With this background it is easy to see how the leaders of many new religions have come to be regarded as gods. Even from the beginning of Japanese religion, the gods have been walking in the street or working in the field.

One of the greatest problems for the new religions is the matter of succession. In many cases the leader is followed by his eldest son, but in other cases a board of directors takes over, and the line of succession is broken. In the case of Ananaikyo, Nakano Yonosuke has adopted a young woman who will succeed to the leadership of this religion. An even more interesting case is that of the Dancing Religion's Kitamura Sayo, who announced that her yet unborn grandchild would be her successor. The granddaughter, now ten years old is known by the title Ohimegami-sama, the Princess-goddess.

Finally it should be mentioned that whereas most of the new religions are centered around one strong leader, there is a notable exception in the case of Soka Gakkai, which started with Makiguchi and later on Toda as the central figure but at present has a number of strong leading personalities. This fact seems to account for some of the success of Soka Gakkai up to now, but may in the future become the source of a splintering-off process in this religion.

7. They Give Man a Sense of Importance and Dignity

Most of the new religions could be called religions of "I-ism."

The new follower is made to feel that he is an important person, that in fact he is the center of his own universe, that he is basically strong and good, not weak and bad.

From the moment he enters, everything is done for his convenience. Services are held at times adapted to his leisure, early in the morning or in the evening; the church, shrine, or temple of the religion is always open to him or his children; the minister or teacher is at any time ready to speak with him and help him with his problems; if he is poor, a minimum of expense is asked from him; and he is told again and again that he is the "master of his own destiny." This optimistic estimation of man, together with the attention paid to the single believer, accounts for much of the popularity of the new religions, but also indirectly has been one of the reasons behind the secession movements that so frequently occur within them.

It can also turn out to be a boomerang and a major stumbling block when the believer meets with difficult problems in his daily life and finds that he is *not* always "the master of his own destiny."

In several religions the believer is given the opportunity to confess and talk things over frankly. On such occasions he tells of his problems and mistakes, and at the same time he receives answers and advice. The best known in this respect is Rissho Kosei Kai. In the headquarters of this religion in Tokyo there is a daily crowd of thousands of believers—mostly middle-aged women—divided into small groups of from ten to twenty people and led by a teacher or counselor. In each group the people are given a chance of presenting their problems and difficulties, while at the same time listening to the problems of others. The leader then gives an answer or solution to the questions, and testimonies are given by the most ardent believers. To Western observers the counselling and the frank testimonies may seem rather un-Japanese; however, what is happening is that the Japanese through this counselling gradually are freeing themselves from the typical Japanese code of behavior imposed upon them during the Tokugawa period. The tremendous success of group counselling is a significant factor in the development of the new religions, and in the further development of the Japanese character. We are perhaps witnessing the first beginnings of a change from national religion into personal religion, a development that could cause drastic changes in the present Japanese religious system.

8. *They Teach the Relativity of All Religions*

Most of the new religions teach the doctrine of inclusiveness and relativity in regard to other religions. The main exception to this is Soka Gakkai, a fanatically intolerant group attached to the equally intolerant Nichiren sect of Buddhism. Otherwise, the traditional religions, Buddhism and Shinto, have always been tolerant, their feelings being summed up in a Japanese version of an old Buddhist thought: We are all climbing Mt. Fuji, some from one starting place, some from others, so we cannot see each other now because the mountain is between us, but we will all see the same moon when we finally arrive at the top.

Consequently most of the new religions regard each other as of equal standing, and have formed the Union of the New Religious Organizations of Japan, in which they are co-operating in various ways. Nevertheless, for the greater number of new religions there is a limit to the inclusiveness, for while they regard all religions as being basically equal, they are still convinced that their own "way to the top" is slightly superior; and their inclusive way of thinking does not prevent them from waging extremely vigorous propaganda in Japan as well as outside.

There is no doubt that inclusive thinking and tolerance are not limited to Japanese religion, but are essential parts of all Eastern religions. Throughout Asia the religious tolerance reflects the inability or reluctance of the Eastern mind to think in exclusive terms. However, it would be of the greatest interest to know to what extent the inclusive attitude of Japanese religion has been molded by the influence of the joining of Shinto and Buddhism, which almost a thousand years ago resulted in the syncretic Ryobu (dual) Shinto. Both of these religions came to be seen as manifestations of the truth, and probably this connection has done much to shape the Japanese religious mind, which so often is quite willing to accept the best of any new thought and combine it with the old—that is, religions do not exist as entities in themselves for the Japanese religious mind, but as parts of a whole which may be united or mixed as one sees fit.

What can be called the selective and combinative religious mind of the Japanese is quite evident in the new religions. Old Shinto and Buddhist doctrines have been mixed with Christian thoughts and Biblical events. To some extent it may even be said that the innovations of the new religions are from Christianity.

It is amazing to see various versions and parts of Christianity embedded in the heart of the new religions. The new religions have actually placed much of Christianity within the framework of Japanese religion as a whole in a different way from that done by the various Christian churches in Japan. Christ is mentioned with the greatest respect and reverence in the majority of the new religions, and it can be said that most of the phases of the life of Christ are to be found in one form or another. There are versions of the stilling of the sea, the Sermon on the Mount, and the Lord's Prayer. Christian terminology is used extensively, and words from the Bible are quoted freely—thus, the official monthly publication of Seicho no Ie uses a Biblical quotation as its motto.

Further, as might be suspected, some of the high-ranking leaders of the new religions are former Christians.

Are the New Religions Here to Stay?

Generally, the significance of the new religions has been underestimated. Until the sensational Soka Gakkai victory in the Upper House elections in 1959, most people did not think too seriously about the possibility that the new religions might turn out to be one of the main developments in the religious history of Japan rather than just a temporary phenomenon. A second look enables one to see that in many ways the new religions have become permanent parts of the social, religious, and now, political picture of postwar Japan.

It is true that a large number of bizarre and rather strange groups appeared after the end of World War II, and that a large number of them have disappeared as suddenly as they came. 1951 saw 156 miscellaneous new religions registered with the Ministry of Education (besides those listed under Buddhism, Shinto, and

Christianity), but after the enactment of the Religious Jurisdiction Law of the same year, the number went down from 156 to 98 by December, and today the number is 30.

Among those that disappeared was Denshinkyo, which worshipped electricity as the main deity and Thomas Alva Edison as one of four lesser deities. Other short-lived religions were Boseikyo, in which sex apparently played a role in healing practices, and Jiyukyo, which established its own cabinet for the country (among them, the famous sumo wrestler Futabayama). Jiyukyo finally was raided by the police and dissolved.

However, those religions that disappeared were the most extreme and bizarre ones, and it can be assumed that the majority of the present 171 are here to stay, at least in the foreseeable future. Some of them will undoubtedly diminish, some of them disappear, but it is just as certain that some of them will develop and may in the future be counted among the strongest religions of the country.

Even at present the numerical strength of the new religions is anything but negligible. The three largest count between them ten percent of the population of Japan, and the largest one, Soka Gakkai, is at present the fastest growing religion in the world, with a monthly increase of up to 100,000 people.

Japan's established religions, particularly Buddhism, are aware of the threat of the new religions to take over the leading position in the religious arena of the future. The General Secretary of the Soto branch of Zen Buddhism, Mr. Sasaki, remarked in his annual report of March 7, 1957: "Buddhism is now beset by a *danger such as it has never known since its beginning*. This danger comes from the new religions and their astonishingly effective propaganda methods. To survive it will take all our zeal and all our financial resources."

Rather than giving the death blow to the established religions it seems probable that the new religions will force the other Japanese religions, particularly Buddhism, into an era of accelerated accommodation and streamlining. This will cause Buddhism in Japan, which even at present differs considerably from continental Buddhism, to deviate even further from its origin. However, without this streamlining process it is doubtful whether Buddhism will be able to survive the challenge of the new religions.

Soka Gakkai

The new religions described in this section are closely associated in one way or another with Nichiren Buddhism, the remarkable sect established by a monk named Nichiren (1222–1282) during the troubled times of the Kamakura period. Nichiren came to believe in himself as the only person who could save Japan from ruin, through his own interpretation of Buddhism. He taught that all the truth necessary to know was revealed in the Mahayana Buddhist sutra *Saddharma-pundarika*—The Sutra of the Lotus of the Good Law. Central among the beliefs of his sect was the importance of saying or chanting homage to the Lotus Sutra as an act of faith. The sutra is known as the Myoho Renge Kyo in Japanese, hence the often-heard invocation *Namu Myoho Renge Kyo* (referred to as the Daimoku). Recitation of the Daimoku plays an important role in Nichiren sects.

This crisis-born nationalistic and fanatical sect coincided with and played a major role during a turning point in Japanese history, and has continued to be a religious force till the present. Nichiren Buddhism is generally considered to be the culmination of the development of Japanese Buddhism—that is, Nichiren's teachings were a final Japanization of the Chinese Buddhist doctrines introduced in the 8th century.

Though the various sects of Nichiren Buddhism may each claim to be the exclusive bearer of Nichiren's "truth," they do not differ in doctrines to any great degree. This is also true of the three new religions that are considered under the heading, "The Nichiren Group."

Strictly speaking, Reiyukai and Rissho Kosei Kai were founded before Soka Gakkai; however, they are handled last in this section for two reasons. First, Soka Gakkai is a lay movement which is actually attached to one of the established Nichiren sects that date from the period following Nichiren's death, so any chronological difference between it and the other two new religions is almost academic. Second, it is easier to see the establishment of all these groups in perspective if this more realistic historical treatment is used.

HISTORICAL BACKGROUND

The lifespan of Nichiren (1222–1282) covered one of the most eventful and dramatic periods of Japanese history. His conceiving and founding of the first distinctively Japanese Buddhist sect, one with such a direct and lasting appeal to the common man, was a major event of this era. The monk Nikko, an original disciple of Nichiren, later became the leader of one of the thirty-one branches that developed out of the original sect. This sect, Nichiren Shoshu (The Orthodox Sect of Nichiren), is the spiritual mother of Soka Gakkai.

Nichiren

Nichiren was a monk at the center of the Tendai sect (a Heian period development of Buddhism based on the continental sect T'ien-t'ai) on Mt. Hiei in the hills above Kyoto. He was dissatisfied with this and other forms of the Buddhism of his day, feeling that none met the needs of the common people. The result of his ten years of study at Mt. Hiei and his subsequent investigation was a firm conviction that he, and he alone, could help the Japanese people. He spent the rest of his life in fierce propagation of his teaching, the like of which has seldom been seen anywhere, especially in the religiously tolerant islands of Japan. After thirty turbulent years he died in 1282, leaving the propagation of his teachings in the hands of his six disciples and an indelible mark in the annals of Japanese religious history.

Nichiren's teaching was based on the Lotus Sutra, which Tendai Buddhism and other sects also used but which Nichiren declared to be the final and perfect revelation of truth. He claimed the Lotus Sutra made the use of other scriptures unnecessary or even harmful. Like Christianity and Islam, and in contrast to most Buddhist sects, Nichiren Buddhism may be called the religion of a book.

The main characteristics of his teaching were: identification of religion with national life; a ferocious intolerance of any but his own teachings; and an apocalyptic mysticism drawn from Mahayana Buddhism. These characteristics are continued in the teachings of Nichiren Shoshu, which was founded by one of Nichiren's disciples.

Nikko

Nichiren left the propagation of his doctrines to his six main disciples, one of whom was Nikko. Nikko was left in charge of the main temple of Nichiren Buddhism at Mt. Minobu while the other five went to another district. A quarrel broke out between Nikko and another disciple, and the latter (with the probable backing of the feudal lord of Minobu) won, causing Nikko to leave the temple. Nikko crossed the river into another fief and established a new temple, the Taiseki-ji, at the foot of Mt. Fuji. This was the beginning of Nichiren Shoshu, the Orthodox Sect as it pointedly was called.

Nikko's teaching has been changed slightly several times through the centuries but in the main represents the teaching of his master Nichiren. The present doctrinal structure of Nichiren Shoshu (and of Soka Gakkai) was formulated by Nikkan, who lived from 1665 to 1725. The basis of this teaching is as follows: The absoluteness of the power of the cosmic diagram, a mandala drawn by Nichiren and known as the Gohonzon; the mystical oneness of Buddha, Nichiren, and the believer (*ninpo ikke*); a fanatical intolerance far exceeding that of other branches of Nichiren Buddhism.

Writings and Doctrines

Soka Gakkai, as such, has no teaching apart from that contained in Makiguchi's *An Essay on Value*. However, as a lay movement of Nichiren Shoshu, Soka Gakkai adheres to all the liturgy, doctrines, and philosophy of the parent sect, and thus goes back to the teachings of Nichiren himself. I shall first compare the application of Nichiren's teaching in Nichiren Shoshu and in Soka Gakkai, then add a few words on *An Essay on Value*.

The canonical writing of Nichiren Buddhism, and therefore of Soka Gakkai, is the Mahayana Buddhist sutra referred to in the introduction to this section. It is known as the Lotus Sutra, or the Lotus of the Good Law, and in Japanese as the Hokkekyo (favored over the formal title, Myoho Renge Kyo). Nichiren Buddhism may be termed "the religion of a book"—the Lotus Sutra. This sutra, which in some ways is similar to the Apocalypse, places the historical Buddha in an exuberant, supernatural setting as the center of the universe, surrounded by lesser Buddhas, Bodhisattvas, other deities, and countless hosts of believers. According to the sutra, the teachings imparted in it are the ultimate revelations of the Buddha, and their revelation on Vulture Peak was accompanied by all sorts of supernatural upheavals and other extraordinary phenomena. The Lotus Sutra played a major role in the development of the second phase of Buddhism, Mahayana, and in it is the basis for the Three Mystic Laws of Nichiren, which developed into the Three Fundamental Principles of Nichiren Shoshu.

Nichiren Shoshu divides the sutra into two parts, or rather, interpretations, and explains them in the following way: "The Hokkekyo is the highest doctrine of Buddhism. It consists of two parts: the *shamon* and the *honmon*. It is generally considered that the honmon is superior to the shamon in philosophical value; further, the time during which the shamon could be propagated has passed. In other words, the shamon interpretation is of no use in this age of the End of the Law. Hinayana Buddhism, provisional ["provisional" is a Nichiren term] Mahayana Buddhism, and the shamon of the Lotus Sutra are the teachings of Sakyamuni, the historical Buddha of India, but the honmon of the Lotus Sutra is the teaching of the Great Saint Nichiren, the True Buddha. We therefore practice the honmon alone, and this is the most remarkable characteristic of our sect."

Beatification of Nichiren and Buddha

In chapter fourteen of the Lotus Sutra, Jogyo Bosatsu (*bosatsu* is Japanese for Bodhisattva) is mentioned as one of the four chiefs of the hosts of Bodhisattvas, and in chapter twenty he accepts the commission of the Buddha to preach and promulgate the teaching to coming generations.

It seems that Nichiren grew more and more convinced that he was a reincarnation of this Bodhisattva—that Jogyo and he were one and the same—so therefore it was his responsibility to promulgate the teachings of the Lotus Sutra.

Nichiren Shoshu goes still further, claiming that Jogyo was a reincarnation of the Eternal Buddha, that, in fact, Nichiren and the universe are one.

From the conviction of Nichiren that he was Jogyo Bosatsu stems his tremendous self-assertion and belief in himself, which caused him to say: "One who would propagate the truth of Buddhism by convincing himself of the five principles is entitled to become the leader of the Japanese nation. One who knows that the Lotus of Truth is the King of all Scriptures, knows the truth of religion. If there were nobody who read the Lotus of Truth, there could be no leader of the nation. Without a leader the nation would simply be bewildered." Or his famous words, that brought him a host of enemies: "I will be the pillar of Japan; I will be the eyes of Japan; I will be the great vessel of Japan."

From this belief of Nichiren, which Nichiren Shoshu developed further, comes also the absoluteness with which Nichiren Shoshu and Soka Gakkai regard Nichiren and Hokkekyo. Accordingly Soka Gakkai speaks of itself in terms of uncompromising absolute authority whereas most of the other new religions speak in terms of relative authority, recognizing the values in other religions.

The Three Mystic Laws

According to the *Main Doctrine of Nichiren Shoshu,* the Three Mystic Laws or Three Mysteries are basic. These are: (1) the Gohonzon, or chief object of worship; (2) the Daimoku, or invocation to the chief object of worship; (3) the Kaidan, or place to receive proper instruction. These, says Nichiren Shoshu, are implied in the chapter of the Lotus Sutra that is called the Juryo-bon (one of the two chapters which members of Soka Gakkai must learn by heart).

Gohonzon

The Gohonzon is a mandala, or graphic representation of the universe organized in terms of the Buddhas: the Eternal Buddha at the center and the various other Buddhas and Bodhisattvas arranged in a descending and expanding order as outlined in the Lotus Sutra. In contrast to other Buddhist mandalas—such as those of Tendai and Shingon Buddhism—the Nichiren mandalas contain neither pictures of the Buddhas and Bodhisattvas nor their names in Sanskrit letters. All the names are written vertically in *kanji,* the Chinese characters which are used by the Japanese as well. In the center is the Daimoku.

The mandala of Nichiren is considered to contain the universal power of all the Buddhas and Bodhisattvas whose names are written on it. And it is claimed that the *satori* (enlightenment) which other schools of Buddhism endeavor to attain by profound meditation or strenuous training can be obtained just by gazing at the mandala of Nichiren and repeating the Daimoku in front of it: "The supreme law of Buddha is perceived by everyone in the Gohonzon. People today, although they are not at all equal to Sakyamuni in their penetration of mind or observation of rules, will be able to attain the Buddha's power of faith, action, and intellect, to attain enlightenment, get rid of delusion, and contribute towards the establishment of lasting world peace—all just by earnest chanting of the fundamental prayer, the Daimoku, before the Gohonzon."

Nichiren Shoshu claims that the mandala kept at Taiseki-ji

is a genuine one, drawn by Nichiren himself, and regards the mandala as a proof of the sect's orthodoxy. However, this has been a bone of contention for centuries between Taiseki-ji and Minobu-san, the latter claiming that the mandala at Taiseki-ji was written by one of the disciples of Nichiren. Professional calligraphers have wanted to compare the handwriting of the mandala at Taiseki-ji with other authentic specimens written by Nichiren but have not been allowed to do so as Nichiren Shoshu does not want to show the mandala to non-believers. Whether this is out of reverence for the holy object or for other reasons is a question.

Whereas the power of the mandala has been part of the teaching of Nichiren Shoshu for centuries, the modern application of this power to heal sickness, create wealth, and bring about world peace is due to Soka Gakkai, which strongly emphasizes that acquisition of right faith must be proved by visible facts. Every issue of the *Seikyo Shimbun,* the weekly organ of Soka Gakkai, records stories of miraculous cures by the power of the Gohonzon. These range from claiming the credit for cures of breast cancer and polio to the doubling of rice sales by a dealer who just joined the organization and the awarding of a patent to a Soka Gakkai inventor.

Soka Gakkai has become well known for its emphasis on faith-healing, the practice of which they carry further than most other new religions. Where most only teach the therapeutic side of faith-healing, that is, how to get well again, Soka Gakkai goes one step further and recommends faith in Soka Gakkai as a means of *preventing* disease. They say, "If you join us, you will not become sick," or they go so far as to say that "if you do not join us, you will certainly *get* sick."

It is obvious that the promise of faith-healing from all kinds of diseases will be an extremely effective means of propaganda for some time. Many people will listen to the slogan "Don't waste your money on medicine and doctors, join Soka Gakkai!" And the successful cases of healing, especially from nervous or imaginary diseases, will draw a lot of other people to the Soka Gakkai camp. However, it is equally obvious that if the expected healing does not occur, the promises may boomerang with unpleasant results. In this connection it is interesting to see that the idea of not going to the doctor at all is on the wane and is gradually being replaced by the safer "Consult the doctor first, and if it doesn't help, then come to Soka Gakkai!"

Daimoku

The recitation of the Daimoku is in many ways a parallel to the *nembutsu* of the Pure Land Buddhist sects. This was an act of faith that simply involved calling on the Amida (Amitabha) Buddha by uttering the phrase *Namu Amida Butsu* (Adoration be to Amida Buddha). The Daimoku is regarded as a rallying cry, a prayer containing unlimited power, a way toward the salvation of non-believers, and an expression of firm belief in the doctrines and mysteries taught by the Lotus Sutra.

The effectiveness of this invocation was mentioned above. Suffice it to quote a passage by Nichiren in his essay *The Sole Great Thing Concerning Life and Death*: "To utter the sacred Daimoku with the conviction that the three are one, the three being Buddha Sakyamuni, the Lotus of the Truth, and we beings in all realms of existence. To utter the sacred Daimoku is the heritage of the sole great thing concerning life and death. This is the essence of what is promulgated by Nichiren. If it should be fulfilled, the great vow of propagating the Truth all over the world would be fulfilled."

Kaidan

The Kaidan, or the place for instruction and ordination, is also where the mandala is located. It is regarded as the center of the country and of the universe, and is often compared to Vulture Peak, the place where the Buddha is said to have revealed the Lotus Sutra. Nichiren spoke of it in apocalyptic terms: "When the law of Kings shall merge with the Law of Buddha, when ruler and people alike shall hold to the Three Great Mysteries, then the Holy See shall be established in a place as excellent as the Vulture Peak. Thus the moral law will be established in actual life. In this sanctuary men of all countries in the world will receive the precepts of repentance and expiation, and thither also great gods like Brahma and Indra will descend." Nichiren usually has Mt. Minobu in mind when he speaks of the Kaidan, but sometimes he identifies the Kaidan with himself: "I live in a lonely mountain retreat. But in Nichiren's bosom, in his body of the flesh, is secretly enshrined the great mystery, which the Lord Sakyamuni transmitted to me on the Vulture Peak. Therefore it is in my breast that all Buddhas are immersed in contemplation, on my tongue that they turn the Wheel of the Law, in my throat that they are born, and in my mouth that they attain enlightenment. This place being the abode of such a man mysteriously realizing the Lotus of Truth, how can it be less noble than the Vulture Peak?"

The apocalyptic character of Nichiren's thinking is evident in his elaboration on the Mahayana Buddhist prediction of the division of the history of the world into three periods of a millennium each, starting from the death of the Buddha set at 947 A.D. after the chronology of Chinese Buddhism. The first division is called *Shobo,* the period of the "true law," and this roughly covers the Hinayana period of Buddhism, which was more or less based on the teachings of the historical Buddha. The second division, *Zobo,* or period of the "image law," covers the period that saw the development of Mahayana Buddhism with its pantheon of deities centered around the Eternal Buddha—this period roughly began at the same time as Christianity. The last division is *Mappo,* the period of the "destruction of the law," which, according to Nichiren, started about the year 1000. This was to be a period where the laws of Buddhism were to become corrupted, and Nichiren took advantage of the religious and political turmoil of his time, claiming that these were indeed the evil days of Mappo that had been predicted. Nichiren taught that at the end of Mappo the Kaidan would become the center of the world, and all beings would be saved by the power of the Gohonzon.

Nichiren Shoshu and Soka Gakkai are not so interested in the apocalyptic and mystic interpretations of the Kaidan. To them the Kaidan is Taiseki-ji, where the Gohonzon is located. According to their teaching, Taiseki-ji will become the "national tabernacle" of Japan when Mappo comes to an end, and a bright future under the leadership of Nichiren Shoshu and Soka Gakkai will ensue.

An Essay on Value

The ideas of Makiguchi Tsunesaburo as recorded in *Kachiron* (An Essay on Value) are the only doctrinal writings of Soka Gakkai itself. The following is from an introduction to the essay and shows the importance attached to it.

"The fallacies inherent in the usually quoted conceptions of truth, goodness, and beauty as the substance of value that have existed since the philosophy of Kant are refuted in the *Kachiron,* an epochal philosophical work that explains the difference between truth and value, and advocates a system of value based on new concepts of goodness, beauty, and benefit. It dissolves the confusion existing in the contemporary world and closely examines the sources of happiness."

Makiguchi contrasts the three values of goodness, beauty, and benefit with the three anti-values of evil, ugliness, and harm. There is a deep significance in the substitution of benefit for truth, part of it being the potential popular appeal of a system worked out on this basis. For the man in the street or on the farm, "benefit" has a far better sound than "truth"—a practical, down-to-earth sound without the vagueness or troublesome overtones of abstractions. Later in the essay, Makiguchi points out that what is truthful does not necessarily bring happiness. On the whole it can be said that the *Kachiron* is an attempt to find a new religious philosophy based on man's self-assertion and on popular appeal, not on abstract thinking about truth.

WORSHIP

Taiseki-ji is the scene of the strange service known as the *ushitora,* which takes place from 12:00 A.M. to 1:30 A.M. This service has been carried on for 670 years and has never been cancelled. The Taiseki-ji "police," young men with special armbands, direct the crowds to the worship hall. Worship starts with continuous repeatings of the Daimoku for about twenty minutes. The amplified voices of several thousand people create a mood that must be almost hypnotic in its effect on the assembled. After the recitation of the Daimoku, part of the Lotus Sutra is read by the chief priest, whose far-off voice is accompanied by the peculiar dry sound of the rustling of thousands of rosaries. Ear-splitting beats on the drums usher in another twenty minutes of the Daimoku. This ends the service, and the "police" direct the people to their respective sleeping quarters.

There can be no doubt that the ushitora service gives the believers a strong sense of fellowship, increases discipline, and gives a deep impression of power and strength. Believers returning from this moving experience are unshakably convinced that Taiseki-ji is the future center of Japan and the world.

Homage is paid to the Gohonzon and to other objects, among them some relics of Nichiren. There is a statue of Nichiren which was carved by one of his disciples, but of more significance is the *onikuge,* the tooth of the great founder, about which Nichiren Shoshu teaches the following:

"Records show that when the Great Saint Nichiren was past the age of fifty, he himself pulled out a tooth that had become loose and handed it to Nikko, his favorite disciple, with the words: 'Take this and use it as a testimony in propagating the religion among all mankind in the future.' Since then more than 610 years have passed, but the tiny bit of flesh that was attached to the root of the tooth when Nichiren gave it to Nikko, began to grow and by now it covers practically the whole tooth. It has been said that when the entire tooth is covered with flesh, the time will have come when our religion has reached its zenith.

The growth of the flesh attached to the tooth has therefore been watched in every age with the closest attention. It is carefully kept in a three-layer crystal case, and customarily never shown to people. . . ."

PROPAGATION

The relationship between Soka Gakkai and other religions is based on the *shakufuku* principle. Shakufuku literally means "to break and subdue" (the evil spirits, and make straight the true teaching of Buddha). And the shakufuku principle is the missionary method adopted by Soka Gakkai: to attack every other religion ferociously, using logical reasoning along with simple abuse.

The shakufuku method was originated by Nichiren himself, and the fanatical intolerance of Soka Gakkai and Nichiren Shoshu can be traced back directly to him. Nichiren maintained that to kill heretics is not murder, and that it is the duty of the government to extirpate heresy with the sword. His invective brought him into numerous conflicts with the government and with other religious groups. Some examples of his strong language and firm self-assurance follow: "If Nichiren had not appeared in the period of Mappo, then Sakyamuni would have been a great liar, and all the Buddhas would have been great cheats."

He claimed that every repetition of the nembutsu of the Pure Land Sects would cost those who uttered it ages in hell. And he called Kobo Daishi, the founder of Shingon Buddhism and one of the most revered Buddhist patriarchs, the biggest liar in Japan. He summarily disposed of all existing religions in his country in the following: "The nembutsu is hell, Zen is a religion of devils, Shingon is national ruin, and Risshu people are traitors to the country!"

The shakufuku of Soka Gakkai is no less violent than that of Nichiren, but it is couched in pseudo-scientific wording. The idea is not only to vituperate but to prove the other religions wrong. The teaching of Soka Gakkai on other religions is contained in the book called *Shakufuku Kyoten* (The Book of Purgation), a book that all Soka Gakkai believers must study before they become members. There is a short chapter on each of the main religions of Japan: the main Buddhist sects, various new religions, Shintoism, and Christianity. As the shakufuku conception is vital to the understanding of Soka Gakkai, excerpts of this book will be quoted, most of them on Christianity:

"Since Christ had a physical body, he must have been heavier than air according to the law of gravity. If a heavy body had arisen into light air, it would be contrary to Archimedes' principles. And if you believe this to be a fact and so break one of the laws of the universe, you will have to deny all rules and laws."

"At first the pure teaching of Christianity consisted only of the Sermon on the Mount. The other ninety percent of the Bible is no more than the dogmas of the disciples. Let us first inquire into the words of Jesus: 'My Father in Heaven makes his sun rise on the evil as well as on the good. For if you love those who love you, what reward have you? Do not even the tax collectors do the same? You should be as perfect as your Father in heaven.' The word 'perfect' means perfect love, and in Christianity the Crucifixion is regarded as perfect love, the love of redemption. According to the words of Jesus, love is indispensable for the practice of Christianity. You see how much more demanding and full of conditions Christianity is, when you compare this with Buddhism, where you have only one condition: to believe. It shows the difficulty of practice and the inferiority of the teachings of Christianity. In the second place, regarding 'for if you love those who love you, what reward have you?' and 'you must become perfect as your Father in heaven,' we see ideas that are completely in opposition to the law of cause and effect. There is an effect wherever there is a cause. Even if you love those who love you, the effect of your love never fails to come out. Furthermore, you have in your mind both the nature to love and the tendency to abhor—to love alone is therefore not possible, except in words. In the third place, their claim that they can atone for the sins of others and expiate the sins committed by themselves as well as others is erroneous. The sins of other people belong to them exclusively and even if you forgive them their sin, it is impossible that their sin thereby will be erased. On the contrary, the very Christians who insist that Jesus was crucified for them for the sake of redemption always commit sin, and confess, and sin again—sin does not at all diminish but increases all over the world. In the fourth place the paragraph 'so perfect as the Father in Heaven' is built on the premise that the perfect Father in Heaven exists. There is no explanation of the substance, the nature, and the faculty of this Father in Heaven. There is no cause, by which this Father has been born, and there can be no effect without cause."

"Jesus worked miracles. They say that forty-six miracles have been put on record. However, posterity could have invented these miracles; they cannot be proven just by the fact that they are written in the Bible. Even nowadays Christians call all sorts of unusual phenomena miracles. It betrays their inferiority that they are ignorant of the reason behind these phenomena."

"Christianity overestimates sin. They talk of original sin, a sin that nobody can escape. Hence they regard all human beings as criminals. A true religion must give strong vitality to man and not reduce him to a criminal."

"God is not the Creator. Living things as well as non-living things of the universe are not given birth by other things, but by themselves. Our life is not given to us by our parents, and is not either given by God or Buddha."

"Jesus died on the Cross. This fact shows that he was defeated by opposition, whatever interpretation posterity may have given to this fact. The Great Saint Nichiren shouted to his executor when he was about to be beheaded: 'The time is passing. Be quick; cut off my head.' And as soon as he said so, the gods of the universe gave him all the power of their protection, and meteors shot across the heavens. *He* defeated his opposition. Comparing this vitality with the fate of Jesus we see that Christianity has no power."

Nor is Soka Gakkai silent on the subject of Shinto: "Saint

Nichiren preached that if you revolt against the true and orthodox religion, and if heretical opinions prevail, then the gods will disappear from us, the saints will stay away, and the demons will come into the vacant house. Shinto obstructs the spread of orthodox and true Buddhism, and therefore demons have come and live in the Shinto shrines as well as in society. Shinto is a heretical religion that we must destroy."

Seicho no Ie

WORSHIP AND PRACTICES

Seicho no Ie has thirty-three churches and 1,173 meeting places, mostly in private homes. The believers are mostly from the middle or upper classes, and not a few intellectuals are among them. The great majority are middle-aged women.

The service, or meeting, begins with a unison recital of part of the scripture. Next there is the speech centering on the teaching of Taniguchi as it appears in his *Seimei no Jisso* (The Reality of Life)—often a speech of two or three hours. After that, or in between, come the testimonies, miraculous stories of healing from diseases, narrow escapes from death, and improved family relationships. These are told with an emotion and frankness which staggers the foreign observer who probably will find this entirely un-Japanese. And finally comes the *zadankai,* the important informal gathering with refreshments, where everybody chats and enjoys himself.

The devotional life of Seicho no Ie has been influenced by shamanism to some extent, at least up to and during the war, when mystical communications between the dead and members of their families were held by means of a shaman. Also, though charms do not officially exist in Seicho no Ie, the shorter scripture called *Kanro no Hou* is regarded as possessing the efficacy of a charm, and several stories are told of the miraculous saving of soldiers on the battlefield by this scripture.

Another interesting phenomenon in the devotional life of Seicho no Ie which at least borders on shamanism is the *nempa*, a peculiar term used only by this religion. It refers to a kind of spiritual waves which are said to have the power to influence other people at a distance. Taniguchi says that when a family holds a memorial service for a deceased member the nempa of the family is sent to the soul in the spirit world with the power to save him. An interesting instance of the power of nempa appears in the periodical *Seicho no Ie* of August, 1953 (pp. 35–36).

It says: "The thought waves are far more delicate than those of the radio, and distance will not be a hindrance to receiving them. We have an example of a patient in Manchuria who could neither walk nor sit with his legs folded. He was healed instantly by practicing meditation at the same time that we were praying for the benediction of all the members of Seicho no Ie. You require a delicate radio set to receive radio waves. Likewise, you must keep your mind peaceful by meditating on the perfectness of the Reality of Life in order to receive the benedictory waves broadcast from the headquarters of Seicho no Ie. We are praying for your health, prosperity, and world peace from 5:10 to 5:40 A.M. daily."

The center of the devotional practice of Seicho no Ie believers is the *shinsokan,* defined by Taniguchi as a "prayerful meditation in concentrating the mind." This form of meditation is one of the elements of Omotokyo which Taniguchi took with him and adapted for Seicho no Ie. Immense power is said to lie in this meditation, because "by meditating and praying to Avalokitesvara (the Bodhisattva Kannon) means not only to ask for the help of Avalokitesvara; it means to realize that one's true self and the life of perfect freedom of Avalokitesvara are one. Realize that the self is Avalokitesvara, the self *is* Buddha, the self is one entity with God." By meditating in this way, man attains to unlimited power—evil, hate, and suffering disappear, and only love and happiness remain: "Meditate solely: 'The World of Reality is filled with goodness.' An evil such as resentment may appear to exist; however, it is non-existent. Love is the only real existence. Therefore that person loves me, and I love that person. This is the only true existence. This is the only true Reality."

WRITINGS AND DOCTRINES

The canon of Seicho no Ie is the book written by Taniguchi called *Seimei no Jisso* (The Truth or Reality of Life). It is a huge work of forty volumes, but a few adapted excerpts are given to enable the student of Japanese religions to get a glimpse of the innermost thoughts of Seicho no Ie:

"One day an angel came to the Seicho no Ie and sang: 'God, who is the creator of the whole universe, is beyond the five corporeal senses, even beyond the sixth spiritual sense of human beings. He is the holy, consummate, infinite Spirit that permeates the universe, the life that pervades the universe, the law that regulates the universe throughout, Truth, Light, Wisdom, Absolute Love . . . . Nothing exists without God; God is holding all being in His hand; nothing indeed exists that does not come of Him . . . . When the Divine Mind unfolds itself into "the creative world," then develops the whole universe, and all the creatures come into existence . . . . All the beings are the creative Words of God; they are all Spirits, all of them are Mind, nothing is made of matter, matter is nothing but the reflection of the mortal mind . . . . God never created sin, God is the only being that creates, so there is no sin in the world that has been really committed, hence there is no sin that has to be revenged . . . .' The angel continued, 'Reality itself is everlasting. Reality shall not fall ill, nor shall it get old, nor pass away. To realize this is nothing but to know the Way. Reality we call the Way, or Truth, as it permeates through the universe. The Way or Truth is always with God, and God is the Way and the Truth Itself.

(Man)

" 'A man is the Son of Light, and in pure Light of Reality does he live. He could meet with no darkness, neither could he see any failure, nor find any hindrance whatsover. Just as celestials stroll about in Heaven in perfect freedom, and just as the fishes in the sea can swim to and fro quite freely, so man full of light and spiritual rejoicing strolls about in a world full of bright light.'

(Sin)

"Then has recited our angel, when a cherub appeared and said: 'For the sake of humanity, in order to help them in attaining to enlightenment, pray give me a full account of the real nature of errors.' To this responded the angel, saying, ' "Error" is so called, as we dream false things that have no existence in reality. To be ignorant of the real aspect of beings is called "delusion." ' . . . 'Is our sin of real existence?' asked again our cherub, to which the angel replied, saying 'There is nothing real in the true sense of the word but God, and those that have come of Him. Sins are not perfect, so they are not of reality. Diseases are imperfect, so they are not real. Death is imperfect, so it could never be of reality. Do not take the things to be real, that have not been created by God. Never dream of things in your bad dreams which have no existence in reality, nor be afraid of things unreal. Sins, diseases, and death are not what God has created; they are therefore unreal, they are merely delusions, though they have ever assumed the garb of reality. I have come to unmask them to show that sins, diseases, and death have no existence in reality. Gautama [the Buddha] himself once came into the world for this purpose. Christ also once revealed himself for the same purpose. If sins were of real existence, even the truth that various Buddhas preached in all ages could not have demolished them, and Jesus Christ's crucifixion might have been, after all, ineffective for destroying them. How blessed are you to know that sins are all unreal . . . . Jesus Christ, too, could exterminate our sins by mere dint of the words: "Thy sins are forgiven." I, too, have expressed it in words, the Holy Sutras and Holy books of Seicho no Ie, and merely by dint of the words I unmask the so-called sin. He who happens to read my words may know the true aspects of Reality, and therefore all of his sins shall come to naught and shall recover without fail from all diseases and realize the Life Eternal, forever transcendent above death . . . . God is Spirit, therefore Man is also Spirit. God is Love, therefore Man is Love. God is Wisdom, therefore Man is Wisdom. Man in reality is Spirit, he is Love, he is Wisdom, he is Eternal Life. Therefore he could never commit a crime, he could neither suffer from any disease, nor could he pass away. Who would dare to call men sinners? God has never created sinners, so there could not be a single man on this earth, who is a real sinner. The idea of sin is contrary to the Sonship of Deity. God is the source of Light, and Man is the Light that has come of God.

(The Kingdom of God)

" 'Christ has taught us "Behold, the Kingdom of God is within you." Verily, verily I tell you, here "within you" means nothing but man's real nature or the real-man, as the inner man of man's real nature is nothing but God-Man.

" 'Again, Christ has taught us "My Kingdom is not of this world." The Kingdom of this world is nothing but shadow of reflection, the land of eternal blessing is only to be found within.'

(End)

"When thus had spoken our angel, the celestial chorus of Heaven sounded in the sky, and down came numberless petals of holy flowers from Heaven, showering from where we knew not, as if to pay homage to the Truth that had been preached by the angel."

Finally, before we take up the doctrines, I want to list the Seven Declarations of Light of Seicho no Ie.

1. We should not be prejudiced in favor of any sect or any religion, but believe in the spiritual nature of man, and live in accordance with the spiritual truth of Life.

2. We believe that to bring the great Life Principle into full manifestation is the way to infinite power and abundance, and that the personality of every individual is immortal.

3. We study and make known to all the Law of the Creative Spirit, so that humanity may follow the right path to infinite growth.

4. We believe that love is the best nourishment for life and that prayer and words of love and praise are the creative Way of the Word necessary in bringing love into manifestation.

5. We believe that we, Sons of God, have infinite power and

abundance within us and can reach absolute freedom by following the creative Way of the Word.

6. We publish the monthly *Seicho no Ie* and other books and booklets filled with good messages so that man may follow the creative way of constructive words and live a happy life.

7. We organize actual movement in order to conquer all the pains and troubles of humanity, including diseases, by means of the right view of life, constructive living, and true education, to finally bring the Kingdom of Heaven to the earth.

God and Man

As can be seen from the above excerpts from *Seimei no Jisso,* Seicho no Ie in a sense identifies man with God. This is illustrated by Taniguchi in the following way: "Gautama is not the only incarnation of the Eternal Buddha in flesh. We are all the Eternal Buddha that is embodied in the flesh. Jesus alone is not the only son of God. We are all sons of God. Jesus taught us to pray saying '*our* Father, which art in Heaven.'" This means they say that all humanity are sons of God, and he is everyone's father, everyone has infinite power as they are God's children.

However, at other times Seicho no Ie seems to forget the identity of God with man and treat the two separately. The illustration on this page will serve to bring this out.

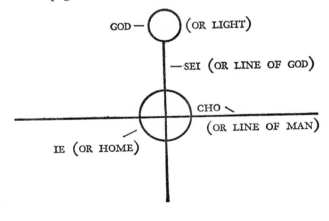

Seicho no Ie preachers often use this diagram to explain how God relates to man. The vertical line, the line of God, and the horizontal line, that of man, meet at one point only. This is called "the true home of man, the center of the world." God's line is called *sei* (life), and man's is called *cho* (growth). The meeting point is *ie* (home), thus they form the name Seicho no Ie (House of Growth). To illustrate the connection between God and man—and this concept is still somewhat blurred—the lines are compared with a water pipe through which water (life) comes to man. The pipe can freeze at times, at which time only the "Light and Love of God" can thaw it. Two different worlds are spoken of: the world of God, with life and love; and the world of man, which depends on God for life by means of the life line that might be cut off under certain conditions.

Sometimes there seems to be a different sort of link between God and man. This one says that sometimes the light from God comes indirectly to man through the scriptures, the nempa, and shinsokan (see above). This is shown in another illustration often used by Seicho no Ie.

SCRIPTURES, NEMPA, & SHINSOKAN

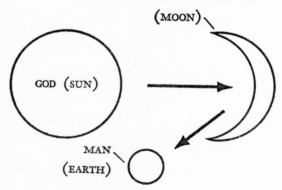

Sin

The conception of sin in Seicho no Ie is a curious parallel to the Buddhist conception of *maya* or illusion.

Taniguchi often speaks of Christianity's doctrine of the Fall or of Adam's original sin and twists it around to the effect that the real sin of mankind is to believe that there is such a thing as sin, and that the fall of man is to believe that there ever was a fall! For Seicho no Ie there exists no sin in the world because they believe that God, being goodness and love, could only create things that are part of the same goodness and love. Taniguchi says: "The idea that 'I am a sinner' is the mother of all kinds of sin in this physical world. On the other hand, the idea that 'I am a son of God' is the mother of all the good things in this physical world."

The application of the nonexistence of everything evil or bad is interesting. Here is an example of how it is applied to the Christian idea of loving one's enemy: "The Bible says we should love our enemy. Seicho no Ie says that originally there is no enemy. You can truly reconcile only when you realize that you have no enemy. If you first recognize the existence of an enemy and then try to love your enemy, you will find it almost impossible because the idea of 'enemy' contradicts 'love.' Only when you realize that you have no enemy will you be able to love anyone without trying to do so purposely."

Another interesting application of the theory of "no sin" is the interpretation of the crucifixion of Christ as an act by God to clear away the sin-consciousness of man: "Christ had himself crucified as atonement for humanity's sin in order to exterminate humanity's sin-consciousness. The crucifixion of Christ meant that he was the humanity of his age, self-bound and self-restricted by the idea of sin, suffering because they believed in Adam's original sin and believed themselves to be children of sin. And although he preached that man is not a child of sin but a son of God, they could not believe it in any way, and therefore he suffered before the multitude, declaring: 'I will be crucified as an atonement for your sins; therefore original sin has disappeared, and there are no longer any sins. I will suffer this much in place of your sins.' What Christ wanted to pacify was not God's anger but humanity's sin-consciousness."

Salvation

According to Seicho no Ie, salvation consists of the realization of the "Sonship"—that man is Son of God, that man is Buddha, and thus born to live in freedom and abundance with limitless possibilities. "To be saved by religion means restoration of the original freedom of life, and does not mean man's deliverance from sin into an exceedingly pleasant world called Paradise, as if man were a mud-smelling carp to be scooped up from the mud and put into pure water."

"Man's salvation by religious truth means the realization of the truth of Sonship, that man's essence of life is originally a perfect Buddhahood, and the originally perfect real aspect of the self should be made manifest and recover the original freedom, original liberation, and original free divinity. Such a truth that delivers and liberates man is true religion; therefore Christ taught in the Book of John: 'Ye shall know the truth, and the truth shall make you free.'"

Usually Seicho no Ie speaks of salvation as something that occurs suddenly, in a moment. Two steps and a testimony, however, seem to be necessary. These are:

1. The reading of *Seimei no Jisso* and other related literature, hearing the speeches of Taniguchi, and attending the services of Seicho no Ie.

2. The practice of shinsokan (meditation), and through this realizing that the individual and God are one, that all people are brothers, and that there is nothing real in the world except love. This experience should generate gratitude, and is an important prerequisite to salvation in Seicho no Ie.

3. The testimony to others to the effect that one has recognized the Sonship and has been saved.

Disease and Faith-healing

To salvation belongs cure from any disease. The problem of disease is solved in the same way as that of sin: as God is Goodness and Love, He cannot create evil things, they reason. Therefore, since disease is an evil thing, it cannot have been created by God, and since all there is in the world has been created by God, disease simply cannot exist. It is just in man's imagination and unenlightened mind that disease and all kinds of suffering exist.

Taniguchi attacks the idea that disease is catharsis. Thus he says of a former Christian who entered Seicho no Ie:

"She had been a very earnest Christian and held the false faith of welcoming sufferings, as is too often the case with Christians. Sublimation of sufferings is a false faith. It cannot be that God is pleased to see man suffer. Yet many Christians think that diseases and misfortunes are given as a cathartic method for sin by God, and that therefore one should be pleased to accept them in order to destroy one's sin. Mrs. Miya was so pious that she thanked God when her eldest son died, but since she began to come to Seicho no Ie, she has begun to understand what the true God is."

Diseases are explained in the following way: "You think that something can hurt you. This false idea arouses anger and fear which creates a negative mental wave (see *nempa* above). And according to the Law of Affinity your negative mental wave will call forth evil mental waves broadcast from the miserable and unhappy people prevailing in the universe. The objectification of these evil mental waves is so-called disease and misfortune." Or: "There is a passage in the Vimalakirti Sutra of Buddhism, where Vimalakirti says 'I am sick because the multitude are sick.' "

Seicho no Ie claims to be able to cure all diseases, to avert all calamities from bed-wetting to atomic burns. The following headlines from the May 1958 issue of *Seicho no Ie* made these claims: "Uterine cancer completely cured in a week; Cancer of the pancreas disappeared in a moment; Stomach cancer cured through reconciliation with mother-in-law."

Many religions lay claim to such cures, but the variety of those with which Seicho no Ie associates itself is such that several follow for illustration. In Taniguchi's words:

"Mr. Matsumoto Jukyo of Ochiai, Tokyo, was in the audience at my lecture given at Hochi Hall on December 19, 1934. His child had the bad habit of bed-wetting, and various treatments were of no avail. To tell the truth, the parents are usually responsible for the child's affliction—the bed-wetting is often the reflection of the parents' mind. When Matsumoto listened to my lecture his mind underwent a sudden change and his child stopped wetting the bed that very night." (That such "miracles" are highly estimated by Japanese mothers appears from the detailed recounting of five such cures in the first four pages of Taniguchi's book.)

"Since she [a little girl] visited Seicho no Ie, she has acquired the firm belief that man is originally perfect, and that therefore her nearsightedness must be imaginary. Telling her doctor so, she persisted in her refusal to wear glasses. Her eyes got well before long, and when she took the entrance examination for school there was nothing wrong with her eyes."

"A young lady came to me and asked for consultation. Her story was that she had been subject to chronic menorrhagia for eight years since the age of fourteen and thus unable to marry and conceive children. Her mental affliction was complicated, so it was necessary to visit me four times before she was cured."

"Mr. Tanaka Ginnosuke, a principal of a primary school in Tatsuno, was in the audience at the Kokumin Kaikan [hall] in Osaka. He was a man of character, but had a big wart in the middle of his forehead which formed a distinctive feature in his physiognomy. As soon as my lecture came to a close, the wart suddenly dropped off. This is a true story and by no means strange because the flesh changes according to the mind."

And this amazing claim: "Lately . . . I revealed true stories of how man has learned to live in harmony with such previous nuisances as mice, ants, ticks, and the like—all these once harmful animals and insects have become unharmful because of the conditions of our minds."

There is no disease or abnormal situation that Seicho no Ie does not claim to have healed. The healing comes about, as claimed above, through the change of people's minds—bitterness turned into gratitude, hate into love, as they listen to Taniguchi, or practice the shinsokan. About the power of the shinsokan Taniguchi says: "It is not always necessary to practice shinsokan in order to meditate on the perfect nature of the person seeking help. If you can concentrate your mind on the perfect nature of the other person while you are carrying on a conversation with him, the illness will disappear." The doctrine of shinsokan may be compared with similar doctrines in other new religions.

Because of the supposed unlimited power of the shinsokan, doctors, diagnoses, and medicine are held in contempt: "I sometimes see a patient suffering from lung disease taking his temperature all the time. Every time he checks his temperature he says to himself, 'I am feverish. I am really ill,' thus making the disease-idea stronger and stronger. This is not the way to be cured. Throw away your thermometer, realize your original true self, which is free from disease. Drive the disease-idea out of your mind and you are sure to recover health at once."

The reader should not believe that Westerners are the only ones who might raise their eyebrows on hearing these accounts—there are countless Japanese as well who do so.

Life After Death

Seicho no Ie does not deny that there is a life after death, but it is not clearly defined. The emphasis on this life is carried to such an extent that Taniguchi claims that paradise and heaven are here: "The pilgrimage of faith does not mean in the literal sense a long journey to the Pure Land of Heaven. We are *already* in the Pure Land of Heaven, without making any laborious trip. We are in reality in Heaven and one with God, though we lead a life in this world. However, we must not be satisfied with mere intellectual understanding of it. We must go ahead and make it our own life and blood, nay, we must endeavour to live daily with this consciousness."

Man of Infinite Potentiality

Perhaps the doctrine that has given Seicho no Ie most of its appeal to people is the idea which can be traced like a thread through all the other doctrines. This is the idea that man, once conscious of his "Sonship," has unlimited resources at his disposal and can live a life of infinite possibilities: "The fundamental principle expounded by Seicho no Ie is that our fate lies in our own hands, that we shape our fate freely ourselves, that we in other words are the masters of our own destiny. The law of destiny is provided by the fundamental truth that man is son of God. Since man is son of God, there is no impossibility, and he creates freely according to his heart's desire the phenomenal world, which is a reflection of the mind."

"There is no impossibility for a person who is united with the life of God and burns with the will to make manifest the wisdom, love, and life of God on earth. Impossibility makes its seeming appearance, because we do not realize God within us. When we make the will of God our will, and cast ourselves into His work, forgetting ourselves in absolute reliance on God, negative words such as impossible vanish from our thinking."

For the sons of God there is no such thing as fear: "Fear is indeed an enemy of life. The negative thought of 'impossibility' and 'all is up' will deprive you of the power of 'possibility' and drive you into an abyss of misfortune which is unnecessary and can be definitely avoided. Then what can we do to break away from fear and arrive at the thought that 'it can be done'? Here is the answer: Pray constantly in your mind saying 'I am a son of God. I will never fail because God is always leading and directing me with His infinite wisdom. God is my wisdom, power, and wealth—He is infinite supply.'"

This theory of man as a being of infinite potentiality is used dexterously in the propaganda of Seicho no Ie. Lavish promises are made for all kinds of occupations: "Medical men will through this be enabled to make accurate diagnoses and prescriptions. Artists will be enabled to transfer to the phenomenal world the truth, goodness, and beauty of God's Kingdom. Scientists will be guided by the wisdom of God and be enabled to make great inventions and discoveries to benefit human life, or again, to discover complex and mysterious laws of the Universe and improve the destiny of man. Again, a technician will be able to make his skill a tool of God, to unite with the great and divine wisdom of God, and proceed one step further than he would be able to do if he relied merely on material knowledge."

Seicho no Ie tells the parents that all problems will disappear. The children's studies will improve if they just close their eyes before each lesson and meditate on being a son of God and on the idea, "I know my lessons well." And a boy who is told often enough that he is a good boy will automatically become a good boy, just as a boy who is always scolded for being a bad boy will become a bad boy. Also, tension in the family, such as between husband and wife, between parents and in-laws, will become a thing of the past, or rather, a thing that never existed, if they apply the shinsokan meditation to their problems and use the unlimited resources waiting for those who realize the Sonship of man.

Similar miraculous stories are told about people who suddenly became able to pay their taxes when before it had seemed impossible; people who through enlightenment were able to find things long lost; people who had narrow escapes from death; and on and on, all due to salvation through using shinsokan, once man has realized his potential as a son of God.

Seicho no Ie and Other Religions

Taniguchi and most other religious leaders of Seicho no Ie study other religions intensely but still claim their own superiority. Many are the stories of people who, by coming to Seicho no Ie, suddenly came to "truly understand" the sutras and doctrines of their *own* religions.

Still, Taniguchi pays the highest tribute to Jesus and Buddha, if not to Christianity and Buddhism: "I have a profound respect for Buddha and Christ. This is because among the other numerous religious founders, these two persons preached the truth; but the followers of their various sects generally misunderstood the truth and could not genuinely transmit what Buddha and Christ taught, and they have consequently preached truth as well as untruth."

It is the religions, Buddhism and Christianity, as they have developed, that are scorned by Taniguchi and regarded as inferior to Seicho no Ie: "There are many religious books, some of which were written by men of high virtue and profound learning. What they say is mostly correct. However, they are merely book-and-church religions, and cannot be applied to practical life because they do not have the realization that now is the time to act, and have not awakened to the truth that 'the Eternal Buddhahood is in me now; the eternal God is in me now.' This realization that now is the time to act turns a religion into practical life. This is Seicho no Ie. The difference between accomplished religion and the new revelation of Seicho no Ie is very slight, but this slight difference is extremely important. When this barrier is broken, religion becomes actual life, but till then it remains a religion of only church and book." This stress on the connection of teaching with life is typical of a large number of the new religions and must be seen as part of the background for their success.

According to Seicho no Ie the present strifes and conflicts between religions will not disappear until all religions have found their way back, away from their founders, to the Eternal God: "When the Christians discover Christ, not in the material form of Jesus in the flesh, but in the eternal Divinity who said 'Before Abraham was, I was'; when the Buddhists discover Buddha, not in Gautama in the flesh, but in the eternal Gautama, who told Ananda 'All Buddhas in the past are my disciples'; when the Seicho no Ie discovers Seicho no Ie not in the house, where Taniguchi in the flesh lives, but in the Seicho no Ie of eternal Reality, who said 'All religions will be rejuvenated by Me'—*then* first will religions no longer have to quarrel over their spheres of influence."

Although Taniguchi has borrowed heavily from Buddhism, it is especially the Christian terms and doctrines he has colored for his own use, and at the same time has misquoted and mixed up some accounts (the above "Before Abraham was, I *was*," for example).

One of the stories in the Bible that Taniguchi most frequently uses is the story of Nicodemus. The following is his interpretation of it:

"If I paraphrase the words of Jesus to Nicodemus, it will be something like this: 'Even if the picture is distorted, do not think that the Real-Man is distorted. Even if the physical man is ill, the Real-Man is not ill. The physical eye cannot see the Real-Man. Can you see, from where the wind blows and where it goes? You can see the Real-Man no more than you can see the wind. To be born of the Spirit means to turn the eye from the physical man to the Real-Man—to come to the realization that you and God are one.' "

Also the crucifixion of Christ, one of the few things concerning Christ that hardly ever is mentioned by Japanese religions, finds a place and an interpretation in the system of Seicho no Ie:

"True freedom lies behind the seeming freedom of being able to do as one pleases, and another name for it is meekness. What are we to be meek toward? It is to the mind of God that we must be meek. Christ prostrated himself in the Garden of Eden [this mix-up of Eden for Gethsemane is another example of superficial Bible study] and repeated twice these words in prayer: 'Oh, my Father, if it be possible, let this cup pass from me; nevertheless not as I will, but as thou wilt.' The bitter wine refers to the fate of Jesus, who was to be placed on the cross to die. Such is a bitter experience, and the mortal mind does not wish for it to happen. But finally Jesus surrendered everything to God's will. Jesus was crucified. Because of the cross the body was killed, but in spirit he was resurrected. He was released from phenomenal bounds and was given true freedom of the spirit. The act of ascending the cross does not symbolize any injunction to be crucified or to imitate any such barbaric practice as burning or torturing the body. It symbolizes the message which Seicho no Ie proclaims: *that his body does not exist, that matter is nothingness.*"

Another phrase of Jesus that Taniguchi often (mis)quotes and gives his own interpretation to is "Before Abraham was, I was." This is how Taniguchi renders it: "Man is an eternal being. As God is immortal, man—a Son of God—is immortal. It is not when he was born from his mother's body that he came into this world as a man. Jesus says: 'Before Abraham was, I was.'"

The words of Jesus and the teachings of Christianity that Seicho no Ie uses—with its own interpretation—are so numerous that they give a distinct Christian coloring to it. One of the most interesting questions in connection with the development of Seicho no Ie, and other new religions, is to what extent and in what way this wholesale adoption of Christian form and content will affect the attitude of these religions towards Christianity in the future.

Summary and Future

Seicho no Ie belongs to the medium-sized new religions. It has been adopted mostly by the middle classes and directs itself toward the intellectual in contrast to most other new religions which have had their great successes among farming classes. His formulation of a teaching that is a mixture of both Buddhism and Christianity has probably been greatly responsible for Seicho no Ie's appeal to the higher classes, but there is no doubt that Taniguchi's personality, his speeches, and the popularity of *Seimei no Jisso* have been mainly responsible for the success of his doctrines.

Seicho no Ie has a large number of devoted leaders throughout the country, and there is reason to believe that it will continue as a fairly prosperous medium-sized middle-class new religion, although its durability and strength will not be truly tested—as is the case with so many other new religions—until it meets the challenge of surviving the death of its creator and present leader.

Glossary

CHINESE TERMS

chai	Curbing physical and mental action. Austerities such as fasting, etc.
ch'eng	Sincerity.
chen jen	Realized man.
ch'i	Life breath, soul.
ch'ing	Feelings.
ching	Book.
chu	Ruler, prince, king.
Chu-tao	Way of the ruler or monarch. The art of ruling.
hsiao	Filial piety.
hsien	Persons of superior morality. Moral aristocrats.
hsing	Nature, either external or inborn.
hsu	Vacuity.
i	Morality. Sensible and prudent behavior. Conscience.
I Ching	*Book of Changes.*
jen	Sympathy and charity for other humans. Benevolence.
kau-yu	Reduction of desires.
kuei	Ghosts.
kung	Temple, sanctuary.
kuo	State, civil authority.

li	Profit, gain. Etiquette, ceremonial.
min	Common man.
ming	Language, orders, decree. Fate.
ming-chiao	Conventional morality.
Shang Ti	"Lord above."
shen	"Stretchers." Spirits of ancestors. Soul.
sheng	Sage.
shu	Principle of altruism.
tao	Road, path, way, principle, doctrine. Doctrine of way in which life should be ordered. The order of the universe.
te	Action or occurrence in human life having necessary consequence of good or evil. Law of ethical consequence. Virtue. Conduct admirable in itself. The power of an orderly, moral existence.
Ti	Ancestor. Universal Ruler.
T'ien	Heaven.
t'ien hsien	Heavenly Immortals.
Ti Hsien	Earthly Immortals.
ting	Calmness.
tso-wang	"Sitting with one's mind blank." Meditative trance.
tzu-jan	Taoist term for one's true self. "Self-so-ness." Spontaneity, naturalness.
wu wei	Inaction.
wu yu	Desirelessness.
yang	Positive principle of action. Light, masculine, active, hot, dry, principle.

yang-sheng	"Nourishing one's life." Enhancing one's own life energies. Caring for one's parents with respect and honor. Sacrifice to ancestors.
yin	Feminine, passive, principle. Malignant principle of action. Negative.
yu	Desire.

JAPANESE TERMS

ashi	Bad.
bushido	"The way of the warrior." Code of chivalry for aristocratic class.
gohei	Folded strips of paper used as symbolic offerings in Shinto shrines.
goryo	Spirits of persons who suffered an untimely death.
harai	Purification.
haraigushi	Wand used in purification rites.
ikoku no kami	God of a foreign country, e.g., Buddha.
Jukyo	Confucianism.
kagura	Sacred dances usually associated with Shinto festivals.
kami	Sacred spirits, gods, objects of worship in Shinto.
koan	Documents of Zen Buddhism. Riddles and stories conveying the essence of Zen.
Kojiki	"Record of Ancient Matters."
magatsuhi	Evil spirits.
matsuri	Worship, performing kami-rites.
misogi	Purification by bathing.

naorai	Sacramental meal.
Nihongi	"Chronicles of Japan."
norito	Prayer.
reikon	Spirits.
saisei itchi	The unity of Shinto worship and government.
sakaki	Sacred tree of Shinto used in all formal rituals.
shinbutsu	Folk religion including such practices as ancestor worship, shamanism, divination, magic, etc.
shinkai	Kami-world.
shinkyo	Sacred mirror. Symbolic of purity of kami and of purity of worshiper who enters shrine.
shinsen	Offering to kami.
shintai	Sacred object symbolizing the kami's presence in a Shinto shrine.
shintai-zan	"Divine body mountain." Mountain housing one or more gods, e.g., Mount Fuji.
Shinto	"The way of the gods." Kami-faith. Spiritual life attained through worship of and communion with the kami. More generally, the Japanese "way" of life reflecting their two-thousand-year history.
sukeisha	Worshipers.
Takama-ga-hara	High Plain of Heaven. Dwelling place of most august kami.
torii	Gateway in shrines symbolically marking off secular, mundane world from sacred world of the kami.
ujigami	Sacred spirits functioning as guardians of clans.
yoshi	Good.

Selected Bibliography

CHINESE RELIGIONS

Creel, Herrlee G., *Chinese Thought from Confucius to Mao Tsê-tung*. The University of Chicago Press, 1953. Available as a Mentor paperback.

——— *Confucius: The Man and the Myth*. The John Day Company, Inc., 1949. Available as a Harper Torchbook.

Eliot, Charles, *Hinduism and Buddhism: An Historical Sketch*, Vol. III. London: Routledge & Kegan Paul, Ltd., 1921.

Fung Yu-Lan, *A History of Chinese Philosophy*, tr. by Derk Bodde. Princeton University Press, 1952, 1953. 2 vols.

Hughes, Ernest R., and K., *Religion in China*. London: Hutchinson & Co., Ltd., 1950.

Latourette, Kenneth S., *The Chinese, Their History and Culture*. The Macmillan Company, 1934.

Liu Wu-Chi, *A Short History of Confucian Philosophy*. London: Penguin Books, 1955.

Moore, Charles A., and Morris, A. V. (eds.), *The Chinese Mind: Essentials of Chinese Philosophy and Culture*. Honolulu: University of Hawaii Press, 1967.

Reichelt, Karl L., *Religion in Chinese Garment*. Philosophical Library, Inc., 1952.

Waley, Arthur (tr.), *The Analects of Confucius*. London: George Allen & Unwin, Ltd., 1938.

——— *Three Ways of Thought in Ancient China*. London: George Allen & Unwin, Ltd., 1939. Available as an Anchor paperback, 1956.

271

———— (ed. and tr.), *The Way and Its Power: A Study of the Tao Tê Ching and Its Place in Chinese Thought*. London: George Allen & Unwin, Ltd., 1934. Available as an Evergreen paperback, 1958.

Welch, Holmes, *The Parting of the Way: Lao Tzu and the Taoist Movement*. Beacon Press, Inc., 1957.

JAPANESE RELIGIONS

Anesaki, Masaharu, *History of Japanese Religion*. London: Kegan Paul, Trench, Trubner & Co., 1930.

Bunce, William K., *Religions in Japan*. Charles E. Tuttle Company, Inc., 1955.

Eliot, Charles, *Japanese Buddhism*. London: Routledge & Kegan Paul, Ltd., 1935.

Hammer, Raymond, *Japan's Religious Ferment*. Oxford University Press, 1962.

Holtom, Daniel C., *Modern Japan and Shinto Nationalism*. The University of Chicago Press, 1947.

Kitagawa, Joseph M., *Religion in Japanese History*. Columbia University Press, 1966.

McFarland, H. Neill, *The Rush Hour of the Gods: A Study of New Religious Movements in Japan*. The Macmillan Company, 1967.

Ono, Sokyo, and Woodard, W. P., *Shinto: The Kami Way*. Charles E. Tuttle Company, Inc., 1962.

Ross, Nancy Wilson (ed.), *The World of Zen*. Vintage Book, Random House, Inc., 1960.

Sansom, G. B., *Japan: A Short Cultural History*. Century Press, 1931.

Suzuki, Daisetz T., *Essays in Zen Buddhism (First Series)*. London: Rider & Co., 1949. Available in Evergreen paperback, 1961.

Thomsen, Harry, *The New Religions of Japan*. Charles E. Tuttle Company, Inc., 1963.